CHARLES
BUKOWSKI

Sunligh

Intervie
1963-19 ɔ

edited by
David Stephen Calonne

2003 Sun Dog Press Northville, Michigan

Charles Bukowski
Sunlight Here I Am
Interviews and Encounters
1963–1993
Edited by David Stephen Calonne

Compilation Copyright © 2003 Sun Dog Press

Designed by Judy Berlinski

Cover design by Grey Christian

Cover photo by Richard Robinson

Thanks to ecco HarperCollins and Linda Lee Bukowski for permission to quote from Charles Bukowski's printed work.

Warmest thanks to John Martin of Black Sparrow Press for his enthusiasm for this project.

A special thank you to Linda Lee Bukowski for providing photos from her personal archive.

Published by Sun Dog Press
22058 Cumberland Dr.
Northville, MI 48167
sundogpr@voyager.net

Library of Congress Cataloging-in-Publication Data

Bukowski, Charles.
    Sunlight here I am : interviews and encounters, 1963–1993 / Charles Bukowski ; edited by David Stephen Calonne.—1st ed.
        p. cm.
    Includes bibliographical references and index.
    ISBN 0-941543-37-4 (pbk. : alk. paper)
    1. Bukowski, Charles—Interviews. 2. Authors, American—20th century—Interviews. 3. Beat generation. I. Title: Charles Bukowki. II. Calonne, David Stephen, 1953- III. Title.

PS3552.U4Z477 2003
811'.54—dc22
[B]

2003060843

Manufactured in the United States of America   First Edition

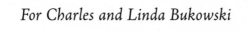

For Charles and Linda Bukowski

Contents

Introduction

Charles Bukowski (1920–1994) was a marvelous talker: engaging, provocative, humorous and wise. He delivered fine lines swiftly, one after another, perfectly timed. Bukowski had perhaps honed some of his formidable skills as raconteur during those happy times spent as a young man entertaining clients in the very lively Philadelphia bar he would later immortalize in *Barfly*. Comfortable with an audience, he performed his side of the tennis match with brio. Bukowski was a master of dialogue's shape and rhythm: question and answer, pause and movement. The surprise hidden between the lines, sparse statement and counterstatement were his forte. His best poems, stories and novels derived from this perfect pitch, from an unerring ear for the music of a sentence, the counterpoint of sentences.

These interviews and encounters document Charles Bukowski's long rise to world renown, beginning in 1963 when he responds to questions from the *Literary Times* of Chicago in his one-bedroom Hollywood apartment, to poolside in San Pedro answering a German journalist in August 1993, just seven months before his death at age 73. These thirty years span a cataclysmic period not only in Bukowski's transformation but also in American cultural and political life. The Cuban missile crisis, birth control pills, war in Vietnam, civil rights movement, assassinations of John F. Kennedy, Martin Luther King Jr. and Robert Kennedy, moon landing, Woodstock, psychedelia, LSD, marijuana, sexual revolution, student revolt, women's liberation, Haight-Ashbury-San Francisco-Southern California hippies, Ronald Reagan, gay liberation, punk rock, AIDS, stock market mania, *Twin Peaks*, sushi, word processors. All these twists and shifts in American consciousness are evident in Bukowski's own trajectory. As we listen to him dutifully answer question after question—a witness and chronicler of the conformist Fifties, apocalyptic Dionysian Sixties and Seventies, and yuppie Eighties—we also observe his journey from obscurity to fame in France and Germany and finally in America following the success of *Barfly*. By the end of his career he counted among his admirers Gary Snyder, Jim Harrison, Camille Paglia, Henry Miller and Jean-Paul Sartre.

Bukowski's life was a long act of self-immolation, a life lived as an experiment in combustion and out of the fire comes the writing, comes the making. By now the facts of his life have been assembled into classic mythic narrative: the tortured artist shaping from his suffering and genius things of profound beauty. Born in Andernach, Germany in 1920, he came to Los Angeles at the age of two. His childhood was devastated by his father's constant beatings and in adolescence an outbreak of terrible *acne vulgaris* required painful hospital treatments. These facial and corporeal eruptions were possibly stigmata of the brutal family drama. Nikos Kazantzakis, the great Greek writer, also endured a spiritual crisis resulting in a psychosomatic skin disease. From this anguished period came his magnificent philosophical meditation *The Saviors of God* (1). Bukowski's later frequent references to Buddhism suggest that he knew deeply the First Noble Truth: All life is suffering. Alice Miller in *The Drama of the Gifted Child* has documented the ways a talented child's sensitivities are brutalized and forced underground by an abusive parent (2).

He soon had his first taste of alcohol, the elixir which took him to freedom, to a place of warmth out of the swing of the sea, the cold of rejection, hurt and lovelessness. The bloody climax of his long binge came at age thirty-five with a ruptured stomach in the charity ward of Los Angeles County General Hospital. But true to myth again, after almost dying he rose from the dead and lived to drink another cold beer. Bukowski loved cats—they are the subject of some of his finest later poems—and it appears he himself had the proverbial nine lives. The torrent of poetry now began in earnest. As he remarked in *Knight Magazine* in 1969: "I was almost dead anyhow and it was kind of like sending a message . . . Sunlight, here I am" (3).

Beginning in 1970, after leaving his job at the post office—he was apparently about to be dismissed; the FBI had assembled a file documenting his "obscene" writings in the underground press and "extensive absenteeism"—Bukowski became a "professional writer." Armed with $100 a month from his publisher, John Martin of Black Sparrow Press, he wrote *Post Office* (1971) and a decade of astonishing creativity followed: *Mockingbird Wish Me Luck* (1972), *South of No North* (1973), *Burning in Water Drowning in Flame* (1974), *Factotum* (1975), *Love Is a Dog from Hell* (1977), *Women* (1978), *Play the Piano Drunk Like A Percussion*

Instrument Until the Fingers Begin to Bleed A Bit (1979), *Shakespeare Never Did This* (1979), *Dangling in the Tournefortia* (1981). By the Eighties, Bukowski's poetry, novels and stories began to be hugely successful in Europe, especially in Germany, and he made promotional tours of Germany and France recounted in *Shakespeare Never Did This*. He married Linda Lee Beighle in 1985 and settled down to life in San Pedro with a pleasant house, garden, black BMW and a steady supply of Concannon Petite Sirah and Bernkastel Riesling.

Bukowski's public persona was that of the drinker, *provocateur*, satyr, clown, bad boy unsettling the staid and bourgeois dead with his outrageousness, continuing in the tradition of Dylan Thomas and John Berryman. Drinking, misbehaving, lusting, we witness a glorious modern Dionysus/Diogenes in Don Strachan's portrait, as well as in Ric Reynold's account of his poetry reading with Allen Ginsberg, Gary Snyder and Lawrence Ferlinghetti in Santa Cruz. Perhaps his most celebrated act of disobedience occurred in Paris on *Apostrophes*, the elegant television literary talk show presided over by Bernard Pivot, a proper and civilized Frenchman, Bukowski's own version of which appeared in *Shakespeare Never Did This*. In Paris it was appropriate that he be the *enfant terrible*, whose proper role after all is *épater les bourgeois*. Although Bukowski tells *Southern California Literary Scene* that Rimbaud and Baudelaire did not thrill him, he followed their wild examples during his time in Paris.

But as in any caricature, this is an exaggeration which obscures the dedicated, inventive literary artist Bukowski had been from the beginning. He was an authentic original who created a revolution in American poetics quietly, persistently, methodically, one poem, story or essay at a time in countless little magazines with small budgets and cool titles: *Approach, Caterpillar, Cerberus, Blitz, Entrails, Sciamachy, Hearse, Dust, Odyssey, Quicksilver, Trace, Nomad, Sun, Coffin, Ole, Schist, Hanging Loose, Experiment, Amphora, Canto, Gallows, Flame, Targets, Avalanche, The Naked Ear, Semina, Matrix, Harlequin, Quixote, Kauri, Spectroscope, Wormwood Review, Klactoveedsedsteen, Abraxas, Painted Bride Quarterly, Epos, Anagogic & Paiedeumic Review, Trace, Coastlines, El Corno Emplumado, Abyss.* He appeared in virtually every major publication of the American underground. Bukowski possessed a natural, untutored literary gift, but he also worked hard at his craft and sullen art, mailing one self-addressed stamped envelope after another in a guerilla raid against whatever is packaged, pre-programmed, false. Ideologies, slogans, cant were the enemy and he refused to belong to any group—Beat, Confessional, Black Mountain, Democratic, Republican, Capitalist, Communist, Hippie or Punk.

Bukowski chronicled his intense inner, psychological, spiritual sufferings in his own inimitable style. He was "confessional" but took a different path than Sylvia Plath, John Berryman, Robert Lowell, Theodore Roethke. He brought poetry out of the academy into the streets where there were few classical allusions, sestinas and famous New England ancestors, but rather L.A. whores, drunks, racetracks, bars, madhouses, roominghouses, and women driving cars towards him on the sidewalk. His language was pounded into pure, raw, American speech with some of the fun and typographical play of e.e. cummings as relief from the heavy existential void he often inhabited. He wanted to stay close to the earth like Hemingway, Dostoevsky, Hamsun, and Lawrence. As he once declared: "I'd rather hear about a live American bum than a dead Greek god" (4). And although he appeared in under-ground publications such as *Evergreen Review* and *The Outsider* along with Allen Ginsberg, Jack Kerouac, William Burroughs, Lawrence Ferlinghetti and Gregory Corso and though he shared many concerns with the Beats—his defiant anti-Establishment jeremiads, obsession with madness and drive towards ecstatic states—he rejected their club-biness, preferring instead the solitary stance of an independent loner.

With independence came visionary fierce clarity for Bukowski's clear eye sees. He places us exactly inside experience, a true phenomenolog-ical writer revealing things in unfettered purity. He looked at life directly, drove it into a corner to see what is there, as Henry David Thoreau did. Then he photographed it. There is no need for additional commentary to the reader because you have had the experience along with the poet. His simplicity and minimalism recall Thoreau's famous saying "simplify, simplify" and his witty Thurberesque line drawings are as spare as his writing: a man, his bottle, a dog, a bird, the sun. Bukowski ritualizes his life, stripping down his self to bare bones.

Although Bukowski says he is no "guru," his vision is essentially reli-gious and his quest is for the sacred. He tells Sean Penn that it is necessary to lie fallow, to "just do nothing at all" for several days and it is difficult not to see in this detachment the wisdom of Lao-Tzu's *Tao Te Ching*. He would like perhaps, like Walt Whitman, to turn and live with the animals to find this integrity, to live wholly naturally. For Bukowski, we are beasts and animals, and therefore as Annable in D.H. Lawrence's *The White Peacock* says, we should be good animals. He is very close to Lawrence in this regard: life should be lived with "the blood" and "the intellect is only a bit and a bridle" throttling us, as Lawrence wrote in a famous letter (5). The prevalence of animal imagery in his titles (Bukowski's *Flower Fist and Bestial Wail* recalls Lawrence's *Birds, Beasts and Flowers*)—run with the hunted, relentless tarantula, cold dogs, dogs from hell, wild horses, mockingbirds—all suggest a continuum of the human and animal. And Robinson Jeffers, one of Bukowski's favorites, also pondered man and hawk, wild swan, roan stallion.

These encounters recorded by American, British, Italian, German and French journalists give us a great deal of Charles Bukowski, perhaps more than we would expect to learn about a writer. They range from the *Berkeley Barb* and the punk 'zine *Twisted Image*, to the august pages of *The New York Times Book Review*. Among the primal Bukowskian themes are classical music, solitude, drinking, admired authors, agonized youth, writing rituals, inspiration, madness, women, sex, love, horse-races. One reads his life directly. One may read interviews with Vladimir Nabokov and find a consummately artful magician who never reveals anything. We learn about chess, about butterfly hunting in the Swiss Alps, about rarefied delights of aesthetic, imaginative, intellectual, combinatorial play. However, in Bukowski's world we enjoy no luscious chocolate, no happy cows, no Alpine honey, no safe banks, no trains that run on time. He celebrates the terrible, raw, bare beautiful truth: the flowers of evil. And he wants to show that truth with no frills, no flights of fancy. Bukowski reveals that he admires plumbers more than writers. They do an essential job by keeping the shit flowing, but unlike writers they do not bullshit. And he remarks that the writers he loves most know how to "lay down the line"—a significant expression since this implies a kind of primal building, or a kind of bedrock painting. As he tells Robert Wennersten: "The hard clean line that says it. And it's got to have some blood; it's got to have some humor; it's got to have that unnameable thing which you know is there the minute you start reading."

In these encounters, he strips away the mask artists often wear. At the close of the *Rolling Stone* interview his sensitive pained yearning is suddenly exposed: the poet at his typewriter looking at people through the window. Yet it is equally striking how much verve and joy Bukowski displays. Achieving this ecstasy is aided by time spent alone, and in many respects he reminds one of the great Canadian pianist Glenn Gould, who shared Bukowski's total dedication to artistic creation as well as his wild imagination, comedic impulse and love of solitude.

His true companions, he tells us, are writers: Carson McCullers, Friedrich Nietzsche, Arthur Schopenhauer, Antonin Artaud, J.D. Salinger, Sherwood Anderson, Franz Kafka, John Fante, D.H. Lawrence, Louis-Ferdinand Céline, Knut Hamsun, Fyodor Dostoevsky, Henry Miller, William Saroyan, Ernest Hemingway, Ivan Turgenev, James Thurber, Maxim Gorky, John Dos Passos, e.e. cummings, Robinson Jeffers, Stephen Spender, W.H. Auden, Giovanni Boccaccio, Conrad Aiken, Ezra Pound, Li Po, Catullus crowd his conversation. And the great composers were equally significant—Bach, Beethoven, Handel, Mahler, Mozart, Shostakovich, Sibelius, Stravinsky, Wagner. Their sublime music played on the radio as he typed.

There is an immense amount of laughter in the encounters here recorded. Bukowski seems unable to speak for two or three consecutive minutes without creating humor. It is great fun to enjoy his associative brilliance, his ability to move from subject to subject and find laughter in unexpectedly juxtaposed connections. He tells Sean Penn about his adventures reading *Journey to the End of the Night* while eating a box of Ritz crackers. And during comments about boxing: "My cat, Beeker, is a fighter. He gets mauled up a bit sometimes, but he's always the winner. I taught him it all, you know . . . lead with the left, set up the right." His titles also give us in microcosm Bukowski's typical fusion of the horrific and humorous, the rough and refined, "low brow" culture up against "high brow," his unique brand of darkest existentialism with a laugh: fingers bleeding/playing the piano; hell/love; flower/fist; rooming-house/madrigals. He places seeming opposites together in a fresh way.

We are told by Aristotle in his *Poetics* that the ability to make metaphors—to find connections between things we might normally not associate with one another—is what makes genius in a poet (6). In his conversation with Marc Chénetier, Bukowski remarks: "I could sit here, thinking about roses and Christianity and Plato and all that. It wouldn't do me any good. If I drive out to the track and get joggled and come back, I can write. It's a stimulus." *Roses and Christianity and Plato*—it's a revelatory thought and completely spontaneous. When one considers the matter, these three things have much in common: they are all pretty structures, beautiful but untrue. Bukowski often quoted Nietzsche on poets as liars and he would also have known Nietzsche's apothegm: we have art so we will not perish from truth.

There are some illuminating moments, as when we hear Bukowski the Moralist. We discover he is indeed a child of the Thirties, of the Depression: a hard, prolific literary worker who saw many of the youth of the Sixties as pampered, lazy, self-indulgent and weak. For a man of the "working class," the problems of soft middle-class kids with affluent parents seemed not to be real problems. Like Henry Miller, who thought the radical, spiritually anarchic Gnostics of the ancient world made the hippies look like "toilet paper," Bukowski wants peace and love but he wants toughness as well (7). For all his protestations about being politically unconcerned, he was a wonderfully nasty, sharp-tongued, irreverent social critic, railing against the frequent falsity, triviality and absurdity of American life.

Bukowski has many voices, and in these exchanges we see how naturally theatrical he was: an actor, a mimic, imitating voices and aware of the implied menace and humor which can be delivered in a single line. The interview itself becomes expression of the very absurdity against which he is fighting a guerilla war of humor and lust and energy and madness. He turns the interview "form" upside down in *Shakespeare Never Did This* as he explodes in an orgy of "answers": "No. Yes. No. No. I like Thomas Carlyle, Madame Butterfly and orange juice with the skins crushed in. I like red radios, car washes and crushed cigarette packages and Carson McCullers. No. NO! No. Yes, of course." Questions and answers, answers and questions, questions and answers: Hemingway's "nada."

And when in conversation with Barbet Schroeder as he finishes a riff about unbearable ordinary life's "snail's pace: 8–5, Johnny Carson, Happy Birthday, Christmas, New Year's. To me this is the sickest of all sick things," he suddenly roars: "Now I sit around and drink wine and I talk about myself because you guys ask the questions, not because I give the answers, OK?" Charles Ives wrote a haunting composition called *The Unanswered Question* in which a solo trumpet speaks a questioning theme against the strings' calm, indifferent, hymn-background of a silent universe. Bukowski wants the truth, and the truth does not come out of questions and answers. The truth is beyond the pairs of opposites, beyond dark and light. It comes from blood, it comes from laying down the line true and level like a good carpenter: the truth is a ferociously simple straight line.

He is in fact not a "nihilist." Rather he strives for a kind of Zen detachment. In his battle scenes with women, for example, in those terrific, memorable emotional exchanges, he often remains mute, silent. Not because he doesn't want to speak but because there is nothing to say and words are not enough. What is Bukowski if not a Gnostic: the ultimate Outsider, alone, thrown into a cosmic mistake of a world, an alien. *Into this world we're thrown* Jim Morrison sang, and Bukowski too felt thrown into an America without soul. The machine is in the saddle but the heart's sustenance may come through solitude, through sexual love, through poetry, through wine, through music, through laughter, through the heart. Henry Miller wrote of the wisdom of the heart and Bukowski also seeks ways into the dark heart of unconscious knowing, D.H. Lawrence's dark gods. He is an underground animal seeking to free the soul strangled by our technological, "Christian," clock-dominated, busy American society. Some readers may be surprised to find that the Dirty Old Man was in fact a tenderhearted man, too shy to make love during the day. He tells *Grapevine:* "There's a lot of puritan in me."

In many ways, the failure of American literati to understand Bukowski comes precisely from an unwillingness to fathom his dark roots, from an ignorance of his true lineage. He derives directly from the German Romantic/Expressionist tradition, in the long line of the mad poet and the *dämonisch*: Hölderlin, Kleist, Nietzsche, Trakl, Kafka, Hesse, Rilke: all moved along the edge of sanity, suffered dark nights of the soul. Interestingly, the German film directors Rainer Maria Fassbinder and Werner Herzog both made their first impact in the United States in the Seventies, about the same time Bukowski began to break through. German artists studied the tortured, isolated, alienated individual, unable to connect. They depicted extreme, surreal emotional states of despair, violence, and sexual combat (captured so superbly by

Robert Crumb in his Bukowski illustrations). It should come as no surprise that one of Bukowski's favorite films was *Eraserhead*: David Lynch's brooding work is an Expressionist masterpiece. Bukowski is as bold an "existentialist" as Samuel Beckett, but he also derives from this German tradition of violent, wrenching, brutal emotion directly portrayed. It is perfectly logical that the Europeans took to him immediately.

Bukowski explored the dark, mad places but he did so as part of his struggling movement towards transcendence. It is war all the time, the fight through to one's authentic selfhood, but there are moments of peace, moments of equilibrium. What emerges from these encounters is an authentic American original, up in his room with Sibelius on the radio, pouring his first glass of wine and waiting for the rush, waiting for the glory, waiting for the line. In a late poem entitled "nobody but you," Bukowski wrote:

nobody can save you but
yourself
and you're worth saving.
it's a war not easily won
but if anything is worth winning then
this is it.

think about it.
think about saving your self.
your spiritual self.
your gut self.
your singing magical self and
your beautiful self.
save it.

don't join the dead-in-spirit
maintain your self
with humor and grace
and finally
if necessary
wager your life as you struggle,
damn the odds, damn
the price.

only you can save your
self (8).

There is plenty of Bukowski's magical singing beautiful self to be
enjoyed in these pages.

When I began this project four years ago, I had little idea Bukowski
had entertained so many journalists. I ultimately discovered more than
sixty interviews/encounters/profiles, and there are more to be found.
For reasons of length, choices ultimately had to be made and several
articles were of necessity excluded. The selections which follow have
been arranged chronologically according to the actual meeting time
rather than by publication date. Errors and inconsistencies in orthog-
raphy have been corrected. The *High Times* interview by Silvia Bizio
includes four sections from her earlier 1981 *Los Angeles Times* version of
the same conversation which I have spliced into the text.

Many people have helped me in the making of this book. I am
grateful to Sanford Dorbin, *A Bibliography of Charles Bukowski* (Black
Sparrow Press, 1969), Al Fogel, *Charles Bukowski: A Comprehensive Price
Guide and Checklist: 1944–1999* (The Sole Proprietor Press, 2000), Hugh
Fox, *Charles Bukowski: A Critical and Bibliographical Study* (Abyss
Publications, 1969), and Aaron Krumhansl, *A Descriptive Bibliography of
the Primary Publications of Charles Bukowski* (Black Sparrow Press,
1999)—all constant and essential companions. I would also like to
thank John Ahouse, University of Southern California, Doheny
Memorial Library, Specialized Libraries and Archival Collections; Ed
Fields, University of California at Santa Barbara Department of Special
Collections, Davidson Library; Roger Myers, University of Arizona
Library, Special Collections; Eric Stanton and Brian Steimel, Eastern
Michigan University, Bruce T. Halle Library; George Washington
University, Gelman Library; University of Michigan, Ann Arbor,
Hatcher Graduate Library. Jamie Boran and Al Fogel gave generously of
their time and knowledge. Several book dealers supplied rare Bukowski
items: Richard Aaron, Michael Artura, David Barker, Thomas Dorn,
Darlene Fife, Simon Finch, David Gregor, Scott Harrison, Kevin Ring,
Ed Smith, Rob Warren, and Jeffrey Weinberg. Thanks to Maria Beye for
everything. Thanks to John Martin who has been enthusiastic about the

book from the outset. Special thanks to Jorge Luis Borges who keeps me up. Al and Judy Berlinski of Sun Dog Press have been wonderfully helpful through the thousands of labyrinthine details encountered in shaping this book. I am deeply grateful to them for their professionalism and friendship. Thanks to my glorious octogenarian parents Pierre and Mariam Calonne who gave me poetry and sunlight.

—David Stephen Calonne
2003

NOTES

1. Nikos Kazantzakis, *The Saviors of God: Spiritual Exercises*, trans. Kimon Friar, New York: Simon and Schuster, 1960.

2. Alice Miller, *The Drama of the Gifted Child: The Search for the True Self*, trans. Alice Ward, New York: Basic Books, 1981

3. Nat Freedland, "Buk—The Bogart of Poets," *Knight*, September 1969, Vol. 7, No. 5, p. 96.

4. Charles Bukowski, *Notes of a Dirty Old Man*, San Francisco: City Lights Books, 1969, p. 207.

5. D. H. Lawrence, letter to Ernest Collings, 17 Jan., 1913, in *The Letters of D.H. Lawrence*, ed. and with an introduction by Aldous Huxley, London: William Heinemann Ltd., 1934, p. 94.

6. Aristotle, *The Poetics*, Cambridge: Harvard University Press, 1965, pp. 88–91, 1459a.

7. Jonathan Cott, "Reflections of A Cosmic Tourist," in *Conversations with Henry Miller*, ed. Frank L. Kersnowski and Alice Hughes, Jackson: University Press of Mississippi, 1994, p. 200.

8. Charles Bukowski, "nobody but you," from *Sifting Through the Madness for the Word, The Line, The Way*, New York: Ecco, 2003, pp. 393–394.

Charles Bukowski Speaks Out

Arnold Kaye
1963

"Charles Bukowski Speaks Out," Arnold Kaye, *Literary Times* (Chicago), March 1963, Vol. 2, No. 4, pp. 1, 7.

To the interviewer, Charles Bukowski is as the yeti to the Himalayan explorer. He's hard to find and when you've found him, life becomes exceedingly dangerous. It has been said by some, that there is no Charles Bukowski. A persistent rumor for many years declared that those gusty poems signed with his name were actually written by a nasty old lady with hairy armpits.

But yes, there is a Charles Bukowski, existing solitarily in a one-room, murphy-bed, (yes, cold water) apartment in the heart of Hollywood, shadowed on one side by the Bureau of Public Assistance, Old Age Security Office, and on the other by the Kaiser Foundation Hospital. Poor Charles Bukowski, looking like a retired junkie, seems to belong there.

When he answered the door his sad eyes, weary voice and silk dressing gown told me that here was, in more ways than one, a tired man.

We sat and talked, drank beer and scotch, and Charles finally, like a surrendering virgin, gave in to his first interview.

From the window, if you stick your head out far enough, and look hard enough, you can see the lights in Aldous Huxley's house up the hill, where the successful live.

KAYE: Does it bother you that Huxley is in a position to spit on you?

BUKOWSKI: Oh, that is a good question. (He dived into the recess behind the murphy-bed and came out with a couple of pictures of himself).

KAYE: Who took these?

BUKOWSKI: My girlfriend. She died last year. What was the question?

KAYE: Does it bother you that Huxley is in a position to spit on you?

BUKOWSKI: I haven't even thought of Huxley, but now that you mention it, no, it doesn't bother me.

KAYE: When did you start to write?

BUKOWSKI: When I was 35. Figuring the average poet starts at 16, I am 23.

KAYE: It has been observed by a number of critics that your work is frankly autobiographical. Would you care to comment on that?

BUKOWSKI: Almost all. Ninety-nine out of a hundred, if I have written a hundred. The other one was dreamed up. I was never in the Belgian Congo.

KAYE: I would like to make reference to a particular poem in your most recent book, *Run With the Hunted*. Would you happen to have the name and present whereabouts of the girl you mentioned in "A Minor Impulse to Complain"?

BUKOWSKI: No, this is no particular girl; this is a composite girl, beautiful, nylon leg, not-quite-whore creature of the half-drunken night. But she really exists, though not by single name.

KAYE: Isn't that ungrammatical? There seems to be a tendency to classify you as the elder statesman of poet-recluses.

BUKOWSKI: I can't think of any poet-recluses outside of one dead Jeffers. The rest of them want to slobber over each other and hug each other. It appears to me that I am the last of the recluses.

KAYE: Why don't you like people?

BUKOWSKI: Who does like people? You show me him and I'll show you why I don't like people. Period. Meanwhile, I have got to have another beer. (He slouched off into the tiny kitchen and I yelled my next question at him).

KAYE: This is a corny question. Who is the greatest living poet?

BUKOWSKI: That is not corny. That is tough. Well, we have Ezra . . . Pound, and we have T.S., but they've both stopped writing. Of the producing poets, I would say . . . Oh, Larry Eigner.

KAYE: Really?

BUKOWSKI: Yeah, I know no one has ever said that. That is about all I can come up with.

KAYE: What do you think of homosexual poets?

BUKOWSKI: Homosexuals are delicate and bad poetry is delicate and Ginsberg turned the tables by making homosexual poetry strong poetry, almost manly poetry; but in the long run, the homo will remain the homo and not the poet.

KAY: To get down to more serious matters, what influence do you feel Mickey Mouse has had on the American Imagination?

BUKOWSKI: Tough. Tough, indeed. I would say that Mickey Mouse has a greater influence on the American public than Shakespeare, Milton, Dante, Rabelais, Shostakovitch, Lenin, and/or Van Gogh. Which says "What?" about the American public. Disneyland remains the central attraction of Southern California, but the graveyard remains our reality.

KAYE: How do you like writing in Los Angeles?

BUKOWSKI: It doesn't matter where you write so long as you have the walls, typewriter, paper, beer. You can write out of a volcano pit. Say, do you think I could get 20 poets to chip in a buck a week to keep me out of jail?

KAYE: How many times have you been arrested?

BUKOWSKI: How do I know? Not too many; 14-15 maybe. I thought I was tougher than that but each time they put me in it tears my guts; I don't know why.

KAYE: Bukowski, what do you see for the future now that everybody wants to publish Bukowski?

BUKOWSKI: I used to lay drunk in alleys and I probably will again. Bukowski, who is he? I read about Bukowski and it doesn't seem like anything to do with me. Do you understand?

KAYE: What influence has alcohol had on you work?

BUKOWSKI: Hmm, I don't think I have written a poem when I was completely sober. But I have written a few good ones or a few bad ones under the hammer of a black hangover when I didn't know whether another drink or a blade would be the best thing.

KAYE: You look a bit under the weather today.

BUKOWSKI: I am, yes. This is Sunday evening. It was a tough eight race card. I was 103 ahead of the end of 7. Fifty to win on the eighth. Beaten half a length by a 60-1 shot who should have been canned for cat food years ago, the dog. Anyway, a day of minor profit or prophet led to a night of drunkenness. Awakened by this interviewer. And I'm really going to have to get drunk after you leave, and I'm serious.

KAYE: Mr. Bukowski, do you think we'll all be blown up soon?

BUKOWSKI: Yes, I think we will. It is a simple case of mathematics. You get the potential, and then you get the human mind. Somewhere down the line eventually there is going to be a damn fool or madman in power who is simply going to blow us all quite to hell. That's all, it figures.

KAYE: And what do you think is the role of the poet in this world-mess?

BUKOWSKI: I don't like the way that question is phrased. The role of the poet is almost nothing . . . drearily nothing. And when he steps outside of his boots and tries to get tough as our dear Ezra did, he will get his pink little ass slapped. The poet, as a rule, is a half-man—a sissy, not a real person, and he is in no shape to lead real men in matters of blood, or courage. I know these things are anti to you, but I have got to tell you what I think. If you ask questions you have got to get answers.

KAYE: Do you?

BUKOWSKI: Well, I don't know . . .

KAYE: I mean in a more universal sense. Do you have to get answers?

BUKOWSKI: No, of course not. In a more universal sense, we only get one thing. You know . . . a head stone if we're lucky; if not, green grass.

KAYE: So do we abandon ship or hope altogether?

BUKOWSKI: Why these clichés, platitudes? O.K., well, I would say no. We do not abandon ship. I say, as corny as it may sound, through the strength and spirit and fire and dare and gamble of a few men in a few ways we can save the carcass of humanity from drowning. No light goes out until it goes out. Let's fight as men, not rats. Period. No further addition.

This Floundering Old Bastard is the Best Damn Poet in Town

JOHN THOMAS

1967

"This Floundering Old Bastard is the Best Damn Poet in Town," John Thomas, *Los Angeles Free Press*, Vol. 4, No. 9, Issue 137, March 3, 1967, pp. 12–13.

Q: The Kennedy assassination and its attendant phenomena are big news once again. Do you favor any of the current conspiracy theories? Are you even interested?

A: I think you guessed it. I am just about not interested. History, of course, makes a president big news and the assassination of one more so. However, I see men assassinated around me every day. I walk through rooms of the dead, streets of the dead, cities of the dead: men without eyes, men without voices; men with manufactured feelings and standard reactions; men with newspaper brains, television souls and high school ideals. Kennedy himself was 9/10ths the way around the clock or he wouldn't have accepted such an enervating and enfeebling job— meaning President of the United States of America. How can I be over concerned with the murder of one man when almost all men, plus females, are taken from cribs as babies and almost immediately thrown into the masher?

But I must admit that Kennedy, like Roosevelt, had an almost creative force of leadership, but political nevertheless and, in this sense, dangerous as a matter of trust and not at all a stimulative factor as to true fire, growth . . . something to make you feel good, better, bigger, more real. The whole assassination thing—Kennedy—the murder of Oswald—the death of Ruby—all the attending things do seem to STINK of something. Yet it is also possible that the whole was simply a continuous error and erring of humans in moil and unworthiness. The Human Being can be very stupid, especially in the half-light of almost 2,000 years of semi-Christian culture where emotionally barbaric ideals are mixed through with educational systems of learning based upon national, regional, economic and status forces. The development of the Pure Mind in America is almost impossible unless a man is fortunate enough to spend the first 25 years of his life in a madhouse or in some other entombed or untouchable state.

Q: LSD is getting a lot of play now, too. Would you care to add to the heap of . . . ah . . . material already in print on the subject?

A: I think that everything should be made available to everybody, and I mean LSD, cocaine, codeine, grass, opium, the works. Nothing on earth available to any man should be confiscated and made unlawful by other men in more seemingly powerful and advantageous positions. More often than not Democratic Law works to the advantage of the few even though the many have voted; this, of course, is because the few have told them how to vote. I grow tired of 18th century moralities in a 20th century space-atomic age. If I want to kill myself I feel that should be my business; if I want to get hooked on mainline that should be my business. If I go out and hold up gas stations at night to pay for my supply it is because the law inflates a very cheap thing into an escalated war against my nerves and my soul. The law is wrong; I am right.

What more can you do with the dead than kill them? Look at our safe, un-drugged populace now in the buses, at the sporting events, in the supermarkets, and tell me if they are a pleasant sight. And why should the M.D.'s be the dolers-out of the goodies? Aren't they fat enough now? Wealthy enough? Spoiled enough? And, really, don't they make as many mistakes as I do? What good are their books? More often than not, a decade later, they find that they were doing the worst possible thing for the patient, while taking all his money.

My objection to the current LSD-craze-phase-blaze is that it has been taken over by the hippies, the swing-kitties, the dull-heads, as a kind of private stomping ground, as a substitute for soul. It works like this: there is a huge Hare Brain Mass halfway between the Artist and the Common Man. This Hare Brain Mass is essentially rejected by the money-making society (the Common Mass), and although they would like nothing better than to be in with the Common Mass, they cannot make it. So, borrowing a page from the Artist, they say that they reject society. And having stolen one page from the Artist they try for the whole book—but they simply lack the talent to create, because they are essentially sprung from the Common Mass. So they are hung between the C.M. and the Artist, unable to make money, unable to create. Now being unable to doing either of these things is not a crime. But being unable to take the truth, being unable to face an honest mirror, they PLAY AT SOUL, at being IN, bop, boot, beard, beret, hip, pop, anything. Long hair, short skirts, sandals, anything, psychedelic parties, paintings, music, psychedelic grapefruit, psychedelic guerrilla front, pop cups, shades, bikes, yoga, psyche light-sounds, disco, girls are Richards, fuzz now Soap, Kid Goldstein the super-pop new boy, The Jefferson Airplane, Hell's Angels, anything, any damn thing to give them identity, to give them a façade of Being to cover the Horrible Hole. Bob Dylan is their soul: "Something's happening and you don't know what it is, do you, Mr. Jones?", the Beatles are their soul, Judy Collins and Joan Baez are their chambermaids, and Tim Leary is their Elmer Gantry.

> "mariwanna was all right
> but acid, man
> that's the fright"

Now you get busted for acid and you're IN, cabman, you're IN. Or a group of them get down on the floor in a circle and pass the grass and talk about Leary and the good old Left, talk about Andy Warhol, and how horrible the war in Vietnam is, and only a damn fool can hold a job, and who wants to drive?—walking is better. And somebody ought to shoot Johnson. And there are candles on the floor. And the boys are mother's boys and the women are twice-married, twice-divorced, gray, bitter and in their mid-forties. Don't think! Freak-in. Freak-out. Lights. LSD. Leary. Guitars. Love. MAKE LOVE! They screw each other like dry rocks rubbing together. March for Peace. March for the Negro. Burn your draft card. Johnson shot Kennedy.

Not all their ideas are totally without merit, but in the essence of all thinking alike on like subjects they cover the Horrible Hole; they imagine themselves objective, lovable human beings. How can a man who hates war, fights for the Negro, loves dogs and children and folk songs, jazz, wants better government, how can a man (or woman or lesbian or homosexual) be anything but a good juicy human being if he or she stands or sits among candles for these things?—but really they are one big shit-mind of jelly grabbing at LSD like the Holy Cross and making me hate it because their footprints, their mindprints are across my eyesight. Maybe when they move on to their next hype I will test a little acid. Until then, let them wallow in it until they get a pigbellyful.

Q: What do you think about Vietnam, civil rights, the recent spasms on the Sunset Strip, or any equally weighty matter? Rant now, Hank! Who knows how long the Bukowski vogue will last?

A: The Sunset Strip matter resides in the same context as the LSD matter, only here the idiots are a little younger. It is one hell of a mellow Revolution. IT IS A COMFORTABLE REVOLUTION. IT IS A BORED AND YAWNING REVOLUTION OF YOUNG MINDS ALREADY LAID OUT TO REST. If baby gets hurt, angry papa and mama will come get them out, and you cops had BETTER NOT HURT MY BABY. These kids don't look angry, they don't look hungry, they don't look ill-clothed or un-housed. They have to stand along Sunset Strip, a former symbol of wealth and lights. I'd have a lot more for them if they gathered in Boyle Heights. I had a lot more for them when they gathered in Watts. These kids want comfortable kicks. These kids are yawning. They have no center, no platform, no voice, no nothing. Police brutality is all they can think of. I've seen police brutality in jails and in the skid rows of cities that they would never believe possible. What they consider Police Brutality is the gentlest of treading on their soft pink toes. See you on television, girls, next Saturday night. WOW!

Q: Yes, this Charles Bukowski vogue . . . it's definitely forming up. How do you view it?

A: I am not aware of a Charles Bukowski vogue. I am too much of a loner, too much of a crank, too anti-crowd, too old, too late, too leery, too foxy to be sucked in and carried away. This appears to be a third interview within two weeks, but I view it more as a mathematical oddity than a vogue. I hope that I never become a vogue. A vogue is damned and doomed forever. It would mean that there is something wrong with me or something wrong with my work. I think that at the age of 46, having worked eleven years in silence, I think that I am fairly safe. I hope the gods are with me. I think they will be.

But I view even these three interviews in an odd light. I cannot see justification for them. I write poetry. Therefore that poetry should be the stand, the base, the platform in itself. And it doesn't matter a damn what I think of Vietnam, the Strip, LSD, Shostakovich, or anything else. Why should the poet stand as Visionary? But look how many of them have, do and will fuck up. Watch them get on stage so the crowd can view them. Watch them opinionate. Watch them orate. Watch them suck into souls of sponge. To me it is still one man alone in a room, creating Art or failing to create Art. All else is bullshit. I answer these questions in an attempt to let the people know that I want solitude and why I want solitude. Perhaps it will work. Not many people come to my door now. I am grateful. Perhaps less will in the future. This doesn't mean women; I will always lay down my work to lay down a woman. I am not good with the soul here and I don't pretend to be.

At work, 1960s (Courtesy of Linda Bukowski)

Q: Why do you piss away so much time and money at the racetrack?

A: I piss away time and money at the racetrack because I am insane— I am hoping to make enough money so I will not have to work any longer in slaughterhouses, in post offices, at docks, in factories. So what happens? I lost the money I have and am further nailed to the cross. "Bukowski," some people tell me, "you just like to lose, you just like to suffer, you just like to work in slaughterhouses." These people are more insane than I am. The track does help in certain ways—I see the faces of greed, the hamburger faces; I see the faces in early dream and I see the faces later when the same nightmare returns. You cannot see this too often. It is a mechanic of Life. Also, being at the track most of the time, it gives me very little time to write, very LITTLE TIME TO PLAY AT BEING A WRITER. This is important. When I write it is the line I must write. After losing a week's pay in four hours it is very difficult to come to your room and face the typewriter and fabricate a lot of lacy bullshit. But I certainly wouldn't suggest the racetrack as the incubator and inspirer of poetry. I just say it might work for me—sometimes. Like beer, or screwing a good woman, cigars, or Mahler with good wine and the lights out, sitting there naked watching the cars go by. My suggestion to all or any is to stay away from the racetrack. It is one of Man's neatest traps.

Charles Bukowski: The Angry Poet

Michael Perkins

1967

"Charles Bukowski: The Angry Poet," Michael Perkins, *In New York*, Vol. 1, No. 17, 1967, pp. 15–18, p. 30.

Charles Bukowski is one of a handful of really important American poets. In some ways he resembles Russia's Yevtushenko, and in Russia he would be more famous. His books aren't reviewed in the *New York Times*, but his underground reputation is gigantic; he's immensely popular with people who usually don't like poetry. He's as far outside the mainstream of modern poetry as 95% of the American public. Consider: a poet who likes women; who'd rather spend his time in a bar or at the racetrack; a poet who instead of teaching or book reviewing, earns his living in a factory. Fittingly enough (although crazy—now there's an award for everything) he was named "Outsider of the Year" in 1962 by the distinguished New Orleans literary magazine, *The Outsider*—which eventually published his two best known books—*It Catches My Heart In Its Hands*, and *Crucifix in a Deathhand* in beautiful editions.

"The old man" (as he refers to himself—he's 47) here gives us an interview that's as different from most literary interviews as you're apt to see, probably because he wrote it himself. Since it is different (meaty, direct, instead of "which kind of pencil do you use, Mr. Frost?") he quickly passes over such interesting items as: he began writing at 25, made a few sales, then quit for 10 years, and why, one day, he sat down at a typewriter and began poems that were long, Hemingway-tough, completely unformal, and relatively easy to understand, about a world of week-long binges, days at the track, shabby furnished rooms—the underbelly of Los Angeles where he has lived most of his life. Poems that have been praised by Lawrence Ferlinghetti and Henry Miller, and most important, read by an ever-growing audience of people who "don't like poetry."

—Michael Perkins

you say you began writing poetry at 35. why did you wait so long?
now listen, don't get too snotty, I just had 6 teeth pulled today and I'll spit a mouthful of blood on that fat beer-gut. Now I wrote short stories, mostly handprinted until I was 25, then I tore all the stories up and quit. The rejects from the *Atlantic* and *Harpers* got too much, got to be too much, the same slick rejects and then I'd pick up the mags and try to read them and fall asleep. Then, too, starvation in little rooms with fat rats padding about inside and religious landladies padding about outside—it got to be kind of madness, so I just picked up and began sitting around in bars, running errands, rolling drunks, getting rolled, getting shacked with madwoman after madwoman, getting lucky, getting unlucky, getting by, until one day, age 35, I ended up in the charity ward of the L.A. County General Hospital, hemorrhaging my lifeblood up outa my ass and mouth, they let me lay around for 3 days before somebody decided I needed a transfusion. Anyhow, I lived, but when I came out of there my brain felt kind of funny and after 10 years of no writing, I found a typewriter somewhere and began writing these poems. I don't know why, the poems seemed less a waste of time.

some still think your poems are a waste of time.
what isn't a waste of time? Some collect stamps or murder their grand-
mothers. We are all just waiting, doing little things and waiting to die.

do you identify with any of the poets or any of the movements?
no, to me the entire poetic scene seems dominated by obvious and soul-
less and ridiculous and lonely jackasses. From the university groups at
the one end to the beat mob at the other, and also including all those in
betwixt and between. The wonder to me is that I have never heard
anybody say this thing the way I am telling it to you now.

why do you call these people "jackasses"? aren't you being ridiculous?
be careful. Red blood upon that shirt would not look nice. The beats
and the university boys are very similar in that they are being sucked up
by the mob. There are run by the mob, the audience, the image-lovers,
the sick, the weak, the starving puking pansies; I mean starving in the
sense that their souls are covered with pimples and that their heads are
these big airy balloons of bad air. These poets cannot resist the live
applause of the half-people. They go from being creators to being enter-
tainers, they get clannish with the mob and clannish with each other
and very horny for fame. I have more respect for the president of a
factory who decides to lay off 50 men from the assembly line. Oh, those
pukers, oh these purple vomiters, hanging from their heels from the
trees and lisping it to the dead mob!

as long as people love it, what does it matter?
the astigmatism of the thing is the result. What matters is to bring each
single individual truly alive, and as long as the so-called poets and the
mob are hand-holding and conning each other it is not, by god, going to
happen. The mob wants to see a name; they want to see if his teeth are
crooked or if his eyes blink or if he urinates down his legs while he
recites. The mob does not want to stop being weak and dippy, they
rather want wrongness justified, they want to be sung to, conned. So
what happens next? Ah, here you get the hip poet, the real hip kitty bard
from eyebrows to toenails. He's for mary, for LSD. He's against war,
war's a damn dirty thing, don't you see? He's for Castro, he might even
be a communist if it weren't so damned much trouble doing the *work*.
Anyhow, he's with them in *spirit*. He likes jazz, sure. Jazz, man, and all
the variants. Yeah, man. Yeah, dad, hip. Groovy. In-there. He might even

have a guitar in his bedroom. But very seldom a woman. Of course, this is mostly on the beat-end. The university boys are a little more careful. It's still easy for them to be against the war but their politics are more guarded. In fact, everything's guarded. But they too run to the mob and chatter, only in a more dignified and dull manner. They'd rather talk about their poems than read them. They can TALK ABOUT POETRY FOR HOURS, parsing words, holy dictionary nuns, saying nothing at all with great and dull dignity. The mob likes this too—they think that they are getting the inside and they are: the inside of a great phony zero.

wait a minute, instead of talking about "them" let's talk about you. Are you for the war?
hell, no. but I don't make gravy out of the anti-thing. I do not march around holy. If I can write a good poem about life or no-life, if I can create a good poem while sitting in a room alone I can do more to end wars or the war in life (if that's what I want to do and I am not sure what I want to do, I don't exactly ask myself) than I can ever do marching in some parade where we are all going someplace, feeling holy, and trick-mate each other.

would you like to tell us something of what your novel is about?
the novel is about 2 years I lived in a faded green hotel full of faded people. It was during the period that I did not write a word and was trying very hard not to commit suicide. The best way for me to commit suicide was to remain drunk as long as possible—drink is a temporary suicide wherein the user is allowed to return to life, most of the time, that is. There were many in this hotel, in fact the whole hotel full, who were living lives that lasted day to day, night to night, the wine bottle bravado, then right back into the face of the ax with empty pockets, giant landladies and ready alleys. I think that I made every woman in that hotel and there were four floor-fulls, and I even went down into the cellar and got one there, and I also cleaned the slate one night by taking on the old white-haired scrub-woman in her tiny closet room. It was insanity and love and the end of the world. Plus sluggings, police raids, plus days of wondering, very painful wondering, the whole world down there in your gut, Christ, Abe Lincoln, Katzenjammer Kids, the faces on the boulevards, and you heaved your gut, you heaved and you heaved and still lived. Terrible. I am trying to record those days as they

happened, not in story-form, novel-form, but as a record of opening and closing of doors, of empty wine bottles falling over in the middle of the night in their bursting sack, of the rats and the horror, and some of the bravery of the single individual facing extinction without the help of society, God, flag, friend, family. This is the hidden world, this is the world you never read about in your daily paper. I'd like to think that it will be a good novel. But it won't be. It will be a recording. But it will do me good. It will help me to remember. It will help me, I hope, from ever becoming a complete phony.

how do you go about writing your poetry . . . do you get a general idea, work from a line or two, or an image?
this sounds more like a question somebody would ask Robert Creeley rather than Bukowski but I'll try to answer it. It works all ways. But the way it works mostly is that there is simply nothing in my head. I mean that I do not *deliberately* think. I move through. I walk down the street to buy cigars. Mostly I don't see anything. I hear some sounds. Somebody says something senseless, something common. Nothing is working or trying to work. I never think, I am a poet, I am recording. If there is any feeling in me it is simply mostly the feeling (now that I must think about it because you are asking me about it), it is mostly the feeling that there is a lot of white hair in my stomach and that at the back of my head there is a strand of hair that shouldn't be there. What I am trying to say is that I am almost always mostly body without mind—and you'll find a hell of a lot of my critics agreeing with me there. I don't know when I write best or how. Many times it is when I have lost at the race track. I come on in here and there is the typewriter. I sit down. The look of the electric light on the sheet of paper looks good. I think, I am lucky to have an electric light. Then the fingers hit the keys. It is the sound of the keys and the electric light. The words arrive by themselves, without thought, without pressure. I don't know how it works. Sometimes there is a pause and I think that the poem is finished, then it begins again. Sometimes it is one poem, sometimes it is six, sometimes ten. But when it happens it usually comes up with four or six poems. I guess from the way I talk that you might presume that I get a lot of action without effort, and this is true in a sense, and although I told you I walk around empty, this is not always so. Sometimes seeing one face suddenly as that face really is—and it can be mine or somebody

else's—can make me sick all day, all night, until I sleep it off. Or some-times saying something or having something said to me can make me sick, tired, off, all day, all night, until again I sleep it off. In other words, it's easy and it's difficult and it's nothing. I can't truly tell you how I write or why or when or where or anything like that. Because it changes day by day too, along with the rest of me.

it appears to us that you are a "loner," that you detest the crowd, that you detest almost everything.
listen, I can't get alone enough. The crowd is always there—in the slaughterhouse, in the factory, at the racetrack, on the streets. I am against an injustice to any single man but somehow you get all those men in a crowd, stinking and hollering petty things, and I sometimes get the feeling that the Atom Bomb was man's greatest invention. If I can't get away from the crowd I'll never know who they are or who I am. I lean toward Jeffers' manner of working it. Behind a wall, carving it. If you live for 45 years and know it you can write for one thousand years. This is where the Dylans and the Ginsbergs and the Beatles fail—they spend so much time talking about living that they don't have time to live. Dylan Thomas should have been a lesson as to what the American mob can do to the artist. But Christ no, they all leap in and follow suit . . . like, like, well, once I worked in this place and I used to park my car outside and I'd watch the man they called The Pig Man, and The Pig Man has this little canvas slapper and he'd make these pig sounds and rap one with the slapper and all the others would run after the one up the runway and into the blade and I'd watch The Pig Man take out a cigarette and light it, holding his damned canvas slapper under one arm. There's some kind of lesson there.

but aren't you doing the same thing you accuse your fellow artists of doing?
watcha mean?

I mean you're flopping off at the mouth, making statements about art, writing, life, just like the others.
you *asked* for an interview. I'm sure that if you run it that it will not make me very popular. But as long as I can still hit the typer, tomorrow or in an hour, as long as I can swallow a beer without swallowing too much blood, everything will be all right.

any final grand statement, oh great master?
yes, friend, poetry is almost dead, has been for a long time. We have the clans, the lonelyhearts, the name-droppers, but no leader, nobody, and it's a little frightening. You know, Cummings dead, W.C. Williams dead, Frost dead, so forth, and I never believed *much* in them, but they were kind of *there* before I arrived, before we arrived, and you kind of took them for fixtures, you swallowed a lot of it anyhow. And now Pound's kind of evaporated somewhere into Europe and we are all thrown pretty much back upon ourselves. It isn't a very nice picture. And no heavy genius showing through. It's like being at a carnival with night coming down. Ginsberg can't write anymore. Lowell is too practiced and, finally, dull. Shapiro talks about what is needed but doesn't supply it. Olson and Creeley are only the extension of a lot of dank and involuted yawn. Say, even Pound's *Cantos* would hardly stop a man from committing suicide, and what good is Art if it can't help a man go on living? What good is—

listen, Bukowski, I think we have enough now. But do you think your writing has helped men go on living?
it has helped *me* to go on living.

pardon me, but you don't look too well.
I told you, I just had 6 teeth pulled. By the way, do you have a car?

yes.
my car won't start. Drop me off at the liquor store.

sure.

Bukowski spit out a huge mouthful of blood upon his rented rug and we moved out.

The Living Underground: Charles Bukowski

HUGH FOX
1969

"The Living Underground: Charles Bukowski," Hugh Fox, *The North American Review*, Fall 1969, pp. 57–58.

Charles Bukowski is the acknowledged King of the Underground. He's been published in such diverse places as *Kauri, Epos, The Beloit Poetry Journal, Evergreen Review* and *Poetry Northwest*. In 1966 he was elected "Outsider of the Year" by *Outsider* mag (then in New Orleans) and ever since then the underground has looked to him as a kind of spiritual leader.

My first contact with him was in 1966 when I came across a copy of *Crucifix in a Deathhand* in the Free Press Bookshop in L.A. I wrote to the publishers (Loujon Press, now in Tucson) and they gave me his address—Los Angeles. I dropped him a line, invited myself over and he responded—OK.

I had the idea of doing a critical study of Buk so I went over with my tape-recorder, scholarly and impractical, only to find out that he didn't open up that way, in front of a mike—and especially when there was a repair job going on in the street outside and his whole little apartment was filled with the whams and bams of air hammers. And besides it was during the day, and as I found out later the Bukowski inner self doesn't operate when the sun's up.

So I came back, left the tape recorder at home and started talking to him man to man. He was born in 1920 and looks about twice his age. The whole lower part of his face is pock-marked from a serious case of acne he had years back, so serious, in fact, that they had to drill into the boils and squeeze out the pus. He works in the post office at night sorting mail, drinks everything that isn't nailed down, and is sagging, broken down, melting. You expect him to keel over—but he doesn't . . . won't!

The thing that most impresses me about him is the absolute clarity and control of his mind. Never misses a trick, knows where and who and why he is at any given moment, never gets disconnected or wanders . . . "drunk." He's always there, watching with his old lion eyes. Relax . . . but not too much.

When women are around he has to play Man. In a way it's the same kind of "pose" he plays at in his poetry—Bogart, Eric Von Stroheim. Whenever my wife Lucia would come with me to visit him he'd play the Man role, but one night when she couldn't come I got to Buk's place and found a whole different kind of guy—easy to get along with, relaxed, accessible. No big "front."

The same kind of duality goes on in his poetry. I hate to say that the "real" Bukowski is a Bretonish surrealist, although there is a Bukowski who gets surrealistic and writes about the day it rained at the L.A. country museum, about the Nor'wester that "ripped the sheets like toenails," about an "Alkaseltzer Mass." The other Bukowski is all 300 pound whores (or any variety of whore), rundown bars, rundown apartments, beer, the D.T.'s, jail, slugging it out, screwing . . . this is the Great American Myth Bukowski, a latter-day Mark Twain (the irreverent Mark Twain) all rolled up into one, and it's this Bukowski that the young poet studs have hooked on to. The other Bukowski, a little scholarly, a little erudite, very "playful" with reality, has been put in the closet.

One night I was over at Buk's house and Darrell (just Darrell, it's all the name he seems to need) of Glendale was over visiting. He was with a friend. Had just published Buk's *Poems Written before Jumping Out of an Eighth Story Window*, one of the best collections of Buk's work ever put together in a single volume. Darrell was talking about "communication." He's an up-tight guy and was especially up-tight that night. He wanted to talk artsy-craftsy and Buk wouldn't buy it, kept saying, "I don't read you man, what the hell are you saying, why don't you say what you wanna say, man, say it for crissake, just say it . . . ." Only Darrell didn't get mad, took it, accepted it. The barroom Buddha was speaking, you had to accept. And that's the attitude of most of the younger poets—

especially those of the "meat" school, guys like Steve Richmond and Doug Blazek (Blaz).

For my own part, though, it's the really hallucinatory Bukowski that I dig, the Bukowski that writes when he's gone beyond pose and is hanging to the reality roller-coaster for dear life. The worst kind of poses are the "real" ones.

The last time I saw Bukowski was in June of 1968. I'd just copied out his fabulous bibliography on cards (he'd lent me all his magazine publications—in suitcases), and I was bringing the last suitcase back. He'd told me about his "old lady," someone he hadn't married, but had had a kid by, a kid he loved a lot. There were toys around his place. A sometimes-kid-presence was there. I knew he'd been bugged recently in the post office because he was writing his "Memoirs of a Dirty Old Man" for *Open City* . . . or at least that's what he told me the cause was. My wife and I had figured out that "the old lady" was putting the heat on and the "Memoirs" were just a pretext for the post office authorities to snoop into Buk's personal life. Anyhow, there she was, long almost-white hair braided, hanging down her back, wearing one-thonged Japanese sandals, kind of hatchet-faced, red, oily-skinned, belligerent.

"I'm Hugh Fox," I said, putting down the suitcase of mags.

"Yeah, that's what I figured," she said and went into the next room.

My wife was with me, and wanted to stay, kind of invited herself.

"We'll just stay a few minutes."

"Come on," I said.

Bukowski didn't say to stay. He looked a little embarrassed, like he didn't know exactly *what* to say. The Old Lady's Control Waves were coming out through the walls. He wasn't fooling anyone, was as meek as a castrated timber wolf.

Finally, I gave Lucia a pinch. And she gave in.

"Take it easy," I said to Buk.

"You too," answered "umble" Bukowski, then added—referring to my critical study of his work, "Try Martin with the book. Don't fart around. He's a good man."

And that was it—we left.

Looking for the Giants: An Interview with Charles Bukowski

WILLIAM J. ROBSON AND JOSETTE BRYSON

1970

"Looking for the Giants: An Interview with Charles Bukowski," William J. Robson and Josette Bryson, *Southern California Literary Scene,* Vol. 1, No. 1, December 1970, pp. 30–46.

This is the first in a series of interviews with established and emerging figures on the Southern California Literary scene. Author and poet Charles Bukowski, perhaps best remembered for his columns in the late Los Angeles underground weekly Open City *and who will see his novel* Post Office *appear in bookstores this month, agreed to be the first interviewee.*

On one afternoon in early November Josette Bryson a former associate editor of the quarterly, ANTE *(and now a Ph.D. candidate and an associate in French in the French Department of UCLA) accompanied me to Charles Bukowski's apartment not far from Sunset Boulevard in central Los Angeles.*—WJR

BR: To start off—when and where were you born?

BUK: Andernach, Germany, in 1920. The FBI asked me that once. I was brought to LA at the age of two. Went to Virginia Road grammar school. I'm an LA guy, really. LA High School. LA City College. I didn't graduate—I just had a good time. I took the courses I liked, you know. The old man never knew. I was there two years—from 1939 to 1941.

BR: Any aptitude for writing show up to that time?

BUK: I was doing some writing but I just didn't feel that I was ready. I knew right then that it was bad. It was not what I wanted it to

be. Right after I had my first story published in *Story* magazine—"Woodbury Nut."

BR: Didn't Norman Mailer publish there?

BUK: Yes—Saroyan—that was the magazine of the day, then. It was
the thing. Once you hit *Story* you were supposed to be "ready." So
I got a letter from an agent—I was in New York at the time—
she said "I want to be your agent on further work," and I said
"I'm not writing. I'm not ready yet. I just happened to hit one
time—and it was a bad story."

BR: How old were you at the time?

BUK: I was 24.

BR: During those years, was there any particular teacher that you
liked—who brought you out?

BUK: No, I disliked them all. I always used to get a D in English. The
teacher liked my writing but the class began at 7 o'clock in the
morning. I always had a hangover and I showed up at 7:30 every
morning. I just couldn't make it. He finally said "Mr. Bukowski,
there isn't any use in you showing up anymore—you'll get your
grade." I said, "alright."

BR: Anybody around then that turned you on to things.

BUK: You mean living people?

BR: Yes.

BUK: No, there wasn't anybody around.

BR: No resident gurus here in the basin at that time?

BUK: No, no, I liked Saroyan—like anybody else, early Hemingway,
Céline . . . Dostoevsky. Kafka . . .

JO: Vittorini—the Italian writer?

BUK: Who's that? Oh, is he the one who wrote dozens and dozens of
novels?

JO: Yes, he wrote the very famous one, *Conversation in Sicily*.

BUK: I could never read his stuff. I used to go in the library and there'd be about 10 or 12 of his books all lined up together. I'd say "how can he do it?" He was either very good or very bad.

JO: I think he's very good, myself.

BUK: Yes, well . . . After I published in *Story* and *Portfolio,* which was edited by Caresse Crosby I gave up writing for ten years and I just got drunk and lived and moved around—and lived with some bad women and ended up in the LA county hospital death ward with blood gushing forth—hemorrhages. And when I came out of there I started writing again. I don't know why. In those ten years I didn't write at all—let's just say I lived. Gathered material, not consciously, though. I'd forgotten all about writing.

BR: What kind of poetry did you write at the time?

BUK: It was personal—action things—things that had happened to me, personally. Rather subjective and maybe a little bit bitter.

BR: Have you been successful in rendering the *major* personal experiences in your life?

BUK: Right now I've been through that although I still write them down as these things keep happening, but my poetry is now becoming—a little bit different. I'm playing with words more but I try to keep them simple—but I'm going more into feeling than experience—my feeling about things rather than direct experience. There's a change—we have to change—we don't *have* to but we feel like it.

BR: Have those experiences you have had affected your craft directly—with force enough to turn your craft into new channels. Have those experiences affected your underlying *mood*— rather than the *subject* of your poetry?

BUK: That's an involved question—you can't separate your experiences from your writing, I don't care who you are. One creates the other—they go together in other words. That's all you have—your experience.

BR: . . . Some of these major personal experiences, did you, say, write sagas about them—or maybe didn't write about them—but maybe they kind of affected the tilt of the ship, so to speak?

BUK: I wrote about them directly to begin with—now I'm tilting the ship, shall we say. In other words now I'm writing about feeling now rather than "I did this or I did that." Now I'm writing more about how I *feel.*

BR: What other poets have influenced you generally, in your life— have turned you on?

BUK: Robinson Jeffers . . .

BR: Some people accuse him of being too severe, too austere—too much by himself, you know, and not "with it" in a way and yet, gosh, I find—what poetry reading I've done recently—that he's just wonderful, that's all.

BUK: Power. He simply had it—has it—well, he's dead. How does one say it? Has it? *Had* it?

BR: He didn't seem to be so much a social commentator, of course, I mean he wasn't—per se—he was more like a dark historic figure, the feeling I get from the poetry I *have* read—but the sense of—if you know anything about the ocean—even walking along it—just the sense—he *knew.*

BUK: All of his figures kind of finally smashed up against the land-scape. Always fascinating—they were very conscious of life. They were blood-filled creatures and they finally, you know, usually came to a bad end. He was better on his longer narrative poems. When he wrote the short ones he tended to preach a little bit. He influenced me a great deal with his simple lines— his simple *long* lines. Using the precise language, you know, not "pretty language"—just *saying* it. And that's what I've been trying to do, keep it simple without . . . keeping it clear. Poeticism. Too much poeticism about the stars and the moon when it's not properly used is a bunch of bad hash.

BR: I've been getting quite a bit of material lately. Some of it I've enjoyed. It's been, what I call—if I can remember Dylan

Thomas—sort of a play on words. Like "ponies mounting the night." You can *feel* the words.

BUK: Thomas was one of the few who could get away with what I call ultra-poeticism. It would be a very rare creature to be a Thomas. He just used everything he wanted to use. And he got away with it. He was poetic but—he got away with it—you know what I mean by poetic.

BR: I've been getting a lot of "bald, crying windows" and that type of thing, which is kind of entertaining and nice. That phrase just came out of my head.

BUK: I have a magazine, too, *Laugh Literary*, and I get some pretty bad stuff.

JO: Were you influenced at all by the French poets and/or German?

BUK: Villon—would you call him French—is that the way you pronounce that?

JO: Villon?

BUK: The thief.

JO: Oh, yes.

BUK: They ran him out of Paris.

JO: Yes, in the Middle Ages.

BUK: He was about the only one. You know, I can't pronounce these names because I have no formal . . .

JO: Baudelaire, Rimbaud?

BUK: I don't care for either one of them.

JO: What about the modern ones like . . . Cocteau, for instance.

BUK: Oh well, he's not too modern.

JO: No, he's not too modern, no.

BUK He wrote a lot of prose, too, didn't he?

JO: Yes. St. John Perse?

BUK: No. I just don't care for the French.

JO: Eluard?

BUK: No.

BR: Rimbaud turned me on.

BUK: He's fairly popular here.

BR: Henry Miller wrote a critique, *The Time of the Assassins*—I thought, wow! The thought of that person being so powerful at the age of 18 or 19 and then dropping it—simply going off into something else.

BUK: I can understand *that*.

BR: Why?

BUK: Writing itself—too many people take it as such a *romantic* goddamned thing. I've known a lot of writers and they're not very—human people I don't think. They're edgy and jumpy and their art is destroying them.

BR: Why is it? It's just like a battery taking off so much juice if you're going to be a good writer—it sucks away the power—the human power and leaves you dessicated. So what are you going to do? Sometimes. Not always.

BUK: Well, *most* of the time I would say writers are not very nice people. I'd rather talk to a garage mechanic who's eating a salami sandwich for lunch. In fact, I could *learn* more from him. He's more human. Writers are a bad lot. I try to stay away from them.

BR: You *do* look in the mirror, though?

BUK: Uh.

JO: What do you think about Jean Genet?

BUK: Genet started very well, didn't he?

JO: Yes, *very* well.

BUK: With his prison stuff. Right now, though, he's become quite a showman. This Black Panther thing. Coming all the way over from France. I know some black fellows and frankly, from the inside, they resent this. It's not known to the press and all that. Big black fellow here, 6'4 280 "killer" sitting on the couch with a bottle of beer and he says "Bukowski, we don't like that Frenchman trotting all the way over here from France and

45

telling us, you know, or helping us or saying what's wrong or what's right. He really doesn't know because he hasn't been here." He's on stage. Well, being homosexual sometimes makes people that way. Or writers start as good writers and then they become politicians or they feel they have to be *leaders* of some sort. The Ezra Pound fascist thing and all that. They become prophets—and they usually become lousy ones.

BR: That's why when I think of Southern California Lit *Scene*—I'm kind of afraid of a sort of literary politics getting into it in some way—I don't want to somehow have readings suddenly pop up you know—or make, or encourage a kind of quasi-showman type of thing. Encouraging it, in other words.

BUK: I don't think that it *needs* much encouraging. When I think of the Southern California literary *scene* nothing much comes to mind.

BR: Why is it—and this always bugs me—but I always had the feeling that Berkeley is a live-wire place. When I was working as a salesman out of town I used to come down to Berkeley and the bookstores and I just grooved on it. Berkeley seemed to be a live, pulsating place the same way as the Left Bank. I don't know if it's because here in LA we're all stretched out geographically, or what, but we lack something.

BUK: You can find a writer anywhere. Well, like Haight-Ashbury. A friend of mine—I won't mention him by name—he was a good writer, when he started. He was back east and he dragged his whole family out here to come to Haight-Ashbury. You know, at the time it was *the* place. I said "Good Lord, man, that isn't the thing for a writer to do. You're going right toward the flame. You're doing the obvious. Stay where you are. Stay in your wheat fields and—you know, in your factory—continue to write." Well, he ran on out there. And that just about ended him. A writer has to be individual, has to—be some kind of a monster thing. You have to hold your own ground. You don't trot *after* things. (We're making rules here).

BR: Of course, if you have a little bit of the journalist in you you're apt to do that, aren't you? To go where the action *seems* to be. Particularly if you're young.

BUK: Yeah. But action is anywhere. You can open the door and it's right there. It'll come to you—it comes to me. I just sit here and it comes through the door. I never go anywhere.

BR: What do you think of workshops and groups and so forth?

BUK: I think they're horrible.

BR: But you do appear at them, don't you?

BUK: I give poetry readings—for money. Strictly survival. I don't like to do it but I quit my job last January 9 and now I've become what you'd call a literary hustler. I do things now that I wouldn't have done before—one of them is giving poetry readings. I don't like to do it at all. As far as workshops go I call them lonely hearts clubs. They're mostly a bunch of bad writers that get together and they—a leader arises, self-chosen, mostly, and they read this stuff to each other and generally they overpraise each other and it's more destructive than it is helpful, because the stuff bounces back when they send it out and they say "My God, when I read that to the group the other night everybody said that it was a work of genius."

BR: Oh, I had things pointed out to me, though, in my own work that was later affirmed by my own agent back in New York. I think that you can get a perceptive leader sometimes.

BUK: You can get good criticism but it's rare in those groups. It's generally a lonely hearts type of thing. People go there for sexual contact and various reasons. The best way to learn how to write is to read good writers and to live. That's all you have to do. You don't need a group.

BR: I was telling Josette, driving over here from UCLA that as far as parts of speech are concerned—breaking up the language—it's always been hard for me, but I used to make A-plusses on my essays and all that. But it was largely because I *read* so much. I got the nuance and picked up seismographically the . . . my writing was just sort of like playing the banjo by ear—if you read a lot of good writing it's bound to get through.

BUK: That's true.

JO: That's not enough, though.

BUK: No, you have to *live*. But there's nothing like reading good writers. When I was first starting I'd find myself writing very badly, I would go out and pick up a book by D.H. Lawrence—who outside of *Kangaroo* and a few other things he wrote very quickly for money—always tightened up my writing and made it less sloppy. I don't need him anymore. In fact, he bores me now. But at the time he didn't. We change our perception about writers, you know, as we go along. I remember when I thought Thomas Wolfe was the greatest thing—you know, when I was young. I'd say: "Good Lord, what a man he was!" Now I read his stuff and I say: "Overdramatic . . . just terrible." I don't even have the words.

BR: Just like an airplane running down the runway and not quite getting enough wind before the flaps to take off—a lot of power but it's just like the propeller blades weren't quite—cutting into it, you know.

BUK: You put it very well, there, yes.

BR: I think that when I first began reading him I thought, gee, he must be 75 years old or 68—his depth and perception and his knowledge—and yet now I feel the same way about him. I think now had he lived beyond 38, or that age—had he gotten through that—had he actually married this character, this gal that he was running around with—had he had some major experience that shot him down—or think had he lived into the second World War or say, still be living today, I think his writing would have changed—it would have *had* to, or—get out of it altogether.

BUK: It *was* changing. His last book—was—not—he didn't wander all over the place, which was interesting at first, you know. But yet it was dull. Even though he tightened it up, it was dull. Well, there's no telling. Some people can only write when they're young.

BR: In your own instance, what's the hardest part about mechanically creating a poem? Does the poem generally begin with you. Do you do the whole draft first—at one sitting, more or less, or does it kind of congeal . . .

BUK: You don't even think about it—one day you come home from the race track—usually it's better if you *lose* a hundred dollars. And you just open up your beer and sit down and you start writing a poem. I usually write ten or fifteen at once and then the next morning I'll look at them and I'll say, well, "these won't do at all and these other six I'll have to drop out certain lines—and the other three are OK the way they are." So it's a kind of trick I've learned as I go along. I never used to change things, you know, when I first started, but now when I—I'm more objective, I suppose—well, that's a *bad line*—that's terrible!

BR: When you say ten or fifteen at the same time, are they all more or less on the same track?

BUK: No, they're all on different subjects. I let the stuff build up and then it takes a certain thing to trigger them and they all come out. Like I say, losing a hundred dollars at the track is a great help to the art.

BR: Do you find that racing is a great help to your income?

BUK: Is the income tax man listening? Let us say that lately, since the harness meet has opened, I've been going out there and making a living at it. But until the last month or so—I'd say for the whole year I'm in the hole, I'm minus. But lately I've been doing quite well—maybe because I *have* to.

BR: Is it actually objectively studying the horses in a situation?

BUK: No, there's a certain method I've learned and . . . I'm not going to tip my hand. But it's very good if I stick with it.

JO: You used to work at the post office, didn't you?

BUK: Yes. I worked three years as a letter carrier and I took two years off at other little odd jobs. I married a millionairess in between—just by accident. When I came out of the hospital you know, I wrote about fifty poems. I said: "What will I do with these things?" So I looked in *Trace* magazine and said "Well, I might as well send them and *insult* somebody." So I looked and I found this magazine called *Harlequin* in this little town in Texas and I said, "this is probably an old woman—she doesn't like dirty words or this type of poetry," you know. She probably likes rhymes and lives in a little rosy hut with canaries—I think I'll wake her up and see what happens." I mailed this big packet of stuff—I always remember dropping it in the mailbox. A letter came back. A big fat one, informing me I was a GENIUS. And they published forty of them. Turned out to be a beautiful young lady who was going to inherit a million or so. I didn't know it, of course. And we corresponded back and forth. We finally met, got married, and *then* I found out when we went to her home town that, uh, she *owned* the place. But it didn't work out. I dropped the million. But you were asking about the post office—I got a little off, there—I did three as a carrier—then I met the lady—and then I did eleven years as a clerk. And I just quit this January 9th and I've turned into a literary hustler.

JO: I know that, because I know somebody who knows you very well. Do you know anybody by the name of Werner? He teaches at UCLA.

BUK: I might.

JO: He's dark, sort of short . . .

BUK: He's French?

JO: Right.

BUK: Yeah. I used to call him Frenchy. Yes, I know him.

JO: He just adores you.

BUK: Oh, he does, does he? He acts like he wants to spit on me. Yeah, I have a beer with him now and then. He's alright. Yes—I had to give up the post office job because it was killing me, really. So I wrote a novel, *Post Office*. It's going to be published here and in Germany. Black Sparrow Press will be the English publisher and Kiepenheuer & Witsch will publish it in the German.

JO: Who's going to translate it?

BUK: Carl Weissner—he translated my book *Notes of a Dirty Old Man* into German—*Notes* originally appeared in the old LA *Open City*. The Germans love me for some reason—they like my stuff. I'm very popular in Germany.

BR: I liked some of your columns in *Open City*—but some were like—ahh, well—then I'd come across one like "The Frozen Man" and it was great.

BUK: Well, you know I wrote one a week whether I felt like writing or not. It was good discipline. *Notes* in book form was quite a thrill to me. Very nicely done. And it was reviewed in *Der Spiegel* which has a wide circulation—It's a kind of German *Newsweek*. Got good reviews. *Post Office* will be out in December, Christmas. It's about fourteen years of hell. But I didn't write it in—what shall we say—a bitchy style. It's mostly humorous, but there's a lot of pain in there—I tried to keep from getting emotional about it—just tried to record it as it happened. Some very funny and tragic things happened in those years.

BR: By the way, this brings me to something else here. What's the best kind of vocational background for a poet today? Do you know any good poets who teach in the colleges? Would you recommend that a young fellow go to a college and take a degree and teach?

BUK: In the old days, I'd say no. But it seems there's a new breed coming up now in the English Departments who are quite good writers. They surprise me. Most of them have just *become* professors. I know one, his name is Bix Blaufuss. He's published in *Laugh Literary*. He teaches English and he writes *very* well. There's also another one teaching at California State College at Long Beach—Gerald Locklin.

BR: He's appearing in this first issue.

BUK: He's *very* good.

BR: Yes, I think he is.

JO: Do you know Hirschman?

BUK: Yes, I know him. He *used* to teach English.

JO: At UCLA.

BUK: His writing varies too much. He's changing styles. Let's see, Locklin—he dresses in ragged clothes—and he looks more like a student than a teacher—he's still very human—Locklin and Blaufuss both.

BR: Same description applies?

BUK: Yeah. They're very loose. More like students than teachers. And they're very human, but I tell them both "they're gonna get at you guys and this is just the beginning, you know. So be careful before you get involved in campus politics and you become swallowed up into a new situation."

BR: They might sort of melt down . . .

BUK: Melt down, yes, that's the word. But so far they're right there. So they're not guilty, yet.

BR: Karl Shapiro—I think he wrote an article in *Library Journal* which was excerpted in the *LA Times*. He thinks that students today really don't read like they used to in an earlier generation and . . .

BUK: *He* doesn't read—or the students?

BR: The students.

BUK: Well, I suppose he knows more about that than I do.

BR: Do you sense that students aren't reading as much?

BUK: I guess not as much, no. I have a friend, Steve Richmond, who was going to try something—he and I wrote poems on boards. Seven feet by three and one half feet. We hung them by ropes. He's a very strange guy, though. I went by his little shop the other night when I went to see my little girl and he'd taken the boards down. The idea was to *get* people to read again—by making it large enough and easy enough for them to *see*. But he's very changeable. He ripped the boards down. I don't know what he did with them—burned them or floated them out in the ocean for the fish.

BR: Does he still have his shop?

BUK: Yeah, but it's empty, there's nothing in there. Very strange sort ...

BR: I was sort of hoping that we'd drop down and see it.

BUK: Richmond's quite a writer too. Or used to be—he's not writing much now.

BR: Speaking of your child ...

BUK: She's six—this wasn't from the marriage to the Millionairess.

Steve Richmond

BR: What's her name?

BUK: Marina. I dedicated one of my books to her.

BR: Does she want to be a poet—or a poetess?

BUK: I hope not.

BR: What do you think of the poetry scene today—generally and locally?

BUK: Well, at this stage of existence this is a very bad time for creation. Very little is being done. It's a very dry, do nothing period. There aren't any giants—there isn't any force—it's very nil. There isn't any power anywhere. That's what I feel about it.

BR: Ward S. Miller, the chairman of the English Department at the University of Redlands says that there's abundant material here in Southern California. "I know many of the writers, some of them quite well," he tells me, and that among his own students "there are a dozen past and present who write quite brilliantly."

BUK: I can't agree with that at all. It just seems to me a very deserted time. We always used to have giants, you know—even a while back. When I was a kid, in my twenties, there was always somebody to look up to—Hemingway, W.H. Auden—he's still alive, but, you know, not writing anymore. Well, there were always these *giants* about. You could pick up *Poetry Chicago* and you'd really get a lift. There was T.S. Eliot at his best—there were always these *powerhouses* around. Now, my God, you look around—it's all flab—there's nothing to look up to—there's nothing around . . .

BR: Do you think maybe nostalgia enters into that, a little?

BUK: No. These boys had it, that's all.

BR: Well, of course, different times, different people. Here we've had sort of an explosion of paperbacks—maybe marketing has had something to do with it, too—so many people have had educations since World War II, so many people coming on and we've gone into a sort of print explosion. Do you think this may have affected . . .

BUK: Well, still it should not "affect" a good writer from being great, you know. Like you take Mailer—he's supposed to be tops. I can barely read him. Somebody put something on me called *Cannibals and Christians*. He's writing about Eisenhower and this and that, and ugh, Good God, it's just terrible.

BR: He did seem, though, to kind of want to probe—when he made the big uproar in *Naked and the Dead* he was in his early twenties . . .

BUK: He *did* write *The Naked and the Dead*.

BR: He did seem to kind of—I did admire him though, for trying to get in and dig and probe . . .

BUK: After *The Naked and the Dead* it was over.

BR: But doesn't he have the prophetic quality about him—the Jewish prophetic quality of—what was it—the Jewish prophet that wails in the wilderness and tries to point out what's happening to civilization—and the Jewish people have *sometimes done* that.

BUK: I don't know.

BR: . . . Although I got the feeling in later years that he might have gotten kind of wrapped within himself, or . . .

BUK: A little bit spoiled.

BR: Yeah, tumbled to the publicity . . .

BUK: Yeah, he got hooked onto the thing. Publicity can spoil a man, really.

BR: Do you think this is what actually happened to Hemingway, that he actually was affected—insulated in some way by his publicity? I often wondered if he might not have been healthier and happier if he had simply (after reading that book, *Papa Hemingway*) . . .

BUK: He tried to get away from that, you know. But also Hemingway had this built-in suicide complex that he was fighting against all of his life. He knew that his writing wasn't what it used to be. *The Old Man and the Sea* was supposed to be a comeback but it wasn't—it was just a recopy of his tighter style. It wasn't as original—it wasn't his feeling at the moment. And that was his attempted comeback and when the critics agreed with him— felt that he'd make it with *The Old Man and the Sea*—I think that he felt a letdown that people were so easy to fool. And, he drank a great deal, you know, and that can make a man depressed, continual drinking.

BR: Do you think he'd been better off simply—getting away?

BUK: There's no getting away, finally. They'll track you down. They told me people bother Henry Miller—Webb told me this—he wouldn't let 'em in and they set a camp on his front lawn, set a *tent* out there. Just camped out for three or four days.

BR: Here, recently?

BUK: Yeah, I don't know how recently. Well—this can be kind of frightening. I consider myself damned fortunate. I've been left alone, and whether my stuff is good or bad, I'm making it, you know—I'm surviving, but so far I haven't been *played* with too much. I consider myself very lucky. Of course, I could use a million dollars and be spoiled!

BR: This is in line with one thing I've thought myself. I've sold advertising as a vocation for many years and I think, well, I'd like to get back into freelance work. Oh, say like a story I'm doing on a Glendale veterinarian who has two-way vest-pocket walky-talkies and a closed circuit TV to benefit his clients and I just groove on that—and I think that this kind of modest, quiet writing is the best way to go. Especially if you enjoy photography as well—to enter it that way—and yet on the other hand that doesn't touch the strings all the way up and down. Awareness—you'd like to do basic essays on consciousness and so forth, you know, if I can be so broad as to . . .

BUK: That doesn't sell too well though, does it?

BR: What do you think the freelance market is generally like now— of course trade and house organs don't have anything to do with you—but have you heard?

BUK: Freelance markets, since we've had this little recession thing have become pretty tough. Lots of editors are writing their own material now and they're using a backlog of material they've already bought or many magazines that used to pay in advance are now paying on publication and things have really tightened up.

BR: Do you think there are more people getting into the market because of the recession—maybe they're sitting around the house with nothing to do and they pick up a camera or a pen or a pencil . . .

BUK: No, I don't think so. It's just that the editors themselves have tightened the thing up.

BR: Not because there are more freelancers flooding the field?

BUK: Now, they might be because they have nothing else to do, it's possible, but you can't call that competition. In other words, that has nothing to do with the situation. I do write for sex mags— I make a little money on the side. I write exactly what I want to—like, you know, *Notes of a Dirty Old Man*. If there's a sex scene in it, I can sell it to them, if there isn't, I can't. I still get little assignments from newspapers. One offered to pay me forty dollars for four columns—forty per column. So I wrote the four columns in one night.

BR: That's the underground press?

BUK: No, it's a kind of "dirty" pink sheet. That's a good night's work. One hundred sixty bucks. I still continue to write poems and *good* stories. They put me in the back because it's really not vile enough.

BR: Do you think we're getting into more of this generally because of being in a sort of dead time? The general trend to pornographic?

BUK: Well, nudism and sex has become kind of a new discovery nowadays. Like it's something we never knew about before. We've discovered it now. Up on Hollywood Boulevard here they have several little places called "adult theatres." Costs five dollars to get in them and I don't know what goes on in there but they're all over the place. Some woman in a liquor store—I was buying my six-pak and she said to me "What's this world coming to—all these little adult theatres around?" and I said "Well lady you don't *have* to go in there—you can walk by them." She didn't like this. I said "I don't go there."

BR: You must still have some family in Germany, don't you?

BUK: I have an uncle in Andernach—he's eighty years old. We wrote for a while and then I told him that *Notes of a Dirty Old Man* was out in German and told him where to get it—and he hasn't written since. I've been glancing through the book here and saw the name Salinger. One I forgot—he's pretty damned good.

JO: What happened to him?

BUK: I haven't heard anything about him—just stopped, I guess. He's very good. Sometimes they do stop. The good ones stop—the bad ones just keep on writing.

BR: When is the next issue of *Laugh Literary* due out?

BUK: Number 3 will be out around February—we have some pretty good poems. I always want to give it up but I keep getting poems that I like and I say, "somebody really should publish these." I'm a romantic, after all.

JO: Well, it's true, these people should be made known . . .

BUK: Well, it's strange, most of the stuff that I get in the mail is very, very bad, you know. I open these envelopes very reluctantly—and once in a while you get that surprise. Like there's a fellow that sent me something called "Barnett's Castle," and I said "my

God, this guy is *good!*" So I wrote him and I said "I've never heard of you" and he said "well I used to write and I've been in business fifteen years and I've started writing again." Well, very strange situation there. There are some strange people out there who *can* write. I mean, they're not great writers but they write very well. So I have to keep accepting that fact and it's OK.

BR: Do you remember your foreword to Steve Richmond's *Hitler Painted Roses*—Earth Poet Series 1—? It was great, and significant. I have a couple of passages, here: "There is just one man thrown upon the earth, belly-naked, and seeing with his eye. Yes, I said 'eye'. Most of us are born poets. It is only when our elders get to us and begin to teach us what they teach us that the poet dies."

BUK: Yeah. That's true. Do you need any explanation?

BR: No. "Our poets and statesmen, our loves have left us very little that we can trust." I also felt that one, in a way.

BUK: It's like children. You know they're very brilliant between the ages of three and four and one half. They can sit and tell you things. They're like ancient philosophers because they haven't been taught anything yet from the outside. They have this knowledge that's already there—they're *born* with it and it hasn't been tinkered with yet. I used to have some marvelous conversations with my little girl when she was three or three and one half. She would *stun* me with the things she would say, and I've heard another friend of mine tell me the same thing. But then you send them to school and they all become alike, you know. Like my little girl drew a picture the other day—somebody sent *her* some crayons. She'd just entered the first grade. So the picture she drew was a little girl and she had an American flag in each hand. I said, "well, they didn't waste much time with her." But she had one of the flags wrong, she had the blue out by the edge instead of by the pole. I'm not exactly anti-American—I'm just saying they didn't waste much time. Give me a three year old kid and I can really have an interesting conversation.

BR: Do you think the world is actually heading through a sort of change—there's a great deal of discussion about the psychedelic revolution yet and some feel, as I do, that there is evidence, in a way, of the splitting of the chromosomes of the generations. That if we're faced with World War III and the threat of a complete blackout through the atomic bomb that perhaps the younger generation is separating themselves—as they seem to be doing sociologically—that maybe this is mother nature's way of separating, here, so that we don't follow the same circuits for ever and ever and wind up . . .

BUK: I follow you. Yes, I know what you mean.

BR: Does the current revolution seem legitimate now, though? It seems kind of ratty, in a way, kind of seamy . . .

BUK: . . . I also have this theory that this same thing has happened before. That the human race begins in a cave and they learn how to build a bridge and somebody creates a pistol and finally you get atomic power. The hydrogen bomb. Then everything is blown up to hell. A few people left in caves. A guy discovers fire. They build the whole thing up and it breaks down again. This thought has occurred to me, too, that it's a continuous cycle. That *would* be a frightening thing, wouldn't it? What would be the reason for it?

BR: Twenty years ago in high school I had a teacher that was discussing the very same thing. He said that some group dug through—were going through archeological digs in the Middle East or some place and they dug through layer after layer, city after city—which means so many thousand years. Got down to the bottom and they found sort of a glaze, a glass-like foundation which was precisely like what they found in the desert, you know, when they blew the atomic bomb, kind of a fusion of glass. And they thought maybe this, you know, interesting thought . . .

BUK: Yes, it's possible.

BR: I kind of wonder if maybe what we're looking for is not to be found in the political realm or even the scientific realm per se but more in your own kind of art, like poetry. What do you think—do you think that poets will have any insights to bring us through the gap?

BUK: Well, there's no final answer you know. There hasn't been. You just do the best you can, that's all. No matter what you're working with, give the best you can.

BR: Do you think the current revolution—psychedelic and all that—is aiming in that direction—what do you think of it—where do you think we're going to come out—with something of value?

BUK: No. I hate to be so cynical but I think it's a fad like swallowing goldfish used to be by the college students or seeing how many could get into a telephone booth. Simply a thing to do. It's a fad more than a reality. I'll tell you how I really came upon this. I was listening to KPFK on this Isla Vista business—those riots up there. So they had some reporters up there and you know, they burned the bank and there was a lot of stuff going on. So the guy on the radio says to the reporter "How was it *tonight?*" The guy says "well, it's very quiet tonight." "Well, why is it quiet tonight?" "The students are all studying for their *finals.*" I thought what the hell kind of revolutionaries are these? They burn a bank, they raise all kinds of hell, throw rocks at the pigs and then they sit down and study for their finals so they can become members of society, you know. Get their grades. And that really kind of exposed it to me right there. There's a lot of faddishness in it. And there are a lot of opportunists, too.

BR: I sense that, somehow.

BUK: And there are a lot of sincere people in it. So you have a conglomeration. But generally with the young it's an expulsion of energy, and it just happens to be that revolution is the thing now.

BR: How do you regard the underground press now—which way does it seem to be swinging. Is it getting richer, in context?

BUK: It's getting to be a bit of a drag. *The Berkeley Tribe* [sic] is kind of juvenile. I would say the only good one that I know of is the one in New Orleans—*Nola Express.*

BR: I've heard of that. I've got to get my hands on one.

BUK: Maybe I like them because they publish my stories and poems!
      That *could* influence my judgement a bit.

BR: Well, we don't want to keep you much longer and we certainly
      appreciate you giving us this much time.

BUK: That's all right. I hope you get something out of all this.

"He's such a nice man!" Josette volunteered as we got into the car and
drove away. "And he's so *lucid!*"

An Evening with Charles Bukowski: A Pulpy Receptacle of Bad Karma, Self-Pity and Vengeance

Don Strachan
1971

"An Evening with Charles Bukowski: A Pulpy Receptacle of Bad Karma, Self-Pity and Vengeance," Don Strachan, *Los Angeles Free Press*, July 23, 1971, p. 4.

Somebody wrote that Sartre and Genet think Charles Bukowski's the best poet living in America today. Outside of southern California he's not as well known as Allen Ginsberg or Rod McKuen, and he's often criticized because he writes only one poem—life is shit. But everyone admits he writes it more powerfully than anyone else around.

Brad, a fellow I work with, is a friend of Bukowski's. He had invited me up to his place in Altadena to meet Bukowski before, but ever since Kathy had told me about the night had brought Bukowski over to her house, I'd been wary of meeting him.

Kathy works with us too. She lives with a filmmaker named Les up in a little house in Silverlake. Bukowski had spent most of the evening calling Les "fat boy" and he pulled up the flowers in the garden when he left.

Since then, Brad or his wife Tully had a new Bukowski story almost weekly. In the most recent, he had taken Tully out for dinner and drinks. "Don't worry," Hank confided in Brad as they left, "nothin's gonna happen to her. I'll see to that." Outside the restaurant, a couple approached them on the sidewalk. "I know you," Bukowski snarled at the girl. "Man, you're fucked up." Her escort made a motion, but Bukowski waved him back. He read her up and down, then told her she had been read out by Charles Bukowski.

This time when Brad invited me to meet him, I felt up to it.

The night I went a few rounds with Bukowski I brought about a gram and a half of Black Primo hash. Brad had seven quarts of wine and a few bottles of Miller's on hand. Since Bukowski's new girl had made him stop drinking, we thought we might get through the evening. Brad had a Pepsi cooling to offer him when he came so we could all tell him how good the wine tasted.

"He'll listen to that for about ten seconds," said Claude. Claude lives with Brad and Tully.

"His new girl's got him dry," said Tully. "I wonder how long that's going to last. He sure does go through women fast."

"Not as fast as me," I said. "It's over already with the triple Sagittarius."

"The one you met this week?" Tully asked.

"Yeah."

"Drown it in this," Claude said wryly, handing me a Pepsi. His wife had just split.

"Here's Bukowski," said Brad. "Oh my God, he's driving up in a car with pink polka-dots on the roof." Brad and his other guests, a couple named Joe and Margie, walked to the door. Bukowski came in wearing a sport coat and slacks. I could imagine the scene the girl had put him through to wear the suit, he at last giving in to please her and because it would amuse people that he came decked out.

He was not as tall as I'd expected—only about my height, six feet at the most—but he was built like a boxcar, a burly hunk of flesh. The regular, rather pleasant features of his face were buried in a great, pulpy, pitted receptacle of bad karma, self-pity and vengeance, capped by the beeriest, most bulbous nose ever to guide uncertain steps through the darkness. The face hung down between his shoulders, giving him the appearance of a massive troglodyte.

His voice was surprisingly soft and not at all deep, and he talked dryly, like W.C. Fields, letting the final syllables slide down and out. "I'm on the wagon," he said, opening a beer.

His girl was good-looking, in her early 30's, out of her element but seemingly possessed of a lot of spark. She reminded me of a fortyish grandmother I'd known back in the Midwest who danced and drank herself away from her old age every night, but this girl was still young and vital and tragedy looked a long way off. "This is Linda," Hank told us. "She's writing a novel. Pretty good one, too."

Linda. This was the girl Brad had fought with last time they'd visited. He felt she was too negative because she didn't believe in marriage.

We were still standing in the kitchen. "That's a far out car you got," I said, but both Hank and Linda let it lay. I passed Hank the pipe. Linda hadn't smoked hash and Hank told her how to do it. "She's from the hills," he told us. "She don't know nothin'".

They'd obviously gotten beyond this point by now. "That's right, I'm just a dumb hillbilly," she said. "I haven't got much here"—she touched her head—"but I've got plenty here." She touched her stomach. "I have a good time."

"You have been through some rough ones, though, baby. You can't deny it."

"Aw-w, Hank . . ."

"But you do, you have some good times too."

A joint was going now, and Hank began explaining dope terms to her. Tully hit the roach and Hank said, "There's a crow for you. A real crow."

"What's a crow?" I asked.

"A crow," he said, letting the word slide down. "A crow smokes it right down, lets that smooth smoke at the end roll over her lips and her tongue without letting them get burned."

Linda passed on the roach, and so did Hank. "Too hot for me, man." He handed it to me. I swallowed it.

"He swallowed it, Linda. Did you see there? He swallowed it, fire and all."

Tully served us chili and the eight of us adjourned to the living room to eat by the fireplace. I'd made a good move, but I still felt intimidated. If he started sparring with me, I thought I might go down. I sat on the sofa opposite him, as far away as I could get. "I can't hear," Bukowski said after a minute. He rose and sat next to me.

"Well, how's the weather, Claude?" he asked after a pause.

"You know I'm going to Florida in a few months," Claude said.

"After her?"

Claude giggled. "No-o."

Hank laughed. "Good."

"Come here," he said to Linda. She sat by him and he put his arm around her. "She wants to dance and feel happy," he said. Brad got sick from the chili and went to bed.

Bukowski started explaining to Linda the logic of committing suicide until she got upset; then he stopped. The Grateful Dead was playing on the stereo. "This dance music is all right, but it only takes you so far," he said.

I felt sufficiently adjusted to his style to venture some conversation. "I sat down good and loaded one night with the Rolling Stones and a Beethoven string quartet, and I found out Beethoven was better."

"What's that?" he said. "You talk so low I miss half of what you say."

I repeated it. "Yeah," he said. "This dance music is OK to start off on but it just goes so far and then you're ready for something more. I learned that one week when I was way out there and I sat down in the dark and listened to Bach, the same piece, over and over again. About the hundredth time it dawned on me. He had all those melodies going, one over the other. He started off with the basic, then he came in with the second, and a few bars later with the third, and the fourth—I said he couldn't do any more. He just kept going, right on up to ten melodies I think it was."

"Bach," said Linda. She got up and walked around.

"She likes to dance," said Bukowski.

"Don't you like anybody popular?" she asked him.

"Dizzy Gillespie!" she said.

"How's Chapter Two coming?" he said. She sat in a chair across the room.

The music changed to something real sweet and syrupy. Hank turned to Claude. "She'll be back, Claude."

Joe filled in most of the silences with long, spontaneous raps on peace and brotherhood, religion and good vibes in general. He wasn't Krishnamurti but he was an affable sort with a light heart. He rapped now about how good it would be if the whole world got it together and began living in a spirit of loving brotherhood. When he finished, Hank said to Linda, "There's the dope crowd."

I told about the animals found inside the Great Pyramid that had not decomposed. "The secrets embodied in the pyramid that allowed the animals to mummify have been discovered in Czechoslovakia. They think that that shape of space resonates cosmic energy. The Czechs have built miniature models that they use to sharpen razor blades."

Bukowski looked at me. "Do you believe that?"

"If you're aesthetic, you don't question miracles," I said.

"You don't believe that," he said.

Linda went to the bathroom. "She doesn't think anyone's having fun," Hank explained, "because they're not up and making noise and dancing. She doesn't understand that people can prefer to spend their time in more introspective activities. She's a good kid but I don't think we're going to make it. We make it great in one place—on the bed—but other ways it's not as good."

I was floating into the music when she came back and sat in her chair. "Come here," he said. She looked angrily ahead. A minute later when I glance toward her chair, I saw a baby in her lap. It had a head like a troglodyte. "Oh, Hank—all right," she said. They got up and crossed back to the sofa, she under his arm.

"There's nothin' can be said against dope," Joe went on, making a long, rather more vague than eloquent defense of it.

"I guess anything that lets you get out of your head, it's good to take it," Hank allowed.

"It sure is. Only I think dope takes you further into your head." Joe went off on another burst.

"I think you smoke dope because you think your balls are too small," said Bukowski.

Joe laughed—it was as much a sputter as a laugh—but Bukowski cut him short. "How big are your balls?"

"No, it ain't that," Joe said. "I got no worries about my balls."

"Well, then, how big are they?" Bukowski asked. How big are your balls?"

"No, it ain't that," Joe said. "I got no worries about my balls. Well, I don't know. I don't go around measuring them with a ruler, you know."

"How long is your cock? How big are your balls?"

Suddenly Bukowski whirled around to me. "How big are yours?" he said.

Needles shot through me and my head filled with blood. My pulse beat at my temples. "Oh come on," I said. "Sure, people in the dope crowd are up in the air about sexual roles, but it's overdoing it to make it personal with every doper you meet."

"I'm not talking about every doper," Bukowski said. "I'm talking about you. How big are they?"

"They're cannonballs. My ancestors used them in the War of 1812."

"How big? Let me see them," he said.

Somewhere during this Linda got up and walked into the kitchen. Bukowski finally got up and went after her. My head was swimming but I was still on my feet. Joe and Margie split for the bedroom to dress the baby for leaving.

Bukowski came back in. "Looks like we're gonna pull down the shades early, folks. Linda wants to leave." Linda was trying to look cordial. "She's got a stomach-ache." He really leaned on it.

They left. Joe came back in the living room. He said he hoped he hadn't offended anyone by talking, but he thought a person had the right to say what was on his mind. We assured him his raps were OK, and he left with Margie and his baby.

Charles Bukowski Answers 10 Easy Questions

F.A. Nettelbeck

1971

"Charles Bukowski Answers 10 Easy Questions," F.A. Nettelbeck, *Throb Two*, Summer-Fall 1971, pp. 56–59.

Saturday

Hello Nettelbeck:

I answered your ten easy questions a few days ago but am just getting them in the mail. I hope I don't turn out as serious as your boy Blazek who seemed to take himself as quite a seer.

Regarding your letter, poets are not the only fools but you'll find more fools among them.

very well, yes, then,

1.) Do you think poetry will be valid in a hundred years from now?

No, and it's not valid now. I'd rather drink buttermilk. Poetry has disgusted me more than any other art-form. It's held all too damn high and mighty holy. It's a pasture for fakes. Even when the boys try to talk straight they talk over-straight, rather borrowing a stance which is as bad as the roses and moonlight stance, the obtuse stance, the clever stance, the concrete stance, all the stances . . . To expect power out of garbage is to expect too much in one hundred years. In fact, poetry has gone back. Some of the early Chinese boys around the hub of B.C. and A.D. had it down quite clearly and honestly & with natural force. 100 years from now buy me a beer and I'll tell you.

2.) What do you feel the purpose of a poet should be during a time of revolution?

Drink and fuck, eat and shit, sleep, stay clothed, stay alive, stay away from guns and mass-ideals and mass-history and find whatever single truth might be found in a single man so that when the so-called mass-truths and ideals and ideas decay again that he (the poet) and they (the tricked) can have more to hold to than rubble and rot and tombstones and treachery and the waste of hysteria and Time.

3.) Do you think the small press scene really does any good?

It's a crutch for 9th rate talents, allowing them to build their prejudices and hatreds and dreams and to continue their bad writing. By "small press" I mean little magazines and little magazine editors who push publication of 9th rate talents into book form, mimeo or otherwise. The small press scene is particularly difficult upon wives and mothers who must support these 9th rate talents while they write 9th rate poetry. Of the poets I knew personally, 19 out of 20 are supported by either a wife or a mother. If these "poets" didn't have their little books and their little magazines to point to, they'd be out digging ditches or pimping or doing something far more healthy than they are doing now. It's time for the wives and mothers to find out that their darlings have shit in their drawers.

4.) Who has been the most influential poet in regards to your own work?

Robinson Jeffers, especially in his longer narrative poems. However, poets really don't lift me too much. Some wild bird like Céline is really much better—he knew how to laugh through the fire and the stink.

5.) How come you're so ugly?

I presume you're talking more about my face than about my writing. Well, the face is the product of 2 things: what you were born with and what has happened to you since you were born. My life has hardly been pretty—the hospitals, the jails, the jobs, the women, the drinking. Some of my critics claim that I have deliberately inflicted myself with pain. I wish that some of my critics had been along with me for the journey. It's true that I haven't always chosen easy situations but that's a hell of a long ways from saying that I leaped into the oven and locked the door. Hangover, the electric needle, bad booze, bad women, madness in small rooms, starvation in the land of plenty, god knows how I got so ugly, I guess it just comes from being slugged and slugged again and again, and not going down, still trying to think, to feel, still trying to put the butterfly back together again . . . it's written a map on my face that nobody would ever want to hang on their wall.

Sometimes I'll see myself somewhere . . . suddenly . . . say in a large mirror in a supermarket . . . eyes like little mean bugs . . . face scarred, twisted, yes, I look insane, demented, what a mess . . . spilled vomit of skin . . . yet, when I see the "handsome" men I think, my god my god, I'm glad I'm not them. There you go.

6.) Who would you say are the 3 worst poets alive today?

Rod McKuen, Rod McKuen, Rod McKuen.

7.) How come you're a poet anyway?

How come you ask so many stupid questions?

8.) Does your cock still get as hard as you would like it to?

Nobody's cock gets as hard as they would like it to. But, being 51 this August 16th, I can't complain. I still go 2 pieces a day sometimes, maybe 4 pieces in 3 days, then a couple of days off. Of course, there are dry periods when I don't have a girl friend or don't look for one. I don't search women out. If they don't come to my door then it doesn't happen. A writer, of course, should have experience with women. There's much pain involved with me as I am sentimental and get quite attached. I am not much of a lady's man and unless I get some help from the lady, not much happens. I'm not married now, have one child, 6. I've been lucky to have 4 long term relationships with 4 unusual women. They all treated me better than I deserved and they were very good on the love bed. Should I stop loving, fucking right now I believe I have been far more fortunate than most men. The gods have been good, the love has been fine, and the pain, the pain has arrived in boxcar loads.

9.) What is your definition of poetry?

How come you ask so many stupid questions?

10.) What would you say is the best brand of American beer on the market today?

Well, that's a bit difficult. Miller's is the easiest on my system but each new batch of Miller's seems to taste a bit worse. Something is going on there I don't like. I seem to be gradually going over to Schlitz. And I prefer beer in the bottle. Beer in the can definitely gives off a metallic taste. Cans are for the convenience of storekeepers and breweries. Whenever I see a man drinking out of a can I think, now there is a damn fool. Also, bottled beer should be in a brown bottle. Miller again errs in putting the stuff into a white bottle. Beer should be protected both from metal and from light.

Of course, if you have the money it's best to go up the scale and get the more expensive beers, imported or better-made American. Instead of a dollar 35 you have to go a dollar 75 or 2 and a quarter and up. The taste is immediately noticeable. And you can drink more with less hang-over. Most ordinary American beer is almost poison, especially the stuff that comes out of the spigots at racetracks. This beer actually stinks, I mean to the nose. If you must buy beer at a racetrack it is best to let it sit for 5 minutes before drinking it. There is something about the oxygen getting in there that removes some of the stink. The stuff is simply green.

Beer was much better before world war 2. It had *tang* and was filled with sharp little bubbles. It's wash now, strictly flat. You just do the best you can with it.

Beer is better to write with and talk with than whiskey. You can go longer and make more sense. Of course, much depends upon the talker and the writer. But beer is fattening, plenty, and it lessens the sex drive, I mean both the day you are drinking it and the day after. Heavy drinking and heavy loving seldom go hand in hand after the age of 35. I'd say a good chilled wine is the best way out and it should be drunken (drank) slowly after a meal, with just perhaps a small glass before eating.

Heavy drinking is a substitute for companionship and it's a substitute for suicide. It's a secondary way of life. I dislike drunks but I do suppose I take a little drink now and then myself. Amen.

—Bukowski

Issue 486 December 6-12, 1974   PUBLISHED EVERY FRIDAY   204   Copyright Berkeley Barb 1974   Bay Area 25c Elsewh

Partying with the Poets

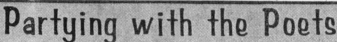

"People who go to poetry readings aren't interested in poetry. They want to see what you look like, they want to see you vomit, they want to see you die. People who go to poetry readings are peep freaks. They want to fuck the poet or tame him or read to him from their own inept works."

--Charles Bukowski

The party where the great poets were finally going to vomit and die after the 2nd Annual Santa Cruz Poetry Reading was a long ways out, near the ocean, and the house had been stripped clean of moveable furniture before the guests arrived. The only thing left in the house above knee-level were the see page 5

Partying with the Poets

RIC REYNOLDS

1974

"Partying with the Poets," Ric Reynolds, *Berkeley Barb*, December 6–12, Issue 486, 1974, pp. 1, 5.

The party where the great poets were finally going to vomit and die after the 2nd Annual Santa Cruz Poetry Reading was a long ways out, near the ocean, and the house had been stripped clean of moveable furniture before the guests arrived. The only thing left in the house above knee-level were the light fixtures and below that, a few pillows scattered around the linoleum floor.

Charles Bukowski was the first of the great poets to arrive. Bukowski came through the door and tossed his dufflebag into the air. As it landed on a woman's shoulder, Bukowski screamed, "Come on you bastards, we're going to party." He rushed over to the bar and started to pour himself another drink. Someone laughed behind Albert and me, "Isn't he a scene?"

A lot of people had gone to the reading to see Bukowski, Ginsberg, Ferlinghetti, Gary Snyder and others. In Bukowski's case, he promised a good show. If people wanted a scene, then he was glad to oblige. As props he had brought along a thermos of Vodka and orange juice which he killed off after the first three poems of the reading.

But there were too many poets, and Bukowski got tapped off stage before the booze had taken hold. Linda King, introduced by Jerry Kamstra as "Bukowski with a cunt but a fine poet regardless of sex," was pushed out on the stage. She did a poem to Bukowski and then flashed off with "A Cock is still a Cock and Nothing More."

Not only was the reading the first fund raiser for Americans in Mexican Jails (AIM-J) but it was also the bright star on the winter social calendar. The reading had been talked up by the Santa Cruz literary set for weeks in advance at the Catalyst, an unhealthy coffee shop where every other table was staked out by fledgling poets and writers and where at least a dozen manuscripts were being written or passed around. A few of the Catalyst crowd seemed to be at the party.

Unlike most poets, Bukowski was accessible. He didn't stand in a corner watching others with sad or cold poetic eyes. He pushed himself on you and covered you with drunken hands. But while everyone watched Bukowski make an ass of himself, his mind was churning up the scene. Behind his glazed eyes and drunken cockroach body he watched you when he knew you were off guard.

Bukowski grabbed Albert by the bar and turned him around. "You're worried about your wife. You should be worried about this guy," he leaned over close and pointed at me. "You're used to all this? Taking it in huh? An intellectual no doubt, Dostoevsky, Tolstoy, Turgenev. What do you do? Teach? Work in a car wash?"

"Don't let him get away with that," Albert said. So I finally told Bukowski that I made pizza and that one of his poems was wrong. There was no macaroni in pizza.

"Pizza?" Bukowski said. "Pizza! Blah." Bukowski about vomited and turned away and was in a fight about twenty seconds later with some man who kept pulling his pants down while he danced.

When Allen Ginsberg arrived at the party, Bukowski latched on to him and buried him under his shoulder. "Ladies and Gentlemen," Bukowski shouted. "We've got Allen Ginsberg as guest of honor tonight. Can you believe it? Allen Ginsberg!"

His voice wouldn't carry above the music. "I wish somebody'd unplug that machine. Cut it, you bastards." He drew Ginsberg up tighter. "A man of genius, the first poet to cut through light and consciousness for two thousand years and these bastards don't even appreciate it. Have a drink Allen."

Someone was trying to introduce William Burroughs Jr. to Ginsberg and Bukowski. Burroughs Jr., one-time author and now a cook in Santa Cruz was looking for work, and for a minute or two Bukowski looked at him trying to figure out why Burroughs looked twenty years too young and was at the party at all. In literature, it was a fine scene. Ginsberg, Bukowski, Burroughs Jr. in arms and Lawrence Ferlinghetti against the wall in the background. Bukowski hugged Ginsberg closer and he rubbed Bukowski's back. "That feels good Allen, real good. No lie."

Ginsberg had been taken in by all the flattery, but when he saw that Bukowski was going to force some booze down his throat he slumped in a fake drunken drawl and said that he had been drinking all night. "God, it's good to see you Allen, really. I don't care if you are a fake. Did you hear that folks? Washed up. Everybody knows that after *Howl* you never wrote anything worth a shit. How about that folks, a vote, Has Allen written anything worth a shit since *Howl* and *Kay'dish*?"

As the booze ran lower, one of the 19-year old Santa Cruz groupies that filled the place came around with her surfer boyfriend picking up change for a run. About two hours later it was pretty clear that they weren't coming back with that hat full of dollar bills. I looked at the woman standing with her back to the wall right next to me. "What nationality are you?" she snapped.

"Well I'm from here. You know, America."

"Well, I'm from Egypt," she snarled. She was very unhappy. She hated Americans for hating Arabs and wanted to fuck everyone at the party.

"Kah' dish," Ginsberg said, correcting Bukowski.

Bukowski backed up, fending off the blow. "Allen, you're tearing me apart. You're a barracuda Allen. Eating me up with your tongue. Hey, why don't you have another drink?" and Bukowski grabbed a drink out of someone's hand, drank half of it, stuck it in Ginsberg's hand. Ginsberg took a sip of the Jack Daniels straight and nearly vomited, thinking it was wine. As Bukowski turned, he dashed for it slipping away through the crowd.

"Where'd he go?" Bukowski asked. "Oh well," and he grabbed a young woman who had been standing quietly against the bar all night. Until Bukowski grabbed her she had been propelling people away with a sense of class which circled her like cattle prods. Inside Bukowski's grip, however, the style didn't work anymore and you could see she was a very young person really, wondering how to get away from Bukowski without hurting his feelings or without looking too prudish or setting off a curse. Bukowski pushed his face down into hers and touched his face with short sweeps of his fingers. "Does this face bother you?" He touched his face again, softly touching the blotched warty jowls, cupped nose, "I mean you find it revolting?"

The woman looked at him, and her heart melted. Underneath all this bullshit, this hunchback cockroach has a heart and he only acts this way because he's been beaten down since childhood by insecurity, she thought. She could relate to it.

"No," she said with a heart of melted Hershey Bars, "I think you should judge a man by the inside of him."

"Well, good," Bukowski said, "Let's go out and fuck then."

Linda King, the poetess introduced as Bukowski with a cunt, was watching all this. She was Lily, she said, in a lot of Hank's columns and stories. She wasn't like the Santa Cruz jet-set, and she was a mature woman. Looking at her made your fingers and chest warm.

The party went on till 3 am. Bukowski was finally talked into leaving after he tried to smash one of the swinging light fixtures, and the floor was covered with broken glass and your feet stuck to the linoleum because of all the drinks he had dropped. As the party thinned, people were worried about who they were going to spend the night with and everywhere you looked men were bouncing from one desperate pitch to another. It was a very old fashioned kind of party.

The sound of a telephone ringing five or six times woke me up at eight the next morning. One of the women who had invited me home had answered it and was talking to her boyfriend. I could just see her blond hair and part of a white nightgown. Her boyfriend was calling long-distance from somewhere, and wanted her to visit for the holidays. She was making excuses. The airlines were all booked up. She didn't have any money and didn't want to borrow it. Yes, she missed him too.

I stared at the back of her head and wondered what her face was like. I looked around the place. The room was paneled in pine or cedar. Karson was brushing her teeth in the bathroom and you could see and hear the waves break a hundred yards or so away. The woman on the telephone started to tell her boyfriend about the reading.

"It was so American," she sighed. "I couldn't believe all these American poets talking about America."

Charles Bukowski

William Childress

1974

"Charles Bukowski," William Childress, *Poetry Now*, Vol.1, No. 6, pp. 1, 19, 21, 1974.

"WE STARTED punching at ten in the morning of a Saturday, and we'd still be fighting at sundown. Or trying to. Our arms would be so tired we couldn't lift 'em. We'd be bloody and blue and black, but the only way we ever gave up was if we got knocked unconscious and even then we knew we'd get stomped so we fought like goddamned Romans as long as we could stand. Parents would sit on their slum Los Angeles porches and watch, dulled by hunger and the Depression. I guess they figured that if we killed each other there'd be one less to feed."

The speaker is Charles Bukowski. He is seated on a crippled sofa in a quiet suburb of Los Angeles, one big hand holding a can of Ballantine Ale.

"Green death," he says, inhaling the brew with satisfaction.

Bukowski is a big man—chunkily built, almost bull-like, nearly six feet tall. Born in Andernach, Germany, August 16, 1920, he is 54 years old. His shoulders are somewhat stooped by years, but still powerful. He weighs two hundred twenty pounds, with perhaps twenty in a slightly overhung gut. The rest of him looks solid—and mean.

There is something wolf-like about his features—fringed from crown to chin with long, fading brown hair. His face is pocked and pitted by a thousand scars of barroom brawls. It is a long face, with a forehead that is very broad and high. Bright green eyes peer out from under thick brows. Even when he is being friendly, his eyes have a way of cooling when he looks at you.

Bukowski is a poetic genius, yet it is his brawling that, perhaps, has brought him the most recognition—at least in the sense that people who know him talk first about his penchant for fighting.

"He's a truly great poet," says Harold Norse, a longtime friend.

"But he is always wanting to fight. To stay around him long is to invite disaster."

"I'M NOT A boxer," Bukowski explains, hefting his beer can. "Just a brawler. At least I was. I'm too old for that stuff now. I once put the gloves on with a pro. We danced around a bit and I got lucky and stuck him with a stiff left jab. I knocked him down. Then he got up and went to work on me like a goddamn piranha. I looked like a side of fresh beef when he got through."

"I got, well, used to brawls during the Depression, when I was a teenager. I hadn't heard crap-all about poetry then, and never had any desire to. On the slum streets of L.A. it was balls-up in those days, and only the tough survived. I was a big, rawboned, tough kid. I made it. Trouble was, I liked it. Liked the impact of knuckles against teeth, of feeling the terrific lightning that breaks in your brain when somebody lands a clean one and you have to try to shake loose and come back and nail him before he finished you off."

"But I fought more as a bar-hopping adult than I did as a kid. My home life prepared me for the roughness of the streets. I was an only

79

child, and only children are usually pampered and spoiled. Not me, baby. I was cuffed and kicked."

HE IS THE child of a German fraülein and an occupation soldier, and he first saw America when he was two years old. His father became a milkman in Los Angeles, then a museum guard, who, in Bukowski's words, "... always brought his goddamn job home with him. To this day I'm terrified of the eight-hour day. I go crazy in such jobs. It's killed too many people, my old man among them. Watching him gab incessantly about his job, watching it slowly kill him, cured me of ever wanting to have a job like that. My typewriter is my job."

His was a loveless home life.

"My old man was an unfeeling bastard. We were total opposites, and he rarely knew or cared if I was even around. Did he love me? Hell, he never knew the meaning of the word. If it caught his fancy he would grab hold of me and beat the hell out of me while dear old mom cheered him on. I dunno, maybe it helped me to a certain discipline, facing life totally unloved. It was a good military stance anyway. It made you a Spartan if you survived it."

He stares at the green ale can, moody and brooding, thick brows lowered. His face is averted.

The room we are in has a lived-in but not sloppy look. There are books and magazines in abundance. I notice some barbells stacked in one corner, and ask him if he lifts weights.

"Lift them?" he half grins. "Hell, sometimes I throw them. I put a whopping big hole in the wall of one apartment once, which I thought improved the place but which the landlord didn't. I dunno if you realize it, but a 20-pound barbell weight makes a great discus if you're drunk and feel like sending something sailing."

BUKOWSKI has been drunk a lot in his life. "I guess the longest drunk I was ever on ran ten years," he says simply, glancing at me with his cool green eyes and crumpling an empty ale can. "I call it my ten-years-off-with-no-writing phase. I sat in one bar alone for five years, opening the place at 5 AM and closing it at 2 AM. Sometimes I slept in and was late and never got there till seven or eight. But I always got there.

"Even drunk, I had a certain wit, a clownishness—and people tend to like a fool. They can study a fool and laugh at him, knowing deep inside that they're really seeing themselves, but without the risk of public exposure. That was my world and I was welcome in it. I was terrified at the thought that I might have to enter the drab world of nine to five."

He had written a few poems and one short story before hitting the booze trail. The short story won a prestigious *Story* award in 1944 when Bukowski was 24. The future looked bright. An agent in New York asked to meet him, to buy drinks, dinner, and talk about his writing future.

Recalls Bukowski, "I told him I wasn't ready yet. And promptly hit the skids. My sole reason for being became the bars. In the five-year one, it got to where, if things were full, the bartender—a big ox with a cruel streak—would challenge me to a 'boxing' match. The schtick, of course, was to let him beat me up for the entertainment of the customers. But once I got tired of that game and decked the bastard and they promptly 86'd me. There I was, on the streets and out of a job just like that."

Bukowski soon landed another such position, where he continued playing the buffoon, and running errands for sandwiches and drinks. From 1945 to 1955, he listed his occupation, he says, as "Drunk."

SOMEHOW, he came out of the haze, and by 1956 he was writing. Still drinking, but writing. "I may have written some stuff in between," he says, "but I'm not sure."

Some of the stuff he may have written in between attracted an unlikely fan—a young, rich, lovely Texas girl of about twenty.

"When she first wrote to me, I thought it was a gag," he grunts, taking a slug at his ale. "But she kept insisting that she loved my poetry, and through it, me, and could she come out and meet me. I guess I must've said Yes in a drunken moment, because the next thing I knew, there she was."

He is somber for a moment, his long, pocked face with its greying halo of hair lost in thought. "She was beautiful," he murmurs. "That much I remember. She hung around for quite awhile, but we never really hit it off. She couldn't stay drunk and I couldn't stay sober, and never the twain shall meet. She finally took off back to Texas, and that's the last I ever saw or heard of her."

Bukowski's first serious writing was at about the age of 22, a couple of years before the big binge. And somewhere along the way, he remembers enrolling in a Los Angeles City College Creative Writing Class.

"The teacher turned me off immediately," he says. "The guy was a goddamned DORK. Tea and cookies and students at his feet on a soft rug. If that's poetry I'm a striped-ass baboon!" (In a high falsetto, he imitates the teacher's defense of a poem called "Red Spider Poem" by a student he calls William Class Member. It's a funny impersonation that cracks me up, to which "Buk" says, "Good, you know when to laugh!")

"Anyway, that did it for me. My first and last class in writing. So I said to myself, OK, if it's acting they want, then I'll act Bukowski. I know him best of all."

Does he have any nostalgia for those lost days. "Hell, no!" he snaps, his bearded face split by a tight smile. "I like the present. I don't know when I've felt better or worse at the same time."

He belches loudly. "Green death," he grunts, hefting the ale-can.

THE BUILDING of Bukowski's poetic reputation has not been a sudden thing; it has been slow and erratic. As with many other poets, his first publication was in the Little Magazines. His first poem to see print, "Hello," appeared in *Matrix* in 1946. Two other poems also appeared in *Matrix* later that year, and a fourth in 1951. Then came the "long drunk," and he published no other poems until 1956, when one poem appeared in *The Naked Ear* and two in *Quixote*. His first group of poems—eight of them—appeared in *Harlequin* in 1957. He then began to publish with increasing regularity in other Little Magazines; the years 1958-59 saw new Bukowski poems in a dozen or more Littles, among them *Hearse, The Beloit Poetry Journal,* and *Epos.*

Bukowski's first collection—the Hearse Press chapbook *Flower, Fist and Bestial Wail*—appeared in 1960. Two other chapbooks followed in 1962: *Longshot Poems for Broke Players* (7 Poets Press) and *Run With the Hunted* (Midwest Poetry Chapbooks).

In 1963, two of Bukowski's strongest early supporters, Jon and Louise Webb, hand printed at their Loujon Press *It Catches My Heart In Its Hands*. A second Loujon Press book, *Crucifix in a Death Hand*, appeared in 1965 (aided by Lyle Stuart). The two Loujon efforts, printed on multi-colored, deckle-edged book papers, won awards as among the most beautiful books produced in their respective years, and are now prized collector's items.

Two further chapbooks followed in 1965 and 1968: *Cold Dogs in the Courtyard* (Literary-Times Cyfoeth) and *Poems Written Before Jumping Out of an 8 Story Window* (Litmus). In the meantime, Bukowski had met John Martin, who was shortly to launch a new publishing venture, Black Sparrow Press. Black Sparrow became Bukowski's "official" publisher, and issued his subsequent poetry volumes: *At Terror Street and Agony Way* (1968), *The Days Run Away Like Wild Horses Over the Hills* (1969), *Mockingbird Wish Me Luck* (1972) and *Burning in Water Drowning in Flame* (1974).

NOT ONLY is Bukowski a poet, he is also a gifted writer of short stories. His stories are hilarious, reverent and beautiful, not necessarily in that order. His prose books include *All the Assholes in the World and Mine* and *Confessions of a Man Insane Enough to Live With Beasts*, published in chapbook form by Douglas Blazek's Open Skull Press in the mid-1960's; *Notes of a Dirty Old Man* (Essex House, 1969), a collection of columns which he wrote for the Los Angeles underground newspaper, *Open City*; and *Post Office* (Black Sparrow Press, 1971), a novel based on his experiences as a postal worker for the Los Angeles Post Office—one of his few 8-5 jobs. More recent are two other collections of short stories: *Erections, Ejaculations, Exhibitions and General Tales of Ordinary Madness*, published by Lawrence Ferlinghetti's City Lights Books in 1972, and *South of No North* (Black Sparrow Press, 1973), drawn from the column which Bukowski now writes for the underground newspaper *Los Angeles Free Press*.

Bukowski's books now total 22, and his underground admirers are legion. But official "honors" by the Literary Establishment have been grudging or absent. He has been honored by a full-fledged bibliography (*Bibliography of Charles Bukowski*, edited by Sanford Dorbin), and he has received (in 1972—and to the surprise of many) a grant from the National Endowment for the Arts. But his poetry has not, as yet, been included in a single major poetry anthology.

BUKOWSKI has one child, a daughter named Marina. He and the child's mother, with whom she resides, have never been married. "The girl is nine," he says, a softness entering his tone. "We really dig each

83

other. She's so cool and calm inside, but with a bubbling sense of humor. Yeah, she's OK, that kid, and I'm glad she's around."

How does he feel about poetry today?

"I would say disgusted but revolted is better," he says. "A lot of taught-poetry is going around. I get sent books or mags by students that have very little strength."

He pauses reflectively.

"Youth today is open, gentle, understanding," he continues. "But it doesn't have the fire or the madness. Congenial people don't create too well. That doesn't apply just to the young, either. A poet of all people needs forging in the flames of hardship. Too much mama's milk won't do it. If that kind of poetry is any good, I've not seen any. The theory of hardship and deprivation may be an old one, but it got to be old because it was good."

William Childress with Bukowski, 1974

IT IS MANY beers later, and Bukowski is holding forth on his theories of poetry and the poetic process. He is obviously aware that he himself has had an influence on many young poets, and the kind of poetry they are writing.

"My contribution was to loosen and simplify poetry," he says. "To make it more humane. I made it easy for others to follow. I taught them that you can write a poem the same way you can write a letter, that a poem can even be entertaining, and that there need not be anything necessarily holy about it."

"See," he says, gesturing with a hamlike hand, "I never got into poetry writing because of any early urge. I started writing not because I was so good, but because others were so bad at the time. They were running a poetry con—little boxed-in poems with all the impact and interest of an enema. I started in to pluck poetry out of that mold, at least my poetry. I hate goddamned formalism. It's still with us and it's been going too long. I just lay the words down.

"See that typewriter? That's an old Royal Standard. You can hit a big typewriter and hit it hard. Hate won't come through on a dinky portable. I literally dramatize the act of creating. I play powerful symphonies and smoke powerful cigars when I write. These days I send Black Sparrow Press a copy of everything I write, good or not. John Martin has a drawerful of my stuff that's never been published. I guess he'll bring it out after I'm dead, maybe, but it's his baby now."

"Do you feel any particular way when you're ready to write a poem?" I ask.

Bukowski lofts an empty ale can towards a wastebasket in the kitchen, misses with a clatter, and turns back.

"I feel a tightness," he says. "Actually, I feel bad—like I'm about to get into a fight, sort of. Then I play footsy with the goddamn chair and type-writer and table. Finally, I sit down, drawn to the machine as if by a magnet, against my will. There's absolutely no plan to it. It's just me, the typewriter, and the chair. And always I throw the first draft away, saying 'that's no good!' Then I enter into the act with a kind of fury, writing madly for four, five, even eight hours. Next day I'll write for two or three. Then I'm spent and exhausted and won't touch the typewriter again for at least a week, when the whole cycle starts over."

Bukowski writes what amounts to a short story a week, besides any poems he turns out. This by virtue of his *Los Angeles Free Press* column. "I call 'em short stories," he says, "because by god that's what they are. So you can say my literary output is 50-60 short stories a year, and five or six poems a week when I'm not hung up on broads or booze."

Are they all good?

"I won't say it's all Grade-A," he replies, "but a lot is. My only writing rule is You Gotta Write Bad Shit In Order To Write Good Shit, and please quote me."

THE INTERVIEW is over, and I am again outside. The smoggy dusk is turning the streets grey-purple. And all up and down the streets, people from the eight-to-five jobs that terrified Bukowski are coming home, stationwagons pulling in drives, men getting out with shiny plastic briefcases.

Paying for Horses:
An Interview with Charles Bukowski

Robert Wennersten

1974

"Paying for Horses: An Interview with Charles Bukowski," Robert Wennersten, *London Magazine*, December 1974-January 1975, pp. 35–54.

Charles Bukowski was born in Andernach, Germany. When he was two years old, his parents brought him to the United States; and he was raised in Los Angeles, where, after a long period of bumming around the country, he still lives.

Bukowski, mostly self-educated, began writing in his early twenties. Ignored, he stopped. Ten years later he started again and since then has published about

twenty books of poetry, hundreds of short stories and one novel, Post Office. *Bukowski's writing is about an existence he once sought out for himself, so knows firsthand: he writes about the lower classes paddling as fast as they can to avoid drowning in the shit life pours on them. His characters, if they are employed at all, hold down dull, starvation-wage jobs. Off work they drink too much and live chaotically. Their attempts to make it—with women, at the race track or simply from day to day—are sometimes pathetic, sometimes nasty, often hilarious.*

On the day of this interview, Bukowski was living, temporarily, in a typical Los Angeles apartment building: low and square with a paved courtyard in the center. He was standing at the top of the stairs that led to his second-floor rooms. Broad, but not a tall man, he was dressed in a print shirt and blue jeans pulled tight under a beer belly. His long, dark hair was combed straight back. He had a wiry beard and moustache, both flecked with grey. "You didn't bring a bottle," he said slowly, chuckling and walking inside. "My girl was afraid you'd bring a fifth and get me so drunk that I wouldn't be able to take care of business when I see her tonight."

In the living room, he sat down on a bed which also served as a couch. He lit a cigarette, put it in an ashtray and clasped his hands between his knees. Aside from reaching for that cigarette or lighting another one, he seldom made a gesture. To the first questions, his answers were taciturn, just one or two sentences; yet he frequently accused himself of being long-winded. Reassured that he was not, he gradually became more and more talkative.

When the interview ended, Bukowski rose and walked to a table on the opposite side of the room. He picked up a pamphlet, flipped it open and said, "Look at this. Something's going on." The pamphlet turned out to be an autograph dealer's catalogue, and it listed about a dozen Bukowski letters for sale. He stared at the list a moment, tossed the catalogue back on the table and mumbled, "I'll make it, man. I'll make it."

—RW

Robert Wennersten: *What were your parents and your childhood like?*

Charles Bukowski: Oh, God. Well, my parents were of German extraction. My mother was born there; and my father's people were German, although he came out of Pasadena.

My father liked to whip me with a razor strop. My mother backed him. A sad story. Very good discipline all the way through, but very little love going either direction. Good training for the world, though, they made me ready. Today, watching other children, I'd say one thing they taught me was not to weep too much when something goes wrong. In other words, they hardened me to what I was going to go through: the bum, the road, all the bad jobs and the adversity. Since my early life hadn't been soft, the rest didn't come as such a shock.

We lived at 2122 Longwood Avenue. That's a little bit west and little bit south of here. When I first started shacking with women, I lived near downtown; and it seems like through the years each move I make is further west and further north. I felt myself going towards Beverly Hills at one time. I'm in this place now, because I got booted out of the house where I lived with this lady. We had a minor split, so all of a sudden I came back south a bit. I got thrown off course. I guess I'm not going to make Beverly Hills.

RW: *What changes have you seen in Los Angeles during the years you've lived here?*

CB: Nothing astounding. It's gotten bigger, dumber, more violent and greedier. It's developed along the same lines as the rest of civilization.

But there's a part of L.A.—you take it away from Hollywood, Disneyland and the ocean, which are places I stay away from, except the beaches in wintertime when there's no one around—where there's a good, easy feeling. People here have a way of minding their own damned business. You can get isolation here, or you can have a party. I can get on that phone and in an hour have a dozen people over drinking and laughing. And that's not because I'm a writer who's getting known a little. This has always been, even before I had any luck. But they won't come unless I phone them, unless I want them. You can have isolation, or you can have the crowd. I tend to mix the two, with a preference for isolation.

RW: *One of your short stories has this line in it: "LA is the cruelest city in the world." Do you believe it is?*

CB: I don't think LA is the cruelest city. It's one of the least cruel. If you're on the bum and know a few people, you can get a buck here and there, float around and always find a place to lay up overnight. People will tolerate you for a night. Then you go to the next pad. I put people up overnight. I say, "Look, I can only stand you for one night. You've got to go." But I put them up. It's a thing people in LA do. Maybe they do it elsewhere, I just haven't seen it.

I don't get the feeling of cruelty here that I get from New York City. Philadelphia has nice rays, too; it has a good feeling. So does New Orleans. San Francisco isn't all they say it is. If I had to rate cities, I'd put LA right up on top: LA, Philadelphia, New Orleans. Those are places where somebody can *live*.

I've left LA many times, but I always come back. You live in a town all of your life, and you get to know every street corner. You've got the layout of the whole land. You have this picture of where you are. When I hit a strange town, I seldom got out of the neighbourhood. I'd settle within an area of two or three blocks: the bar, the room I lived in and the streets around them. That's all I knew about a town, so I always felt lost; I was never located, never quite knew where I was. I was raised in LA, I've always had the geographical and spiritual feeling of being here. I've had time to learn this city. I can't see any other place than LA.

RW: *Do you still travel a lot?*

CB: I've done my traveling. I've traveled so damn much, mostly via buses or some other cheap mode, that I've gotten tired of it. At one time I had this idea that one could live on a bus forever: travelling, eating, getting off, shitting, getting back on that bus. (I don't where the income was supposed to come from.) I had the strange idea that one could stay in motion forever. There was something fascinating about constant motion, because you're not tied down. Well, it was fascinating for a while; and then I got un-fascinated or non-fascinated. Now I hardly travel; I hate going to the drugstore.

RW: *What turned you off about New York?*

CB: I didn't like it. I didn't have a taste for it. I don't think I could ever like New York, and there's no need to go there. I guess New York was almost the beginning of American civilization. Now it's the top of our civilization. It represents what we mean. I don't like what we mean, what New Yorkers mean.

I landed there with $7 and no job. I walked out of the bus station into Times Square. It was when all the people were getting off their jobs. They came roaring out of these holes in the ground, these subways. They knocked me about, spun me about. The people were more brutal than any I'd ever seen anywhere else. It was dark and dank, and the buildings were so damned tall. When you only have $7 in your pocket and look up at those huge buildings . . .

Of course, I deliberately went to New York broke. I went to every town broke in order to learn that town from the bottom. You come into a town from the top—you know, fancy hotel, fancy dinners, fancy drinks, money in your pocket—and you're not seeing that town at all. True, I denied myself a full view. I got a bottom view, which I didn't like; but I was more interested in what was going on at the bottom. I thought that was the place. I found out it wasn't. I used to think the real men (people you can put up with for over ten minutes) were at the bottom, instead of at the top. The real men aren't at the top, middle or bottom. There's no location. They're just very scarce; there aren't many of them.

RW: *Why was San Francisco a disappointment?*

CB: You get the big build-up, you know, in literature and movies and God knows where else. I got up there and looked around, and it didn't seem to live up to it. The build-up was too big; so when I finally got there, there was a natural letdown. And when I hit San Francisco, I knew I had to hustle a job. I knew some guy would hire me, pay me a bit of money, and I'd have to bust my ass and be grateful that I had a job. It was the same as everyplace else.

Most cities are alike: you've got people, a business district, whore-houses, police who hassle you and a bunch of bad poets walking around. Maybe the weather is different, and the people have slightly different accents; that's about it. But, like I said, LA has a spiritual and geograph-ical difference which, because I've been hanging around it, I've picked up on. I have an acquaintanceship with LA, you might say.

Now, women are a lot different than cities. If you're lucky, you do all right. You've got to be lucky with women, because the way you meet them is mostly through accident. If you turn right at a corner, you meet this one; if you turn left, you meet the other one. Love is a form of acci-dent. The population bounces together, and two people meet somehow. You can say that you love a certain woman, but there's a woman you never met you might have loved a hell of a lot more. That's why I say you have to be lucky. If you meet someone up near that possible top, you're lucky. If you don't, well, you turned right instead of left, or you didn't search long enough, or you're plain, damned unlucky.

RW: *Did you do much writing while you were on the road?*

CB: I got some writing done in New York. In Philadelphia, St. Louis and New Orleans, too, in my early days. St. Louis was very lucky for me. I was there when I got rid of my first short story—to *Story* mag, which was quite a mag in its day. (They discovered William Saroyan and reprinted top-class writers.) I don't remember if I wrote the story in St. Louis, because I was moving pretty fast then; but I was there when it got accepted.

You've got to have a good city to write in, and you've got to have a certain place to live in to write. This apartment is not right for me; but I had to move right away, and I got tired of looking around. This place isn't rugged enough. The neighbours don't like any noise at all. It's very constrictive, but I'm not here most of the time. I'm usually over at Linda's big house. I write and lay around. This place is for when things go wrong with her. Then I come running back here. I call it my office. You see, my typewriter isn't even here; it's over there. I used to pay rent over there. Then we had a split. Now I still live there, but I don't pay rent. That was a smart move.

RW: *How did you end up, at one point in your life, on the bum?*

CB: It just occurred. Probably through the drinking and disgust and having to hold a mundane job. I couldn't face working for somebody, that eight-to-five thing. So I got hold of a bottle and drank and tried to make it without working. Working was frankly distasteful to me. Starving and being on the bum seemed to have more glory.

There was a bar I went to in Philly. I had the same barstool—I forget where it was now; I think it was on the end—reserved for me. I'd open the bar early in the morning and close it at night. I was a fixture. I ran errands for sandwiches, hustled a little. I picked up a dime, a dollar here and there. Nothing crooked, but it wasn't eight to five; it was 5 a.m. to 2 a.m. I guess there were good moments, but I was pretty much out of it. It was kind of a dream state.

RW: *What poets do you like reading at the moment?*

CB: Auden was pretty good. When I was young and I read, I liked a lot of Auden. I was in a liking mood. I liked that whole gang: Auden, MacLeish, Eliot. I liked them at the time; but when I come back on them now, they don't strike me the same way. Not loose enough. They don't gamble. Too careful. They say good things, and they write it well; but they're too careful for me now.

And there's Stephen Spender. Once I was lying in bed, and I opened this book up. You know what happens when a poem hits you. I was thinking of that one with the touch of corn about the poets who have "left the air signed with their honour." That was pretty good. Spender got them off. I can't remember them all, but I know that he set me off three, four, five, six times. The more modern poets don't seem to do this to me.

It could be that I was more spiritually available to be turned on at that time and that I wasn't as much into the game. To be sitting in the stands as a spectator and see a guy hit a home run: Holy God, that ball goes flying over the fence, and it's a miracle. When you get down there and play with them and hit a few over yourself, you say, "That wasn't so hard. I just seemed to tap that ball, and it went over the wall." When you finally get into the game, miracles aren't as big as when you're looking on from the sidelines. That has something to do with my lack of appreciation now.

Then you meet writers finally, and that's not a very good experience. Usually, when they're not on the poem, they're rather bitchy, frightened, antagonistic little chipmunks. When they get turned on, art is their field; but when they get out of their field, they're despicable creatures. I'd much rather talk to a plumber over a bottle of beer than a poet. You can say something to a plumber, and he can talk back. The conversation can go both ways. A poet, though, or a creative person, is generally pushing. There's something I don't like about them. Hell, I'm probably the same way, but I'm not as aware of it as when it comes from another person.

RW: *Do the classical poets—say, Shakespeare—do anything for you?*

CB: Hardly. No, Shakespeare didn't work at all for me, except given lines. There was a lot of good advice in there, but he didn't pick me up. These kings running around, these ghosts, that upper-crust shit bored me. I couldn't relate to it. It had nothing to do with me. Here I am lying in a room starving to death—I've got a candy bar and half a bottle of wine—and this guy is talking about the agony of a king. It didn't help.

I think of Conrad Aiken as classical. He's hardly Shakespeare's time, but his style is classical. I feel it was influenced by the older poets way back. He is one of the few poets who turns me on with classical lines. I admire Conrad Aiken very much. But most of the—what shall I call them, purists?—don't pick me up.

There was one at the reading the other night. William Stafford. When he started turning on those lines, I couldn't listen. I have an instinctive radar, and it shut me off. I saw the mouth move, I heard sounds; but I couldn't listen. I don't want to take castor oil.

RW: *What do you look for in a good poem?*

CB: The hard, clean line that says it. And it's got to have some blood; it's got to have some humour; it's got to have that unnameable thing which you know is there the minute you start reading.

As I said, modern poets don't have it for some reason. Like Ginsberg. He writes a lot of good lines. You take the lines separately, read one and say, "Hey, that's a good line." Then you read the next one and say, "Well, that's a fair line"; but you're still thinking of the first line. You get down to the third, and there's a different twist. Pretty soon you're lost in this flotsam and jetsam of words that are words themselves, bouncing around. The totality, the total feel, is gone. That's what happens a lot. They throw in a good line—maybe at the end, maybe in the middle or a third of the way down—but the totality and the simplicity are not there. Not for me, anyway. They may be there, but I can't find them. I wish they were there; I'd have better reading material. That's why I'm not doing all the reading I should, or like people say you should.

RW: *How much reading should you do? I've always thought that writers who don't read are like people who always talk and never listen.*

CB: I don't listen very well, either. I think it's a protective mechanism. In other words, I fear the grind-down of doing something that's supposed to have an effect on me. Instinctively, I know ahead of time that the effect won't be there. That's my radar again. I don't have to arrive there myself to know that there's not going to be anything there.

I hit the library pretty hard in my early days. I did try the reading. Suddenly, I glanced around, and I was out of material. I'd been through all the standard literature, philosophy, the whole lot. So I branched out; I wandered around. I went into geology. I even made a study of the operation of the mesacolon. That operation was damned interesting. You know, the type of knives, what you do: shut this off, cut this vein. I said, "This isn't bad. Much more interesting than Chekhov." When you get into other areas, out of pure literature, you sometimes really get picked up. It's not the same old shit.

Anymore, I don't like to read. It bores me. I read four or five pages, and I feel like closing my eyes and going to sleep. That's the way it is. There are exceptions: J.D. Salinger; early Hemingway; Sherwood Anderson, when he was good, like *Winesburg, Ohio* and a couple of other things. But they all got bad. We all do. I'm bad most of the time; but when I'm good, I'm damned good.

RW: *At one point in your life, you stopped writing for ten years. Why was that?*

CB: It started around 1945. I simply gave up. It wasn't because I thought I was a bad writer. I just thought there was no way of crashing through. I put writing down with a sense of disgust. Drinking and shacking with women became my art form. I didn't crash through there with any feeling of glory, but I got a lot of experience which later I could use— especially in short stories. But I wasn't gathering that experience to write it, because I had put the typewriter down.

I don't know. You start drinking; you meet a woman; she wants another bottle; you get into the drinking thing. Everything else vanishes.

RW: *What brought it to an end?*

CB: Nearly dying. I ended up in County General Hospital with blood roaring out of my mouth and my ass. I was supposed to die, and I didn't. Took lots of glucose and ten or twelve pints of blood. They pumped it straight me into without stop.

When I walked out of that place, I felt very strange. I felt much calmer than before. I felt—to use a trite term—easygoing. I walked along the sidewalk, and I looked at the sunshine and said, "Hey, something has happened." You know, I'd lost a lot of blood. Maybe there was some brain damage. That was my thought, because I had a really different feeling. I had this calm feeling. I talk so slowly now. I wasn't always this way. I was kind of hectic before; I was more going, doing, shooting my mouth off. When I came out of that hospital, I was strangely relaxed.

So I got hold of a typewriter, and I got a job driving a truck. I started drinking huge quantities of beer each night after work and typing out all these poems. (I told you that I didn't know what a poem is, but I was writing something in a poem form.) I hadn't written many before, two or three, but I sat down and was writing poems all of a sudden. So I was writing again and had all these poems on my hands. I started mailing them out, and it began all over. I was luckier this time, and I think my work had improved. Maybe the editors were readier, had moved into a different area of thinking. Probably all three things helped make it click. I went on writing.

That's how I met the millionairess. I didn't know what to do with these poems, so I went down a list of magazines and put my finger on one. I said, "All right. Might as well insult this one. She's probably an old woman in this little Texas town. I'll make her unhappy." She wasn't an old woman. She was a young one with lots of money. A beautiful one. We ended up married. I was married to a millionairess for two and a half years. I blew it, but I kept writing.

RW: *What happened to the marriage?*

CB: I didn't love her. A woman can tolerate that so long unless she's getting some other type of benefit out of it, either fame or money from you. She got nothing out of our marriage, neither fame nor money. I offered her nothing. Well, we went to bed together. I offered her that, but that's hardly enough to hold a marriage together unless you're a real expert. I wasn't at the time. I was just some guy dressed in clothes who was walking across the room, eating an egg and reading the paper. I was tied up with myself, with my writing. I didn't give her anything at all, so I had it coming. I don't blame her, but she didn't give me much either.

She was arty and turned on to artistic types. She painted badly and liked to go to art classes. She had a vocabulary and was always reading fancy books. Being rich, she was spoiled in that special way rich people are spoiled without knowing it. She had this air that the rich have. They have a superior air that they never quite let go of. I don't think that money makes that much difference between people. It might be in what they wear, where they live, what they eat, what they drive; but I don't think it makes that much difference between people. Yet, somehow, the rich have this separation value. When they have money and you don't, something unexplainable rises up between you. Now, if she'd given me half of her money so that I could have had half of her feeling, we might have made it. She didn't. She gave me a new car, and that was it; and she gave that to me *after* we split, not before.

RW: *In a short story you made a sort of self-pitying remark that went something like this: "Here I am, a poet known to Genet and Henry Miller, washing dishes."*

CB: Yes, that's self-pity. That's straight self-pity, but sometimes self-pity feels good. A little howl, when it has some humour mixed with it, is almost forgivable. Self-pity alone . . . We all fail at times. I didn't do so well there.

I didn't do well as a dish washer, either. I got fired. They said, "This man doesn't know how to wash dishes." I was drunk. I didn't know how to wash dishes, and I ate all their roast beef. They had a big leg of roast beef back there. I'd been on a drunk, and I hadn't eaten for a week. I kept slicing this goddamned leg. I ate about half of it. I failed as a dish washer, but I got a good feed.

RW: *Another time, though, you said you enjoyed anonymity, that you liked the idea of people not knowing who you are. That seems like a contradiction.*

CB: There's a difference between being known by another writer and being known by the crowd. A good workman—if we can call it that— like, a carpenter—wants to be known as a good carpenter by other carpenters. The crowd is something else; but to be known by another good writer . . . I don't find that detestable.

RW: *Do the critics' opinion of your work ever bother you?*

CB: When they say I'm very, very good, it doesn't affect me anymore than when they say I'm very, very bad. I feel good when they say nice things; I feel good when they say unnice things, especially when they say them with great vehemence. Critics usually go overboard one way of the other, and one excites me as much as the other.

I want reactions to my work, whether they be good or bad; but I like an ad-mixture. I don't want to be totally revered or looked upon as a holy man or a miracle worker. I want a certain amount of attack, because it makes it more human, more like where I've been living all my life. I've always been attacked in one fashion or another, and it's grown on me. A little rejection is good for the soul; but total attack, total rejection is utterly destructive. So I want a good balance: praise, attack, the whole stewpot full of everything.

Critics amuse me. I like them. They're nice to have around, but I don't know what their proper function is. Maybe to beat their wives.

RW: *In Post Office, there's an episode about the flack you got from the government because of your writing. Did they actually give you a lot of trouble?*

CB: My God, yes. The whole scene underground: one dim light, the handshake, sitting down at the end of a long table, two guys asking me little trap questions. I just told them the truth. Everything they asked, I told the truth. (It's only when you lie that you get your ass in a wringer. I guess the big boys have found that out now.) I thought, Is this America? Sure, I'll back it all the way as really happening. I wrote a short story about it, too.

RW: *You've been published a lot in the underground press. Those newspapers, now, seem to have lost their original vigour. What happened to them?*

CB: They've turned it into a business, and the real revolutionaries were never there. The underground press was just lonely people who wanted to get around and talk to each other while putting out a newspaper. They went left wing and liberal, because it was the young and proper thing to do; but they weren't really interested in it. Those newspapers were kind of a lark. They were a sign to carry around, like wearing a certain type of clothing. I can't think of one underground newspaper that meant anything, shook anybody.

RW: *You mentioned your problems with women. Didn't one of your girlfriends recently try to kill you?*

CB: She found me on my way to another lady's house. I had already been there and gone and was coming back with two six-packs and a pint of whiskey. I was quite high at the time. Her car was parked out in front, so I said, "Oh, jolly. I'll take her up and introduce her to the other one, and we'll all be friends and have drinks." No chance. She rushed me. She got those bottles out and started smashing them all up and down the boulevard—including the pint of whiskey. She disappeared. I'm out sweeping the glass up, and I hear this sound. I looked up just in time. She's got her car up on the sidewalk, rushing it towards me. I leaped aside, and she was gone. She missed.

RW: *Many of your stories read as if they're written off the top of your head. Do you write that way, or do you rewrite a great deal?*

CB: I seldom revise or correct a story. In the old days, I used to just sit down and write it and leave it. I don't quite do that anymore. Lately I've started dripping out what I think are bad or unnecessary lines that take away from a story. I'll subtract maybe four or five lines, but I hardly ever add anything.

And I can't write except off a typewriter. The typewriter keeps it strict and confined. It keeps it right there. I've tried to write longhand; it doesn't work. A pencil or a pen . . . it's too intellectual, too soft, too dull. No machine-gun sounds, you know. No action.

RW: *Can you write and drink at the same time?*

CB: It's hard to write prose when you're drinking, because prose is too much work. It doesn't work for me. It's too unromantic to write prose while you're drinking.

Poetry is something else. You have this feeling in mind that you want to lay down the line that startles. You get a bit dramatic when you're drunk, a bit corny. The symphony music is on, and you're smoking a cigar. You lift the beer, and you're going to tap out these five or six or fifteen or thirty great lines. You start drinking and write poems all night. You find them on the floor in the morning. You take out all the bad lines, and you have poems. About sixty percent of the lines are bad; but it seems like the remaining lines, when you drop them together, make a poem.

I don't always write drunk. I write sober, drunk, feeling good, feeling bad. There's no special way for me to be.

RW: *Gore Vidal said once that, with only one or two exceptions, all American writers were drunkards. Was he right?*

CB: Several people have said that. James Dickey said that the two things that go along with poetry are alcoholism and suicide. I know a lot of writers, and as far as I know they all drink but one. Most of them with any bit of talent are drunkards, now that I think about it. It's true.

Drinking is an emotional thing. It joggles you out of the standardism of everyday life, out of everything being the same. It yanks you out of your body and your mind and throws you against the wall. I have the feeling that drinking is a form of suicide where you're allowed to return to life and begin all over the next day. It's like killing yourself, and then you're reborn. I guess I've lived about ten or fifteen thousand lives now.

RW: *Just a minute ago you mentioned classical music, and you make remarks about it in lots of your stories. Are you seriously interested in it?*

CB: Not as a conscious thing. In other words, I have a radio—no records—and I turn that classical music station on and hope it brings me something I can align with while I'm writing. I don't listen deliberately. Some people object to this in me. A couple of girl friends I've had have objected that I don't sit down and *listen*. I don't. I use it like the modern person uses the television set: they turn it on and walk around and kind of ignore it, but it's there. It's a fireplace full of coals that does something for them. Let's say it's something in the room with you that helps you, especially when you're living alone.

Say you work in a factory all day. When you come home, somehow that factory is still hanging on your bones: all the conversation, all the wasted hours. You try to recover from those eight, ten hours they've taken from you and use what juice you have left to do what you really want to do. First, I used to take a good, hot bath. Then I turned on the radio, got some classical music, lit a big cigar, opened a bottle of beer and sat down at the typewriter. All these became habitual, and often I couldn't write unless they were happening. I'm not so much that way now, but at the time I did need those props to escape the factory syndrome.

I like a certain amount of interruption when I'm writing. I do a lot of writing over at Linda's. She has two kids, and once in a while I like to have them run in. I like interruptions, as long as they're natural and aren't total and continuous. When I lived in a court, I put my typewriter right by the window. I'd be writing, and I'd see people walking by. Somehow that always worked into what I was doing at the moment. Children, people walking by and classical music are all the same that way. Instead of a hindrance, they're an aid. That's why I like classical music. It's there, but it's not there. It doesn't engulf the work, but it's there.

RW: *There's a certain Bukowski image that's been created: drunkard, lecher, bum. Do you ever catch yourself deliberately trying to live up to that image?*

CB: Sometimes, especially, say, at poetry readings where I have a bottle of beer by my hand. Well, I don't need that beer, but I can feel the audience relating when I lift that beer and drink it. I laugh and make remarks. I don't know if I'm playing the game or they're playing the game. Anyway, I'm conscious of some image that I've built up or that they've built, and it's dangerous. You notice that I'm not drinking today. I fooled you. Blew the image.

If I drink two or three days in a row, I get pretty bad. Like I said, I've been in the hospital. My liver is not in great shape, and probably neither are several other organs. I heat up very much; my skin gets red-hot. There are a lot of danger signs. I like drinking, but it should be alternated; so I take a few days off now and then, instead of running a string of drinking days and nights together like I used to. I'm fifty-three now; I want to stay in the game a while longer, so I can piss a lot of people off. If I live to be eighty, I'll really piss them off.

RW: *Are poetry readings as bad an experience as you make them out to be in a couple of your short stories?*

CB: They are torture, but I've got to pay for the horses. I guess I read for horses instead of people.

RW: *How much time to you spend at the track?*

CB: Too much, too much, and now I've got my girl friend hooked. I never mention the track to her, you know. We'll be lying down, and morning will come around. Or we'll be writing. (She writes in one corner of the room, and I write in another. We do pretty well that way.) We've been at the track all week, and I'll say, "We'll get some goddamned writing done today at last." All of a sudden, she says something about the race track. It could be just a word or two. I'll say, "All right, let's go. You said it." That always happens. If she'd keep her mouth shut, we'd never go. Between the two of us, we've got to solve that problem of one wanting to go and the other not.

Races are a drag-down. There are thirty minutes between races, which is a real murder of time; and if you lose your money on top of it, it's no good. But what happens is that you come home and think, "I've got it now. I know what they are doing out there." You get up a whole new system. When you go back, either they changed it a little or you don't follow your nose: you get off the system, and the horse comes in. Horses teach you whether you have character or not.

Sometimes we go to the thoroughbreds in the daytime, then we jump over and play the harness at night. That's eighteen races. When you do that, you've had it. You're so tired. It's no good. Between her and me, we've had a rough week; but track season closes in a few days, so my worries will be over. Race tracks are horrible places. If I had my way, I'd have them all burned down, destroyed. Don't ask me why I go, because I don't know; but I have gotten some material out of all that torture.

Horse racing does something to you. It's like drinking: it joggles you out of the ordinary concept of things. Like Hemingway used the bull-fights, I use the race track. Of course, when you go to the track every day, that's no damned joggle: it's a definite bring-down.

RW: *What do you think about the Supreme Court's recent decision on pornography?*

CB: I agree with almost everybody else. It was silly to relegate it to the local area, the town or the city. I mean, a man makes a movie; he spends millions of dollars on it, and he doesn't know where to send it. They're going to love it in Hollywood and hate it in Pasadena. He'll have to sense how each city is going to react. My idea on obscenity is to let everything go. Let everybody be as obscene as they wish, and it will dissipate. Those who want it will use it. It's hiding things, holding back that makes something so-called evil.

Obscenity is generally very boring. It's badly done. Look at the theatres that show porno films: they're all going broke now. That happened very quickly, didn't it? They lowered the price from $5 to 49 cents, and nobody wants to see them even for that. I've never seen a good porno film. They're all so dull. These vast mounds of flesh moving around: here's the cock; the guy has three women. Ho-hum. God, all that flesh. You know, what's exciting is a woman in clothes, and the guy rips her skirt off. These people have no imagination. They don't know how to excite. Of course, if they did, they'd be artists instead of pornographers.

RW: *I understand that* Post Office *might be sold to the movies. If it is, will you write the screenplay?*

CB: I would tend to back away from it. I'd rather put any energy I have (I almost said "left") into a piece of paper: beginning a new novel or finishing the one I'm at or starting a poem. I'm like any other guy who's doing what he wants to do in his own way.

It's such a whole new field that, unless I have total control, I don't want to enter it; and I'm not well enough known to get total control. Unless they gave me my own head, I wouldn't want to do it; and if they gave me my own head, *they* wouldn't want to do it. I don't want to fight all those people to get my thing across. Once again, the radar tells me there'd be too much trouble.

RW: *What are you working on now?*

CB: I'm putting a novel together. A book of short stories is coming out, and some of those are similar to chapters in the novel. So I'm pulling all these chapters out, patching it up and putting it back together. It's a good exercise. The novel is called *Factotum*. Factotum means a man of all trades, many jobs. It's about many of the jobs I've had. I took the glamorous chapters out, which is just as well. Now I can have the everyday humdrum thing of the alcoholic, low-class, as they call them, workers trying to make it. I got the idea, kind of, from *Down and Out in Paris and London*. I read that book and said, "This guy thinks something has happened to him? Compared to me, he just got scratched." Not that it wasn't a good book, but it made me think that I might have something interesting to say along those same lines.

RW: *One last question: Why do you put yourself down so much in your stories?*

CB: It's partly a kind of joke. The rest is because I feel that I'm an ass a lot of the time. If I'm an ass, I should say so. If I don't, somebody else will. If I say it first, that disarms them.

You know, I'm *really* an ass when I'm about half smashed. Then I look for trouble. I've never grown up. I'm a cheap drunk. Get a few drinks in me, and I can whip the world . . . and I want to.

The Free Press Symposium:
Conversations with Charles Bukowski

BEN PLEASANTS

1975

"The Free Press Symposium: Convesations with Charles Bukowski," Ben Pleasants, *LA Free Press*, October 31–November 6, 1975, pp 14–16.

Ben Pleasants

Ben Pleasants: Does lifestyle really matter? I mean, William Carlos Williams was a doctor; Stevens, an insurance man; Locklin's a professor.

Charles Bukowski: Lifestyle can matter finally. It can catch up with you. Sometimes it takes a while. Lifestyle's important. What you do is important. Like if you catch a dog and saw off his leg for breakfast, that's important.

Pleasants: That's lifestyle?

Bukowski: Yeah, that's good lifestyle. Not for the dog but for the hunter. The lonely hunter.

Pleasants: How did Bukowski get you guys going? As a writer? When did you first run into him, and what was the influence he had?

Steve Richmond: I started writing before I ever heard of Bukowski. I was told to send some poems to lots of magazines. The *Wormwood Review* was one of the three magazines along with *Kenyon*, *Partisan*. And there were Bukowski's poems in *Wormwood*. And *Ole* came in there too. This was 10 years ago. I put out a little book, and I sent it to Bukowski (somebody sent me his address); he sent me back a little "thank you" note. One thing led to the next, and there's been some influence.

Ron Koertge: I was writing before I heard of Bukowski, too. Because I was writing at the age of 5, and that's why. At the University of Arizona Locklin showed me a copy of the *Wormwood Review*. And the first time I saw anything by Bukowski was in *Wormwood* magazine. And I can't help but say what Steve says, that it's the same kind of thing. I don't know what the influence is, but the influence is there. There's no question about it.

Locklin: Yeah. This is going to sound like a commercial for *Wormwood Review* pretty soon, but that's where I first saw Bukowski's things. I was publishing, too. And I saw a couple of his poems in there. Actually, the first couple of things I saw, I didn't even like them that well as poems. But I did like what he was doing and I thought it was something different from what a lot of people were doing. I liked the spontaneity, and I liked the closeness to the subject matter, and I liked the honesty of the poems.

And so a couple of years later, somebody in Long Beach wanted me to find someone to give a reading down there. I'd heard a little about Bukowski by then, and I said I'd try to get in touch with him, and I did. He came down for a reading, and since then I've read much more of his work.

Pleasants: What about readings? Is poetry better on the page or on the stage?

Bukowski: I don't think anybody should ever read poetry before an audience unless it's a matter of survival. Getting the rent or getting a new tire for your car, getting a car. I think there's a lot of vanity in reading to the audience. I think the creative act is when it comes out of the typewriter. That's all. I have apprehension about reading. Every time I read, I . . . I guess that's why I have to jostle the audience a bit. I feel like they're the enemy. That they've come to see the sacrifice. Even though I read, I'm against it.

Locklin: I have never made up my mind about reading. Sometimes I enjoy doing them and sometimes I don't. But I certainly do agree with Bukowski that the primary thing is the typewriter. Readings are secondary.

Pleasants: Steve, you read at Chatterton's about six months ago. What are your reactions?

Richmond: That was the first time in five or six years. That's just to push the book I put out, to get some money, to buy a tire. Other than that, they're really a bore.

Bukowski: How about impressing the female?

Richmond: That's the only good reason, really.

Pleasants: How does sex influence good writing, and does women's liberation affect what you say?

Koertge: I think so. If I was pretty sure that I could get laid and I had to read a poor poem to do it, I'd do it in a minute.

Bukowski: Even if the poem was three minutes long, right?

Koertge: And about the women's liberation thing, I seem to be on the side of feminists. I like a lot of women who are feminists. I think it's probably right. It's on the side of angels.

Pleasants: Safe place to be.

Meeting of the "Bukowski Symposium" at the L.A. Free Press, 1975.
(l. to R.) Ron Koertge, Ben Pleasants, Charles Bukowski, Steve Richmond, Gerald Locklin

Koertge: When there are lots of angels. I think that's probably it. None of the poems that I write would be published in women's journals or anything but some tend to be sympathetic poems, to the plight of women. For all I know that's just a fulcrum to bounce into their underwear.

Pleasants: Steve, you do a lot of things in terms of sexuality.

Richmond: There's no place really to explore the planet now except maybe a change of molecules. What's going on inside of that hole . . . You've got your pole, they've got their hole, and all of these emotional things to come from that interaction. What's going on there, so we can explore that . . .

Bukowski: And write about it, right?

105

Pleasants: Why do all young poets, with the exception of Richmond, want to be novelists?

Bukowski: I don't think that's true.

Pleasants: I think it's true of all the people who are here.

Locklin: I have a theory on that. I think it goes back to Hemingway. Hemingway loved his life, which I think has been rather envied. He made it as a writer at a fairly young age, he had a very interesting life; he wrote well in spite of it. But I think he's so envied as both a person and a writer that people, at least in their early years, start out wanting to be Hemingway. And they get started thinking that to be a writer means to be a novelist.

Bukowski: Listen, I tend to disagree with all of that. I find that too many poets are poets and poets only. Not just write the poem but continue to write the poem.

Pleasants: Same one over and over?

Bukowski: No, they usually don't improve. But the idea is they think there's something aside from *the* Hemingway, against *the* Hemingway. They think there's something corrupt about being a novelist. Or worse, a short-story writer is really looked down upon. And most, especially in L.A. or Frisco, many poets just write poetry, and they feel a certain muse arrives for the poet and doesn't arrive for the short-story writer or the novelist.

And that having written the poem and feeling holy about it, they starve to death or have people taking care of them. They O.D. and they beg and they sleep on people's couches because they are the poet and they deserve this special treatment . . . that a novelist or a short-story writer doesn't deserve because a poet's a special type of person. And I don't think they are.

Pleasants: Actually, you brought prose to poetry. Your brought short stories and novels to poetry. A lot of your stuff is really stories.

Bukowski: It's just a line. I could write a poem as a short novel. That's all.

Locklin: I always thought that was true. In the universities, they tend to talk about restoring narrative to poetry and that sort of thing, and as far as I'm concerned, Bukowski did it without even thinking about it.

Richmond: It's easier to get a poem published than it is a novel.

Bukowski: It's easier to get a poem rejected than it is a novel.

Koertge: No, it's not. It just takes longer for a novel.

Bukowski: No, you see, you write a novel and how many pages have you blown to the winds? A poem comes back, and you either send it out again, or tear it up. Then you sit down, put on a new typewriter ribbon, and you get another poem. It's less time consumed.

Pleasants: There's another thing, though. A really good poem is like a stick of dynamite: it just goes off with tremendous force. Whereas a novel is another type of thing. I think in terms of power you can say it better in a poem than you can in a novel.

Bukowski: Yeah, if it works . . . . You mentioned John Crowe Ransom. One of the only good poems he wrote was about the Catholic girls, you know. He was watching them walk by, and he said, "I know a woman"—these aren't the exact lines, but "I know a woman who is now old and so forth and so forth who was once more beautiful than any of you." And that was a powerful . . . a poem can do that . . . I know what you're saying.

Pleasants: I wanted to ask you about the influences that made you think first of all and the influences that made you work. What about those two concepts?

Bukowski: Think and work? I don't even like those words; I don't know what they mean.

Pleasants: O.K., well, the ones that moved you to get to the typewriter and work.

Bukowski: What moved me to the typewriter was just sheer desperation. I had these dog jobs, and my time was being invested in another man's game. He had my life . . . 8, 10, 12 hours . . .

Pleasants: But other writers have done that, too. Didn't you see the possibility of working that con game, too?

Bukowski: I didn't know what other writers had done. I just had to take those extra couple of hours, get the beer out, and to balance what was happening to me.

Richmond: It's got a lot to do with making your own answers to survive. You know, you read a book and there's no answer there. There's nothing worth surviving for in what you read. Nothing worth surviving for in what you see in the streets. So you go to the typewriter and you create something, and it becomes the only thing worth surviving for.

Bukowski: Exactly it.

Pleasants: What do you have to say about that, Ron?

Koertge: I don't think anything. I mean, not that's coherent.

Pleasants: In what Bukowski's done, is poetry prose? What is the distinction? What makes a poem poetry?

Bukowski: I don't concern myself with what's a poem, what's a novel. I just write it down—it either works or it doesn't work. I'm not concerned with "this is a poem, this is a novel, this is a shoe, this is a glove." I write it down and that's it. That's the way I feel about it.

Pleasants: Do you feel that way, Ron?

Koertge: I like having published enough so that I can send things out, and if people say we don't like this 'cause it isn't a real poem, I can just send it out again, and somebody'll say we're gonna publish this and call it prose poems or something. I don't care what they call it. But I like being in the position where I don't have to worry about it.

Pleasants: This is a question to Bukowski. Jeffers was a nihilist, classic definition. Are you a nihilist? And what about the influence of philosophy?

Bukowski: You want to find out if I know what the word nihilist means?

Pleasants: No, you know what it means.

Bukowski: I don't know what I am. But certain people in the marketplace say "he's very negative." This is the put-down. They never read the stuff. It might be a long blonde in a long dress lighting a ciga-rette, talking to a friend of mine . . . "Bukowski's so negative," and that's all I know about nihilism. So maybe I am.

Pleasants: But nihilism is really about antiman, that man is a filthy animal. You don't really feel that way, do you?

Bukowski: No, I don't. Man is a drab animal who's wasting his potential. God, that sounds holy. I get on a bus full of people and I look at them and I get unhappy because I feel that they're not right for certain reasons. Not because they don't have God, not because they're not drunk—there's something else wrong there that disturbs me.

Pleasants: You're really a defender of the little man in many ways. Maybe you don't know you are, but a lot of little men feel that way.

Bukowski: I don't know about that.

Pleasants: I'd like Bukowski to discuss the poets present.

Bukowski: O.K. Richmond, I think, has this wildness that is very attractive. I can open one of his books and read right through it. Of course, I don't start with the first poem . . . I find one here and there. I can open one of his books and no matter which page I land on there is, even with the worst poems, some strength there, and it's this simple, profound savagery.

He has it, and I've always said he's had it, but they haven't found him yet; and even when they find him, like Picasso said, "Even when I was unknown, only a few people knew what I was doing, and now that I'm discovered, and I'm known, still only a few people know what I'm about."

In other words, for Steve, it doesn't matter except for his own ego, maybe getting a little more cash in his pocket, but he's doing his job, and he's doing a damn good job.

And K., if Ron has stolen a little bit of my thunder, I always believe in jostling, getting a little bit of humor into the tragic aspects of whatever we're trying to do—inhale and exhale, survive. I brought out a book like that. The beer's getting to me, tra-la-la.

Anyhow, I think I can speak of Locklin and K in the same fashion that brought humor and looseness into the game. They brought joy into it, you know. They've jostled it. They've opened it up, and it's good. The game has been too dusty and too stodgy and too holy. They've brought in orange seeds, vomit, horse's hooves, laughter, the whole thing. It's a good show. They've done it—they've opened up areas—they've loosened it.

Pleasants: What about publishers? How do publishers get into the whole milieu of writing?

Bukowski: I have to be careful now. How do they get in? I don't know—I can't even answer that. I don't know their motives—I don't know—I'm not them.

Pleasants: How do you deal with them?

Bukowski: I've been pretty lucky. Basically, I leave them alone, they leave me alone. They do what they have to do, and I do what I have to do. The best publisher is the one who doesn't bother you, phone you; you leave him alone. It's kind of an offhand thing at best. It's not chummy. It just works. You turn on the hot-water faucet, it warms up and gets hot, and you use it. You use publishers, and publishers use you. It's a good affair—it has to be a good affair. That's the way it's set up.

Pleasants: Faulkner said his books were his children. Are your books your children?

Bukowski: I'm sorry Faulkner ever said that.

Pleasants: Which one do you like best?

Bukowski: Of Faulkner's?

Pleasants: No, of your books.

Bukowski: Oh, I don't have any preference. It's all similar. It's all one line.

Pleasants: Which are the poets you most admire from days gone by?

Bukowski: Oh, way back? Jeffers, to begin with. In his short stuff he tends to preach. But there haven't been many good poets. They don't pick me up. I don't have any influences. Maybe Jeffers, a long time ago; and at a time, there was Stephen Spender. He had some flowing lines, you know—"This man's dead life, that man's life dying." Then there was Auden for a while—there was always somebody for a while, and then it flattens out and you move to another. There's really nobody.

Pleasants: How do you like working on a deadline as you do at the *Free Press?*

Bukowski: Actually, I got three columns ahead the other week, before I got all messed up. But it works both ways. You can write some awful bad stuff. I have had some luck, too. I've sat down, I just put the page in, and I say, "Well, you don't even feel like writing, you have nothing in your head, and all this stuff comes out. It just clicks. I've gotten quite a few stories that way. I've gotten on to a book of stories later on. So it works both ways. You get the bad and the get the miracles sometimes when you don't even think it's there . . . it arrives.

Pleasants: What about Bukowski the cartoonist? Isn't there a Thurber connection there?

Bukowski: I've been accused of that.

Pleasants: You like Thurber.

Bukowski: Yeah, I did. But I think if you compare my drawings to his, you'll see an influence, but there's a good deal of difference. His people are upper middle-class, having their problems, and mine are kind of stark and out of it. They're kind of stunned and they don't quite know what's happening. Even the look of them: no eyes and they're just standing. Things have happened to them that have stunned them into gentle imbecility that might be endearing in its best light.

And I think the whole tonality's a great deal different from Thurber, though maybe the line or the drawing of a dog or something, there's a similarity in that aspect. There's an influence, but the whole tonality is just the opposite.

Pleasants: How do you relate to the problems of writing a novel as compared to writing poetry?

Bukowski: A novel is a real—it's laying down a mattress you can't sleep on. It's hard work, it's work in a factory. But the way to do it, of course, is to write short chapters, and that gives it . . . Most novels bore me—God, that's awful but they do—I guess I write short poems, and they all add up to a big novel, I don't know, I haven't answered that very well . . .

Pleasants: No, that's good.

Bukowski: It bothers your mind. It's like trying to hide a girlfriend from your wife.

Pleasants: I want to get back to politics. I personally think that people can write political things and make them valuable. I won't give any examples of Solzhenitsyn, but how does politics affect good writing, and can a writer be political and artistic at the same time?

Bukowski: I was going to answer that Neruda got away with it. Also, there was this guy in Germany who wrote the song "Mack the Knife." I've heard his stuff over the radio. He has such a powerful clean line, and he's talking about things that are happening during the day: it gets very good and then he throws in, can I say, Marxist lines, and it just deadens me. I say, why did he do that?

Pleasants: Because he's a Marxist.

Bukowski: It's like a guy with one ball, finally, to me. I think you can improve life without being political.

Pleasants: Is Solzhenitsyn's writing of value?

Locklin: Yes, it's of value.

Pleasants: I found a strange thing. He wasn't the first Russian writer to come to America for asylum to be elevated to a certain fashion. I think we spoil the Russian writers. We bring them over . . .

Pleasants: Who was the other one?

Bukowski: There was someone else, I've forgotten . . . It goes back a ways.

Pleasants: Where is the center of American poetry today in terms of location?

Bukowski: Probably east Kansas City, Kan.

Pleasants: The Iowa writers' school? San Francisco? Is it in Los Angeles?

Bukowski: How can I say that?

Koertge: Well, it sort of has to be Los Angeles and New York. That's the easy answer. San Francisco?

Bukowski: But Los Angeles is not looked at as a literary center at all.

Koertge: No, but there's more going on here than people know.

Bukowski: And when they know, it'll be time to move, right?

Koertge: I wouldn't know where to go.

Locklin: Carlsbad.

Bukowski: D.H. Lawrence had Taos; Jeffers created Big Sur, right? A writer creates an area where he creates, and then the mob comes in and there they are. So maybe they'll discover Los Angeles.

Koertge: Well that's the thing about L.A., it's so big. It's such a fucking octopus that you can get away.

Locklin: There aren't literary movements, there aren't literary groups, particularly in L.A. There are lots of creative people who don't see each other that often. I see Bukowski about once every year. Ron and I are very close friends, and I might see him every couple of months.

Koertge: I haven't seen Steve for six years.

Bukowski: Every time I see Ron, it's at the racetrack and he's reading a book out there. He's not even reading the racing form.

Richmond: We don't see each other but we read each other all the time.

Koertge: Oh, sure.

Bukowski: This is our worst day right now.

Richmond: This is good once every five, six years.

Koertge: Like one of those college things. We ought to agree to meet here 10 years from now and also agree not to see each other for 10 years, then we'll all come back.

Pleasants: What are the future plans for Bukowski? Besides survival.

Bukowski: Well, that's the No. 1 thing: Durability is more important than truth. In order to tell the truth, you've got to be durable to begin with. My master plan which probably won't work . . . I decided a long time ago to live to 80 or so and die in the year 2000. I saw Wantling at a reading in Illinois. He decided to die in the same year, and a month later he was dead. So you know the master plan like Adolph's may not work.

But my master plan is to shove it to 'em for another 25 years. I'm going to make them so sick of me that when I die there will be screams of joy. And then later, exaggerations of my greatness. That's it, the year 2000.

Pleasants: What is the possibility of Bukowski winning the Nobel or the Pulitzer Prize?

Bukowski: Go to hell!

Koertge: I don't know what the standards are exactly. But as a kind of guess, it seems extremely rare. Just because he's such a cattle prod, he goads so many people. He's so electric and alive all the time. I think he'd piss off too many people too often that would be on the board for them to put him up to it.

Pleasants: I'd just like to draw up at this point anything you'd like to add.

Bukowski: There are a lot of people who talk about Bukowski who say, "He hates women," or "He's so negative." But they don't . . . it's a word-of-mouth thing that passes around. They don't examine the work. When I started reading at the age of three, I found literature very damn dull and pretensive. I felt it was a hoax. Parts of Shakespeare were very good. I'm not just saying Shakespeare . . .

Pleasants: Well, you didn't like Faulkner . . .

Bukowski: Well, Faulkner, too, Faulkner in the italics—the thought processes. But what I'm trying to say, I got the feeling it's his ego with a big E. That literature had been a grand hoax—a drab, dull, pretensive game, that it lacked humanism. There are exceptions—but I just felt it was a kind of hoax through the centuries. You'd open a book and fall asleep, just dull and contrived. It just seemed to be a damn hoax.

So I thought, let's open up and clear up the line—be able to hang out a clothesline, a simple line, and be able to hang emotion in it—humor, happiness—without it being cluttered. The simple, easy line, and yet having the simple easy line to hang all these things—the laughter, the tragedy, the bus running through a red light. Everything.

It's the ability to say a profound thing in a simple way. And they've been doing it backwards. They've been saying—what? I don't know what they've been saying. It's been very discouraging. So I've tried—it sounds very holy—but I've tried to open up what I thought was wrong with the whole game. And I've had a hell of a lot of help, too—J.D. Salinger and these people sitting around the table tonight.

O.K., that's about it.

Interview: Charles Bukowski

INTERVIEWED BY DOUGLAS HOWARD

1975

"Interview: Charles Bukowski," Douglas Howard, *Grapevine* (Fayetteville, Arkansas), Vol. 6, No. 19, January 29, 1975, pp. 1, 4–5.

GV: I suppose there are many typical questions that you are asked in interviews and that answering them becomes somewhat repetitive.

B: Feel free.

GV: In *South of No North*, you seem to have basically two types of stories. One is the imaginative story and the other is the autobiographical story.

B: That's true. I no longer recall *South of No North*, but basically that's true of all my stories. There are some where the two intermix; so you might say there are three kinds, some in which imagination mixes with reality, half and half.

GV: Do you know which story in *South of No North* would be typical of that?

B: No. I couldn't tell without glancing through the book. (*picks up copy of* South of No North.) Let me see; in this case there might be just the two types. Basically, you're right here; there's either one or the other; there's no intermixture. Most of these are fictional rather than autobiographical.

GV: "No Way to Paradise," the story with the miniature people, do you remember how it originated?

B: No. Oh, yes. I can, because I have to do a column. I don't have to, but I do do a column every week for the *Free Press*, and the deadline was there, and I had no idea of what to write. So I just sat down and started typing, and that's what came out. It was kind of like, you might say, if I can use the word, a lark. But I think it worked. I just wrote something. There was nothing in my head at all.

GV: What about "Maja Thurup?"

B: Oh, that came out of a newspaper. I read where this woman had gone and found a savage and brought him back home with her. I just read a clipping in the paper, and the rest took off naturally from there. So there is one in which imagination and reality to mix up. A lot of people didn't like that story. It upset them.

GV: There's horror in it.

B: I wrote a story once about a little girl getting raped on roller skates. In fact, it appeared in the *Free Press*, and the editor put a long prelude in front of it before he published it: "Bukowski has a daughter; he loves his daughter; if you see Bukowski with his daughter, you'll understand that he's a good man." He had to say all of these things before he published the story. He was frightened of it. What I try to do is to get into the mind of a man who would do such a thing, and try to figure his viewpoint. I write stories about murderers, rapists, all these types. It doesn't mean that I'm a murderer or a rapist. People don't seem to understand that. Or, it doesn't mean that I'm for murder or rape or anything, but I like to explore what this man might be thinking and that a murderer can enjoy a cup of hot cocoa or enjoy a comic strip. This is rather fascinating to me, you know, to explore these things.

GV: Well, one wonders when reading your stories about what kind of person you are because you have a lot of characters who are very macho. There's one called "The Man," in which a woman comes in, and this fellow's a dishwasher, and she tells him what a good man he is. He ends up slugging her and then putting out a cigarette on her wrist.

B: Again, this isn't totally imaginative. There was a guy like that. So I just took off on the memory of him and wrote him up. It wasn't me. I'm very gentle with my women. In my life, of all the women I've known,

I have hit two of them. And that's, that's a pretty good record with all the women I've known. They got to me twice. Generally, I'm very gentle, very tolerant. I try to understand what's bothering them.

GV: When you write your stories are you concerned with meanings, or are you concerned with something that you might call "play." There seems to be a lot of "play" in your stories, writing that is done for the sheer excitement of something very peculiar, very strange, bizarre, different.

B: You're right. I get my kicks out of exploring these areas. You know when I write the poem I tend to stay pretty close to the source of things. In the stories I kick up my heels; I rather enjoy myself in the stories; I get my natural kicks, as you might say. It's a relaxer. Sometimes I might even write stories that might upset people, deliberately, just to do it. Yea, I get my natural kicks writing short stories, a relaxer; then I go back to the poem; I jump back and forth. One helps the other.

GV: Do you revise much?

B: Not stories; usually they just come straight on out. I'll change a line or two that's awkward. I revise poems much more. Stories, they just come out.

GV: Hugh Fox wrote a book on you in which he said that you're basically an underground writer and that you're not accepted by the big New York publishers because of that.

B: No. What has happened is that I'm tied up with Black Sparrow, and actually, I have had some overtures from New York publishers. Doubleday wanted to do a book of my selected poems. But Martin, you know at Black Sparrow, said that he'd rather do them. Also, Viking Press wanted to reprint *Post Office*, but Martin asked too much for the rights; so they didn't do it. I believe it was $40,000 he wanted. So in a sense, I'm underground, and, in a sense, I'm damn glad of it because it allows me to remain fairly level. Poverty is a good cleanser, you know.

GV: Yes, Fox called you radioactive, and I wondered, if you were published by the "overground" press, would that tend to hurt you as a writer?

117

B: There's no telling what that might do, and, of course, there is a gamble that it would be destructive. The women would get younger, better looking, and I would drive a better car, and maybe I would lose my touch through this.

GV: You have a story about a writer who does that.

B: (*Laughs*) Yea, I thought that it might possibly be me, but it doesn't seem to be working that way. The women aren't getting younger.

GV: The writer in the story started out with a thirty-five year old, and by the end of the story he has a seventeen year old.

B: I was really dreaming then. Could still happen.

GV: Are you living off your writing now?

B: Yes, I have been since . . . I quit my job at the age of fifty, and I've been paying my way now for four years. I've been drinking a lot of beer, playing the horses, and I usually eat a steak for dinner.

GV: Are you keeping ahead on the horses?

B: No. But in the last month or so I've been doing very well. I've got a new system. Sometimes these systems do well for a month or two, and then they just simply fall apart. Then I have to invent a new one, you know, to have an excuse to keep playing. I need the horses for my writing.

GV: How's that?

B: Well, you know, you sit around . . . It sets something off in me. I go out there and the people, the action, the drabness of it, everything . . . it's a loosener, I'm able to write that very night, especially if I lose a lot of money. If I lose a lot of money I'll get drunk and really write some poetry. I guess it's fear.

GV: Do you write best when you're unhappy or when you're feeling good?

B: Both ways, when you're feeling real good you write, when you're feeling bad you write, and when you're not feeling anything you write. You write all the time; it doesn't matter.

GV: Fox says that you have said that most of the things that are published by the overground magazines, the poems, are "dullness and poetic pose."

B: Yea, well, I'll back that still. I see poems in *The New Yorker* now, I read a *New Yorker* on the plane coming in, and the poems are still bad, very bad, old stuff with French phrases. And they're playing with words, "The trees fell down; the sun came through," the sun, the moon, the stars, the same old shit. The poetry is still lazy and false; I can't buy most of that stuff.

GV: Do you ever write formal verse?

B: No.

GV: Do you think that formal verse is false because it's formal?

B: It's not false because it's formal, but it's been around too long. It's been overused, and it's become a bore and a drag. No, it's not false because it's formal; it's just dull because it's formal. They've been overdoing it, and they continue to do it. Like I say, I can't use it.

GV: I wanted to ask you about women.

B: Women? Oh, boy, I know all about them. I've been on the earth fifty-four years, and I've lived with many of them.

GV: Do you . . .

B: What the hell are they?

GV: In at least two stories you have men being castrated. In "No Way to Paradise" Anna castrates George because, she says, if she can't have him, she won't let him have anyone else. And then there's another story, I've forgotten which, in which a man castrates himself so that his wife won't have power over him sexually.

B: Yea, I've been wondering about this castration complex of mine. I've written a couple of poems about it too. I just thought of it the other day. I said, "what am I about here? What does this mean?" I really don't know, unless . . . I think it's more symbolic than actual. In other words, it's . . . at times we all try to figure ways to escape the female and the power she has over us. I would never take that route; it's probably a symbolic gesture though. It's the only thing I could think of at those moments, you see, of frustration and panic and dominance and loss. It just happens to my characters. I can't figure it; I can't figure the meaning of it.

GV: In *Post Office*, Henry Chinaski always had a lot of trouble with his women, and it seemed like he was very reasonable generally, but his women took very irrational positions that he just had to put up with.

B: Chinaski just happened to stumble on a bad run of women. All women in the world aren't like his women.

GV: You have another escape from women in "Love for $17.50," where a man buys a mannequin and falls in love with it.

B: That's totally imaginary. I was driving by this place, and this mannequin was standing out front of the store, and she looked very fine. Had on high heels, a real class doll, you know. In fact, I even asked my girl friend at the time, "Why don't you buy me that mannequin?" She never did. So the idea for the story came from that. Perhaps, if I had really let myself go, I might have done the same thing; I don't know. But that's where I got the idea. I drove by and saw that mannequin standing there that looked better than a hell of a lot of women I've seen. A real class mannequin. She held her head so nicely, and all that business. Looked like a teacher of algebra. I'm really not anti-woman. I'm really not pro-woman. I just experience them and write about it.

GV: Do you have any opinions on women's liberation?

B: I suppose I do. Overall, I think, it's a good thing, but also it's weakening. Once you gather in a group and you start using group ideas, you lose your own individual thinking processes. And in that way, it's weakening. So, you get some baddies in that group too, simply man haters. It's like any other group; it has its good points and its bad; it has its freaks; it helps some and destroys others. Overall, I'd say it's a good function.

GV: Have you read Erica Jong's *Fear of Flying*?

B: No, I've heard about it, but I haven't read it. I've almost lost the ability to read. I did all my reading in the twenties and teens, and it's very hard for me to read anything, except my own stuff.

GV: Why is that? Do you get bored with it?

B: I do. I read the lines, I get into the first paragraph, and I just can't . . . I feel some falsity; some bad line or a bad paragraph right away, and it just spoils the whole story. I guess I'm just too critical to read anything. I've fallen in love with myself.

GV: Do you have a central theme in your fiction?

B: Life, with a small "l."

GV: Experience?

B: Some is experience; some is things I hear, envision . . . it comes from everywhere. The more experience you have, the better off you are, of course.

GV: I was going to ask you if you have any favorite contemporary fiction writers, but if you don't read much anymore, I don't suppose you do.

B: I'd have to go way back to an undiscovered guy, well he was discovered at the time. His name was John Fante. He had a great influence on me. I liked his writing style. It was open and easy, and it was clear and it was emotional, and it was just damned good writing. He seems to have been forgotten.

GV: What are some of his books?

B: *Ask the Dust; Wait Until Spring, Bandini.* H.L. Mencken discovered him, and he printed him in *The American Mercury.* He wrote about Italian family life. I just liked his writing style; it was open and clear. And then I liked Carson McCullers. I thought she wrote very well. But the contemporary writers I don't know. Mailer doesn't go down for me. I don't know. I don't read too much, but when I come upon it, nothing happens.

GV: What about William Saroyan?

B: Saroyan, I liked his writing style; it's easy. Fante and Saroyan, I really liked their open, easy style, but Saroyan was so sugary with this love thing, and it was kind of like he built a fairyland in there that didn't quite jive with reality. And this used to irritate me a little bit, but he had this easy, open style, and he filled it with sugar and creampuffs most of the time. I couldn't understand how a man who could write so easily and openly could stumble on the content, on the other part of it. So I decided to take care of the content . . . shit.

GV: I've thought of you and Saroyan as being like opposite sides of the same coin, because you have that openness, that you were speaking of, in common.

B: I really liked his style. I picked up on it right away. He can lay down that easy flowing line, uncluttered, but what he said with it, oh.

GV: He was an idealistic young man.

B: He was. I was never an idealistic young man. There's the difference. I like to think I'm closer to the truth. I have moments of optimism. They are rare. (*New beers are passed out.*)

B: Do you think you'll be able to write this thing up in any manner?

GV: What I'll do is transcribe it and then take out the slow parts.

B: (*Laughs*) Maybe you'll have to take out the whole thing.

GV: There is one other thing I wanted to ask you about, which, simply put, is why you write dirty stories?

B: I don't think I write dirty stories.

GV: Well, let me put it another way. A lot of them concern the seedy side of life.

B: Yea, well, I've lived the seedy side of life. Therefore, I'm able to write about it, skidrow conditions. I've lived with alcoholic women; I've lived on very little money; I've lived a kind of mad existence. So therefore I have to write about it. The sex sometimes got grimy; but actually a dirty story is a very dull story. If you ever try to read one, you know: "the guy took out his throbbing cock; it was eight inches long, and she bent her lips . . ." This is a dirty story, and it's boring. So I wouldn't say I write dirty stories.

GV: The reason I used the term was that it was used, quoting you, I think, in Miller's anthology of contemporary American poets.

B: Well, it's all right. It's a loose term. It doesn't wound me too much. I'm just not a dirty guy. There is a lot of puritan in me. That's what my girlfriends tell me: "God, you're almost a Puritan, and you write that stuff."

GV: Why do they say that?

B: Well, in the sexual act, in making love, I tend not to be too forward. I even hate to make love in the day time; you no, you're looking into her eyes, she's looking into yours. It's kind of embarrassing. There's a great deal of Puritan in me. Luckily, I've met a woman now who's taught me a great deal about love-making, you know, what a woman wants. I've complied and I've enjoyed it. So, I'm learning at a late age. I guess I've been a bad fuck to a lot of women for two or three decades. No wonder I've had so much trouble with women. Now, my God, I can't get rid of them. It's really switched around.

GV: Do you meet more women since becoming a writer?

B: Since I've learned to make good love, which was five years ago, I've had a great deal of trouble, and the writing has something to do with it, but the, shall we call it, the expert love-making has a great deal to do with it too. I've got a saying now about women, "They always come back." It's true. You think they've gone forever, and here they're at the door again. They always come back, sometimes at the same time, two or three of them. That's when it gets rough. Here I've turned into a lady's man, and I've got this big pot belly; I'm fifty-four years old; my shoulders are slumped; my nerves are shot. All of a sudden I'm a lady's man. It's weird.

GV: Are most of the poems you have written in the three volumes that Black Sparrow has published?

B: Yes, with the last one, they got *Crucifix*, and they've selected some poems too, in this last one, *Burning in Water*; it has a great many of the poems outside the two books, *Mockingbird* and *Days Run Away;* they left those out. So you buy those three books, and that's about me, so far as the poems go. That wraps it up. Of course, I intend to write another twenty years. We'll see.

GV: I really liked "What a Man I Was."

B: Oh, yea. People tell me they like that, but I'm not so . . . I think it's a little bit whacky, and a little bit on the corny side, I'm not crazy about it. He shoots out the stars and the moon. Yea, my girlfriend says, "Why don't you read that at your reading?" I say, "Oh my God, no."

GV: Well, he's like Big Bart (a character in "Stop Staring at My Tits Mister").

B: Oh, Big Bart. (*Laughs*) I got that story . . . somebody mailed me a sex magazine, and it had this story about this kid and the evil man, and it was very corny. So I kind of re-wrote it and changed the ending. In the story in the sex magazine the woman shoots the evil guy, Big Bart, but in my story she shoots the kid. Big Bart's the one she really wants. That story was so bad I wanted to re-write it for the fellow.

GV: Do you get nervous before a reading?

B: When I read, usually, I'm a little bit nervous on my first one or two poems, and then it drops away. When I first started reading, I was pretty tense, but hell, after you give twenty, thirty-five readings, it tends to drop away, just by attrition.

GV: You have a soft voice.

B: People meet me and they say, "My God, you got this soft, gentle voice." After reading my stories they expect me to come in the doorway (*shouts*): "Hey, you motherfuckers, let's get on with it." And they say, "Are you Bukowski?" They expect something crude, some guy stomping around with big feet: "Gimme another beer, you son-of-a-bitch!" I always let 'em down. "Are you Bukowski?" "Yea, I'm Bukowski." Oh, God. Oh, I get a little raunchy at times.

Charles Bukowski, An Interview: Los Angeles, August 19, 1975

Marc Chénetier

1975

"Charles Bukowski, An Interview: Los Angeles, August 19, 1975," Marc Chénetier, *Northwest Review*, Vol. XVI, No. 3, 1977, pp. 5–24.

Interviewer: Somewhere You say you are not interested in writing "novels," you just write your life. Is all you write strictly autobiographical?

Charles Bukowski: I think I improve my life with fiction or creative fiction. I shine up the areas that need to be shined up and leave out the parts that . . . I don't know. It's just selectivity. Generally what I write is mostly fact but it's also adorned with a bit of fiction, a turn here and there to make it separate. I guess it's cheating in a way, but you could call it fiction. Is fiction cheating? (*Laughs*) I mix fact with fiction. Nine-tenths fact and one-tenth fiction, to set it straight. So I take all the advantages, that's what.

Interviewer: Is it different when you write a poem or a short story?

Bukowski: It doesn't matter. And I don't know why I do either one. I don't like the narrative poem; when it takes longer to get it down with words, when it takes a totality of words I'll use the short story or the novel; if I tell it with less words I'll use a poem. It has nothing to do with line, shape or anything like that. It has nothing to do with theory or reliability. It doesn't matter. If you break my stuff down and just run it down on one total line it all sounds the same—with minor exceptions. With a poem there might be a little more intensity. If I'm trying to say it short, I brighten it up, try to polish it just a touch, but not too much.

That's where you have this false poetic concept: a poem being something holy and sparkling, which is what destroys most poems: overdoing. Superfluous overdoing. You know, too much imagery and all that bullshit. I'm trying to keep it simple and yet still keep it tight. That's a long answer for a short question.

Interviewer: Since you don't put much store by form . . .

Bukowski: I know. I don't.

Interviewer: . . . can you define the thin line between what, for you, constitutes a poem and a short story?

Bukowski: I'd say the line is a matter of convenience . . .

Interviewer: You talked of novels, in the plural. Is there one besides *Post Office?*

Bukowski: I just finished a novel that will be out in November. It's called *Factotum,* which means a man of all trades, a guy with a lot of jobs. I read *Down and Out in Paris and London.* Ran into it by accident. Read it and I said: "Oh, this lad thinks he's had hard times; wait till I tell mine." And that's how it began. I had fifty, sixty, eighty, a hundred jobs. My original idea was to write about all the jobs, but I just couldn't, there are too many. I had also written about some in short stories and I had to leave *them* out. So the novel was hard because I had to leave out some interesting parts I'd already written in short stories . . . How much tape do you have? *(Laughs).*

Interviewer: Do you feel linked at all to whatever goes on, literarily, in this country?

Bukowski: You mean other writers? No. I ride my own horse, I tend to stay away from writers. See, they always waste an awful lot of time, talking about this guy and that guy. I don't like their conversations. Then I get in there too, you know. I'll say: "Oh hell, X can't write worth a shit," and I've got a drink in my hand and . . . That doesn't do. I stay away from them. Now I seem to be running with musicians. The other night there was this rock star. I look around, look around, and everybody's got guitars playing, singing and arguing about music and the guys say the same thing: "Oh hell, X can't write a song." I said, "Hell, here I am back where I started; I've got to get rid of them too . . ." I don't know. Best people to know are the non-creative. You get more natural words and ideas out of them because they're not talking about the arts, the arts, the arts, you know; they're not gossiping. Or if they are gossiping, it's about a guy who beats up his wife and hangs her upside down from the ceiling—which is interesting. That type of gossip is fine. I can use it; but writers, musicians, no. I stay away from them.

Interviewer: But such scenes don't give you ideas, they give you subject matter; people—at least I—never think of you as working with ideas, but with living stuff . . .

Bukowski: Right. I'm not so much a thinker as I am a photographer. I try to stay away from thinking. It doesn't befit me (Laughs). I have nothing to prove or solve. I find that just photographing is very interesting. Especially if it's people you see and then you write it down; it can get a little bit holy here, but there's a message or sense of direction after you've written it down: It says something which you didn't even quite know. So that works better for me. I'm not a hell of a politician, I'm afraid . . .

Interviewer: What do you mean?

Bukowski: I have no faith in one single source of action or direction. I mean it all crumbles, you know, it doesn't get there: God, Communism, the Gay Party, whatever the name, it crumbles, it doesn't work.

Interviewer: What does?

Bukowski: Young girls, beer, horses, armchairs, smoking a cigar. Oh, what works for me is classical music.

Interviewer: I was going to suggest it did: your stories are constantly referring to it.

Bukowski: Yes. I don't understand it, but I'm hooked on it.

Interviewer: "To understand" is a verb that hardly applies . . .

Bukowski: What I mean is . . . Why, I'm rather crude in my other outlooks! and yet you might call classical music a refined feeling or art form, as that's always described. Yet it appeals to me. So? It confuses me and it confuses other people I know. Here's a guy with a bottle of beer in his hand, a cigar, and he's just banged a 25-year old girl in the ass and they've had a big fight and there's a broken window and she runs out the door and he goes up and he turns on Mahler . . . *(Laughs)* Maybe it does fit, I believe it fits, but from the standard concept of a person put together as a total person, it doesn't fit—you know what I'm trying to say?

Interviewer: Is that saying that besides the instant, the moment, there's nothing that's worth caring for at all?

Bukowski: Nothing worth caring for? I think I care for many things. And that's what bothers me. But I don't know how to line them up. I can't find any guiding element to tell me how to set these things up I care for into a fashion that will make them more durable, or grow better, or whatever . . . Oh, that's enough . . . Jesus! *(Laughs)*. Oh, I care, almost everything gets to me. Things affect you. But I can't buy outward resolving formulas, cure-alls. I'm not saying this well. In other words, I have to figure it out alone. I can't have any help. But I'm moving very slowly. *(Laughs)* The writing helps, and the drinking. That's about it.

Interviewer: Horses fill your writings. Is this an old thing with you?

Bukowski: The racetrack? It's not so much the horses. There are lots of things at the racetrack. To begin with there is a crowd. There's humanity in total there. They're all there and the guards are off. They've entered the arena and they're betting money and this is their blood. Most of them can't afford it, and if you've ever been to a racetrack when the races were on, as you look at the faces, you arrive at some unwritten truth about things. It registers. Especially if you lose, and most of them lose. And I've been out there looking at faces. You know, the moment of truth, when they're on the cross there . . . Well, that's not the word, but something similar to the cross. I have this horrible feeling about them; and then, I go in to urinate, or to piss, or both, and I look in the mirror afterwards and I have the same face as they have. But also it joggles you out of your ordinary response. I could sit here, thinking about roses and Christianity and Plato and all that. It wouldn't do me any good. If I drive out to the track and get joggled and come back, I can write. It's a stimulus. I think Hemingway used to do it with bullfighting. He would see the bullfights . . . The same thing happens with boxing matches. What it does is set life up on some sort of a stage platform and you view it and you join it; especially with racing you join it because you bet your own money. You become a part of it. I don't know, it just brings you there in a way—subconsciously mostly, but actually it brings you there. It's very very real.

Interviewer: The gambling—lose or win—aspect of it?

Bukowski: Yes, and the life of the characters . . . I have certain ways of betting. Sometimes I get off and my horse comes in. You test your own character. I don't know. It just sets my writing off. Sometimes I can't write for a couple of days. I'll go to the race track. Win or lose, I come back and that very night and maybe write six, eight, ten, twelve poems, or a short story or something. So I need it for some reason. I'm not quite sure. If I was sure I probably wouldn't need it, you see . . .

Interviewer: I am going to ask you a question specifically because I am French.

Bukowski: What? You want to know how to beat them or something? (Laughs)

Interviewer: No . . . Have you ever read or heard about Céline?

Bukowski: Oh, yes. But only one of his books. What is it called? *Journey to the End of the Night*. I just come across books, by accident. I was in bed reading that and I just started laughing. I laughed all through it. Not a, you know, a "ah,ah,ah." It was just a joyous laughter. What he wrote was real. It had this very humorous piece and I said "Oh, my God!" I remember it starts out with men who are marching down and he marches with them and they're discussing the war and the officer is standing in the middle of the road and the officer gets shot. It's very funny even though it's happening and it's running all through there and that's always been the way I wanted to write. Even if it's tragic you say, "Oh what the hell! Tra la la! We go on." And it's very strong and funny and good and I really admired him in that novel. But afterwards, you know, he got cranky; his publishers were gypping him, and they broke his motorcycle or they stole his bicycle or something and he went on and on just bitching all the time, you know: "This isn't right and this isn't right." He lost whatever he had in the first book, really lost it.

Interviewer: What triggered my question was in part the fact that you mentioned earlier your having planned your life so as to die at the age of eighty in the year 2000. You told me you had seen that in a dream. It made me think of another book of his, *Death on the Installment Plan*.

Bukowski: Yes, I planned to read that but I couldn't get through some of his later stuff. It just got too . . .

Interviewer: Paranoid?

Bukowski: Yeah. So I just couldn't. If he only could have kept it up. The guy with durability was that Knut Hamsun: he just kept going. He was a Norwegian or something. His first book was *Hunger*, which is his best, a little thin thing. Then he started writing these big, huge . . . make you think you could never read them, and you go through it and you read the whole huge thing. He's lived all his lives or imagined them, and he just kept it all together all the time. That's what I'd like to do. Just keep writing at a good pitch instead of giving way. So many give way. You know about J.D. Salinger? Short stories, *Catcher in the Rye*. He's practically vanished, this guy. He just disappeared.

Interviewer: No one has ever seen him as far as I know.

Bukowski: No. A friend of mine claims to have seen him in a skid row hotel, but I don't know. *(Laughs)*

Interviewer: Do you feel akin at all to the Beat Generation writers?

Bukowski: Oh no. I said that real fast, didn't I? But I don't. I find a certain type of phoniness about them.

Interviewer: Even those who have survived, that is, who kept writing and producing even though the so-called Beat period was over?

Bukowski: You mean people like Ginsberg, Ferlinghetti, etc.?

Interviewer: Yes, and Kerouac in his day.

Bukowski: Yes. I don't like the whole gang of them. There was something too chummy about them. They gathered together and they'd do this and they'd do that, but I guess the artists have done that for a long time. Just gather and read some poems and all that; but this has always irritated me. I like a man who makes it on his own, without having to join, sitting around. I was in Frisco, you know, in some cafe, and this guy then drove me home and said: "Well, some times, any time of the day, you'll find them in there drinking coffee." I mean . . . Hell!

Interviewer: It's the institution that bothers you, right?

Bukowski: Yeah. The Beats were always like that: they would chum together, hang together, get photographed together; then the big acid trip, Timothy Leary got in there, and marijuana.

Interviewer: But that was another period.

Bukowski: Oh it was? Leary wasn't mixed in there? I don't know much of this. I was on my ten-year drunk at the time.

Yeah. I stopped all writing for ten years and just got drunk. While the Beats were beating, I was drinking. So I didn't know what was going on. I started drinking—real heavy drinking—at the age of 25 and didn't stop until I was 35. I didn't write at all for ten years.

Interviewer: Had you, before?

Bukowski: I had, a little, in a magazine called *Story Magazine*. Not well-known, but it discovered William Saroyan, discovered a lot of American writers. It discovered me, tra la la. Anyhow . . . Then I got in . . . There was a magazine called *Portfolio* by Caresse Crosby, the Black Sun Press. It was quite a thing in those days. I was living in New York at the time. I came out in *Story*, which was *the* literary mag of the day. I got a letter from this lady agent; she said, "Come out and I'll buy you dinner and drinks at such and such a place and I'll be your agent." So I wrote her back, "I'm not ready." And I wasn't ready. So I just got drunk and gave it up. Of course, during this ten-year drunk I gathered all types of material that I never would have gathered if I had been a literary type pumping out stories. You see, a lot of them appeared later in *Notes of A Dirty Old Man*. In this sense it happened to me while I was on my drunk. But I don't think I was consciously gathering materials. I just gave it up, just tried to . . . who knows what I was doing? I ended up in the hospital, spit my stomach out and started over again and then here I am. It's quite simple.

Interviewer: Do you do much rewriting of what first comes out or does it remain the way it came into existence?

Bukowski: They used to come out quite a bit. Now I tend to rewrite just a little bit, especially when I write drunk the night before. I take out whole lines or paragraphs, and when I get sober I insert a new line. I buck it up. I don't think I help it. I used to be very ashamed to rewrite anything. You know, it came *out* like that, so it was supposed to be pure or something. But now I say, "Well, it can come out a little bit impure, it could use some help," so I do a little rewriting but not a hell of a lot, because I'm lazy, very lazy, yeah, God's lazy one. No, I'm not God's lazy man; I'm just a lazy man.

Interviewer: Is writing so linked to what you do and experience that you cannot envisage the one without the other? Does "no experience," "no special event," mean "no writing?"

Bukowski: I have to keep—I see what you're trying to say—I have to keep living in order to write. I can't go to the top of the mountain looking down, observing. I have to get burnt in order to write at all, to intermingle; and that means women, jails, various strange spots, you know, whatever happens. I have to taste it before I can write. I can't lose contact. Just memory alone I can't work on.

Interviewer: It's the violent, immediate part of the experience that you translate then?

Bukowski: An experience is usually violent or unpleasant. That's a cynic's remark. No, that's a realist's remark. OK . . . (*Laughs*)

Interviewer: Is the short story you write just after a particular experience the most intense thing you do? Does the recollection of it make it more intense? Do you then feel the need for adding things on top of what happened really?

Bukowski: As I said, I do cheat a little; I brighten it up. It may be mostly true, but I can't help improving it with one thing that will make it sparkle a little more. The idea is that the story need not be about me. It could be about one thing and this thing could have happened or it should have (*Laughs*) somehow. So I put it in. It makes me feel good. In a sense it's cheating and in another way I feel it's not. Even if I write in the first person. Oh, I mean, the hell with those morons. I'm really telling it exactly as it is. Most writing is so damn boring. I think it needs help.

Interviewer: Let me rephrase my question then . . .

Bukowski: OK. Trap me! (*Laughs*)

Interviewer: All right. You said earlier that what you write is autobiographical . . .

Bukowski: *Mostly*, I said.

Interviewer: Right. Mostly. Well then, where does the new name come in? Why is a Henry Chinaski the "hero" of all you write, instead of you?

Bukowski: Oh, that's just kind of playing with them . . .

Interviewer: Who is "them," the readers?

Bukowski: Yeah, just a bit. They know it's Bukowski, but if you just give them Chinaski they have a sense of saying, "Oh, he is really wonderful. He's calling himself Chinaski, but *we* know it's Bukowski." So, it's just goosing them a little bit. They love it. And Bukowski would be too holy anyhow; you know, "I did this." Especially if you do something good or great or seemingly great, and your own name is there. It makes it too holy. Now if Chinaski does it, maybe I didn't do it, see, that could be fiction.

Interviewer: But you don't *have* to do this; you can't mean for a minute that it's "fear of the ego trip," or something, considering what Chinaski is really up to in the stories . . .

Bukowski: I'm terribly mixed up, you know.

Interviewer: Most of your stories, in their day-to-day appearance, in their plainness, their simplicity, don't give you such heroic dimensions that you should fear them in the way you said.

Bukowski: Most of the time, I degrade myself a bit . . .

Interviewer: Does Chinaski help?

Bukowski: He helps, yes. Oh, Bukowski would help more. I could really degrade him. I don't know what Chinaski is really; I really can't answer why I do that.

Interviewer: Does he provide you the distance that allows you to add things on top of what really happened?

Bukowski: Actually I think there's less added to Chinaski than there is to Bukowski. Maybe it keeps me from adding. I can't answer the question. I don't know what Chinaski is, why I put him in a novel; I mean, if it was Charles Bukowski in *Post Office*, why, somehow they would have these dripping bleeding hearts over "this great poet, this great writer sitting in a post office." You know, there *are* those types. And if you say Henry Chinaski, that takes some of that off. That could be a reason. They couldn't quite nail me you know. God knows why. Some things we do without ever knowing why but we've got to do them or you would turn purple or green and die and that's all. They are that important but we don't know why. So that's one of them.

Interviewer: What place do established, famous recognized writers have in your mind? Are some particularly useful to you?

Bukowski: I can't use them. One reason I took to writing was because I'd be doing some reading of the great works of the centuries and I thought, "Good God! This is it? This is what they're settled on? Shakespeare? Tolstoy's *War and Peace*? This stuff? Chaucer?" Chaucer isn't too bad. But I mean, all the big boys they drag across you. It hardly sparkles or heightens. It didn't do it for me; so I said, "Something's wrong here. I have to keep going." I guess you call that ego or misinterpretation or lack of insight, but it simply bored me, they made me yawn. All the great minds of the centuries. Most of them made me yawn.

Interviewer: Who doesn't?

Bukowski: Friedrich Nietzsche, Schopenhauer—that's great, good stuff—and Céline's first book, and two or three others I can't think of. so I was dissatisfied with what was being done. The main thing that bothered me was the lack of simplicity; and by simplicity I don't mean just bare bones without meat, I mean a good way of saying. I think genius is the ability to say difficult things in a simple way. What they did is say simple things in a difficult way. They're doing it all wrong for my money and I just like the simplicity and easiness without losing the profundity, or the glory or the flash or the laughter. That's what I've been trying to work on, to get it easy without losing the blood. That's been my plan.

Interviewer: One of the very many remarks that come from people who don't like your work . . .

Bukowski: There are a number, yes . . .

Interviewer: A couple . . .

Bukowski: Battalions!! But go ahead . . .

Interviewer: They find your work appallingly simple. You used the "flesh and bones" metaphor. As far as I'm concerned, it's all flesh and hardly any bones, but some are bothered by it because what you do doesn't answer any of the normal literary criteria. It's besides the point of most of what's being done. So your critics ask themselves: Can one describe *Post Office* as a novel, or else is it a *good* novel, or even is it literature?

Bukowski: You see, they are victims of their training, their literary training, their literary heritage. Unless something sounds literary, they think it can't *be* literary. By literary I mean the accepted high form of saying something above journalism. So I think they're confused rather than me, and I think they're just defeated by the centuries. So many poets will be writing a good poem playing it simply, and just have sunlight and they don't have to throw in this . . . It's almost like they're begging or saying, "Well, I should have written this, therefore, I'll throw in a soft poetic line and you will forgive me for these other lines which I have already done." And when I hit that line, I almost puke. As I said, they've given it up, they've quit, they are victims of their heritage. So I think I've gotten away from that heritage, because it never interested me. Maybe, it's brain damage, whatever that is, but I've gotten away from that heritage, a lot of it. So I have a certain advantage. In other words, I needn't sound like that something. Unless you sound *like* something they think it's untrue; but that's *their* problem.

Interviewer: You said "above journalism." In that case, on what side of journalism do you situate yourself?

Bukowski: I hope I've gotten rid of the weather report; but of course, Hemingway, Gertrude [Stein] told him that in a sense journalism was the way out. Begin to use journalism, she said, use that simplicity, you know, break away from what's being done; and she helped him make that step; which I understood; and of course, he didn't write what I call journalism. He wrote a very serious melodrama with a lot of humor, and it often had a lot of soul. But it was taught, and it was interesting and it was readable, simple, and I think it was moving in my direction. What I'm trying to do is move in that direction and still have the content of humor, blood, sparkle. Hemingway's was too much wood. As I say, I think it should be very simple and still have more power than those who abuse the word and go back to their heritage and throw them a flowery line or the delicate subtle phrase or turn of phrase. We're all tired of the turned subtle phrase and the riddle in the middle of the line. It's just been going on too long, for me it has. I want the bacon in the pan and burning. We might be running out of time. Oh, they've said that for centuries too, but how many nations have the hydrogen bomb now? 45? 68? *(Laughs)*. Hey, I almost stopped bullshitting . . .

Interviewer: What would be the form that gets down to essentials then?

Bukowski: There is no final form, there are no final essentials, there is no final bone, because we never know everything or anything. All we can do is the best we can. It's just a working away of surpluses that boggled us, that we've been carrying too many years. Say it, simply say it. Of course, without cliches, platitudes, and with some originality. Simply say it profoundly! *(Laughs)* That's a hell of a program! That's why I get worried sometimes. But see, when I'm talking to you, I talk about these things, but when I write, I do them without program or rule, so that's a little different. But you've got me thinking about them. So that's different too. Next time I write I won't be thinking those things I've said, I'll just be writing.

Interviewer: Do you still write those columns for the paper?

Bukowski: Yeah, there's one due tomorrow I haven't written yet.

Interviewer: What sort of a reception do you get for those columns?

Bukowski: Got all kinds of them. I get love letters from young girls who want to fuck me. I seldom bother with them because they bring a lot of trouble. Then I get real hateful hate letters.

Interviewer: People bother to send you hate letters?

Bukowski: Oh, yes. One guy especially sent me one. I was writing for *Open City* at the time; the people with the hate usually write on lined paper; it's short note-book paper with the blue lines on a clear . . . and they use a heavy black ink that reminds you of blood, and they have a very heavy stroke and their grammar is very bad and their line of thought breaks off and starts in again, you know, they'll jump lines of thought, they'll jump from here to there, you hardly know what they're saying but you feel this heavy black hatred in there. All of a sudden they'll curse you. They don't do it well, they do it so badly it makes you sick.

I was on the way to the racetrack and I had just received a hate letter and I opened it and I stopped on the other end of a tree at Wilton Place, and I almost puked. It wasn't that I thought he was right; it's just this contempt crawling, this creepiness, all this . . . he could have written it to anybody. He found me as the one to write it to. I was available. And he got to me because the next column I wrote—he'd told me where he lived, he'd told me he was going to teach me how to write; you know, that was funny after that letter! So I wrote the column, and I ended it by discussing hate letters, hate, hate, and then I said, "Oh, by the way, baby, one more hate letter from you and I'm going to come to your hotel and kill you." I was almost sure I was. He had me . . . I thought—you know, Crime and Punishment—there are people always killing . . . I was in that state of mind! I would dedicate myself to erasing him from the earth. He got to me all right! So I wrote the column and I got no more letters. He sent no more letters. I got rid of him. The guy didn't want to die! (*Laughs*). Oh, I get to them . . . ! I get letters from madams of whorehouses: "Come up, I'll give you free drinks or anything else. We run a fine house up here." I have some strange readers. I'll go to the race track. I guess there are a lot of horse players who read my column. Not too often, though. Maybe I'll go ten times, and maybe twice in these ten, a guy will come up and say, "Are you Charles Bukowski?" So horse players read me, and the whores. Mad men. College professors . . .

Interviewer: Do you pay that much attention to what is being written here and there on your work in "the groves of Academe?"

Bukowski: (*Laughs*) I pay a little. I don't mind what they say. But sometimes I get completely misquoted. You know, especially when they put it in quotes, a line from a poem that's not in the poem, to prove a point. I dislike that. That's all that bothers me, when they misrepresent my actual words. There was one critic there . . . I was writing about a trash man who came by and I was writing about myself being a writer, but anyhow he put a quote in there: "Here I am sitting behind these blinds. I'm a genius and the trash man doesn't even know it." Quote. The line isn't even in the poem! Things like this are done. I don't know why they're done. Maybe they read the poem and forget it. That's their idea of what I said. Then they put it in quotes, which shouldn't be done. It's just snotty. But I don't mind being rigged up. It helps sell books. It's made me interested in certain poets a long time ago, especially when they're under attack; they would quote certain lines as being a very bad poem and I'd say, "Well, this is a very good poem and I must get the facts on this."

Interviewer: What's a good poem?

Bukowski: For me, or when I read one?

Interviewer: When you write one. What is it that makes you think that it's a good or a botched one?

Bukowski: Oh, it's an instinctive thing. I mean, it's all together. It does it. I gave a reading the other night. I was reading along. It was a fairly serious poem. I was drinking beer. I finished the poem. It was quiet. So that was a good poem. They knew it said something they had a little reverence for.

Interviewer: What did you expect them to do? Hoot?

Bukowski: I wouldn't mind. I thrive on adversity, you know. Some adversity, not total adversity. It's destructive. We all know that. A little adversity is good for the soul. Total adversity is impossible. Did somebody say that? Sounds all right.

Interviewer: You said it anyway . . .

Bukowski: What did Dostoyevsky say? "Adversity is the main spring of self realism."

Interviewer: Do you write with a certain category of people in mind? Do you direct your work to anyone?

Bukowski: Well, if you do, you're doomed. I am doomed, let's change it. Because it's my nature to remain as I have become and if I worry about them I stop being what I've become. I have never worried about them except as my murderers, my landlords, my jailers. But as readers of my work I have never worried about them.

Interviewer: What on earth were you jailed for?

Bukowski: Which time? (Laughs) Wandering around in the street drunk, drunk driving, fights with women. What happens to me with women is always violent for some reason. They make a lot of noise and attack me, break things and scream. I bring out the best in them. So the police arrive, you know, and the man is usually wrong in America when . . . Maybe they've grown up in France, but in America, when a man and a woman are fighting, they'll think the man is the instigator. Jesus, even if the female has gone completely insane, babbling and screeching, saliva pouring out of her mouth, grabbing butcher knives, rushing towards one. I think that in Europe they realize that a female often gets this way. Here in America they think the man is the evil one. They take the man away when these things happen. They take the wrong one. (Laughs) The woman is the poor helpless one in the eyes of our law, our controls. God, one day I went to see a lady and my girl friend caught me outside, began screeching and vanished. First she broke all the beer in my sack, broke my whiskey bottle, she went up and down the street, she must have smashed a pint of whiskey, sixteen or eighteen bottles of beer. She missed a couple, but, as I was sweeping up the glass, I looked up, heard this sound: She has her car up on the sidewalk trying to run me down. Now, that's love . . . I have had many narrow calls with the females. They all seem to . . . I don't know if it's love, they become possessed with me.

I do something for them that they don't like to lose. At any rate, we just had a scene not too long ago. I was with a 24-year-old girl. This one came back to town and knocked on the door. Made a wild scene. Hair-pulling, animal moans, screams, it was terrifying. I tried to separate them. And I fell down, I slipped, and I wrenched my knee and couldn't get up. I was drunk, you know. They went down this court, whirling and screaming. God, it was terrifying. Blood and piss flying through the air, hair. Horrible. *(Laughs)* And the police came and the police wanted me too. Everybody wanted me that day, and none of them got me.

Interviewer: Do you like the work of Antonin Artaud? I know City Lights put out a collection of his translated writings some years ago.

Bukowski: Oh, yes. He is a good poet. I've read quite a bit of his stuff. I don't know how it translates over but he sounds to me entirely crazy. Now maybe I don't understand what he is saying, but his moments of clarity become my moments of clarity. You see, then he is very, very, very good, it is so beautiful. "How come people are so disgusting and the sick people are the real ones . . ." This is true. I read the whole thing. It was all broken up but it really makes sense. But there are good parts that are just wasted for me, where he may know what he is saying but I don't always. He was in the madhouse a while, wasn't he for some years? Trying to cut off his pecker on a boat going to Africa or something like that. He was a very interesting sort. He has it. He had it. He's dead, but he has it.

Interviewer: You work with a number of underground papers?

Bukowski: No. Just *Free Press*.

Interviewer: Do you feel strongly about politics? Do you care?

Bukowski: Oh, I care, but I don't think there's any use in me caring. I mean, I think all the parties contain their own evils and their own goodnesses and I don't know what to do about them. You know I can vote for this but I don't know what's gonna happen.

Interviewer: You vote?!

Bukowski: I never voted. I said, "I can vote." I should say, "I could have voted," but I've never voted. Nothing has ever interested me.

They're all rabbits in the hutch. They're all alike; they're different, but they're all alike. I guess certain parties have more benefits for the rich, others have more benefits for the poor. But I can't get fired up about this. That's all. I mean, take the Democratic Party and the Republican Party: What difference does it make? It doesn't matter. The Democrats are usually better souls, I'd say they are more interested in what happens to everybody. The Republicans are just more tied up with money interests and that's it.

Interviewer: Is Wallace a "better soul?"

Bukowski: Wallace . . . He might be Vice-President for all I know. This Wallace thing is very strange. He is a part of the Democratic Party. But I don't quite understand it because I just don't follow it that close. But this is for the Southern votes; people will vote for a guy because he doesn't like blacks. I don't have enough left of me to get into that area, figuring that out. I just record what happens and that's it.

Interviewer: You keep an eye on it?

Bukowski: Closed, a half-closed eye. It could burn you out you know; they'd believe you don't believe this or that and then it all turns on you. Whether they call it betrayal or . . . These intellectual writers, you know, they'll just comment on betrayal; it just falls apart, I don't have time for it. And nobody bothers me with it—you know, "Hey, Bukowski, would you like to . . . ?"—because I don't claim to be more than I am. I'm working at remaining what I am.

Interviewer: Did you ever go back to Europe after you came over to America?

Bukowski: Never. I'll probably never make it.

Interviewer: You wish to?

Bukowski: I'd like to . . . That's a silly thing. I'd like to go back to Andernach, Germany, to walk through the town, that's all, that's all I want.

Interviewer: Because you were born there?

Bukowski: Yeah. You know I am a romantic fellow, I'm very sentimental. I am a softie. I'd just like to do that. I'd stay there maybe overnight.

I wouldn't want it to go past that, just to have done it. The street you were born in . . . and after all these years, come back. It's probably been all bombed to hell and probably all been rebuilt, but it's something. If I could only know the corner it was, you know. Oh I'm soft, I'm sentimental. That's why I have trouble with women, I get attached. All my women all say "Oh you write this hard stuff but you're soft, you're all marshmallow inside" (*Laughs stupidly*) and they're right. I don't have it . . .

Interviewer: Your novel comes out in November, you said?

Bukowski: Yes and it's called *Factotum* and pretty thick.

Interviewer: Who brings it out?

Bukowski: Black Sparrow. It went on and on and it took me . . . I wrote my first novel, *Post Office*, it took me 20 nights . . . either 20 or 21. I'd just gotten out of the post office and I thought I just couldn't make it without that big mother there giving me my pay check. But I had not made enough out of my writing to be able to quit my job. I tried to be a writer and I was fifty years old. You don't have a trade in America and you drop out at the age of 50 . . . It's almost impossible, having tried. So it was a hell of a gamble and I was a bit shaken. Oh! I quit! I would have died if I had stayed. Anyhow, I wrote the novel. It was 20 nights. I had plenty of whiskey, the radio was on to classical music, and some bunch of cheap cigars and a lot of typing paper, a bright light overhead and beer. Beer, the cigars and classical music . . . Every night . . . I didn't think I'd finish it in 20 nights. I set a goal; I said, "I'll write ten type-written pages singlespaced," and I was used to working my night's work. But I would never remember going to bed. I'd wake up in the morning, sick, go and puke . . . God! Papers would be all over the couch and I'd say, "Let me see if I made my ten pages last night. I'd pick them up. 10 . . . 12 . . . 14 . . . 18 . . . 23 pages!! Good God. If I just do ten tonight I'll be thirteen ahead! I always kept exceeding. Of course what I'd have to do the next morning, you know, some of these end pages . . . when I got very drunk the writing got out of hand, sort of . . .

Interviewer: Shaky?

Bukowski: Yeah! I'd have to tighten that up a little bit! The last pages I'd say, "Wow! What was I saying there?" (*Laughs*) And this one took me four years. A very slow process.

Interviewer: *Factotum?*

Bukowski: Yes. For the last period it just sat in a drawer there. I was hooked up; I had just two or three chapters to go and the ending; I couldn't open that drawer. I'd take it out, say, "Shit, I don't know . . ." Only one night I came back from the track. I had a few beers, just walked in and typed up two or three pages and it was all done, it was so easy. So I wrote one novel in 20 days and another one in four years.

Interviewer: You want to write more novels or keep to poetry and short stories from now on?

Bukowski: I want to write one more novel, but I don't think I'm mature enough to write it. Maybe it'll take 20 more years. I'll call it *Women*. It should be a laugher if I write it. It really should be. But you have to be very honest. Some of the women I know now must not know that I write this. Some things I really want to say . . . But I'm not going to report it! It would get me into all kinds of trouble (*Laughs*)! I've said enough!

The Pock-marked Poetry of Charles Bukowski—Notes of a Dirty Old Mankind

GLENN ESTERLY

1976

"Buk: The Pock-Marked Poetry of Charles Bukowski—Notes of a Dirty Old Mankind," Glen Esterly, *Rolling Stone*, June 17, Issue 215, 1976, pp. 28, 30–31, 33–34.

In preparation for tonight's poetry reading, Charles Bukowski is out in the parking lot, vomiting. He always vomits before readings; crowds give him the jitters. And tonight there's a big crowd. Some 400 noisy students—many of whom have come directly from nearby 49'rs tavern—are packed into an antiseptic auditorium at California State University at Long Beach on this fourth night of something called Poetry Week. Not exactly the kind of event calculated to set the campus astir, as evidenced by the sparse audiences for readings by other poets on the first three nights. But Bukowski always attracts a good crowd. He has a reputation here—for his performances as well as his poetry. Last time he was here, he had both an afternoon and an evening reading. In between, he got hold of a bottle and slipped over the edge. Too drunk to read at the evening performance, he decided to entertain the students by exchanging insults with them. It developed into quite a show. Backstage, Leo Mailman, publisher of a small literary magazine and coordinator of tonight's reading, peeks between the stage curtains for a look at the audience and says: "A lot of these people are repeaters from his last reading. Some of them were disappointed by his drunkenness; they thought they got ripped off. But a lot of others were perfectly satisfied because they felt they got a look at the real Bukowski—you know, the legendary gruff, dirty old man, the drunk who doesn't give a damn and goes around looking for fights. They saw Bukowski in the raw.

"At the other extreme, when I called him to make arrangements for this reading, he was completely sober and fell all over himself apologizing for the way he acted last time. He was very soft-spoken, telling me how sorry he was he got drunk and how he hoped to make it up to us this time. I was amazed. So who's to say which one is the real Bukowski—the hostile drunk who makes a spectacle of himself, or the humble, diffident guy who's worried that he might have let somebody down?"

A few minutes later, Bukowski, clad in an open-necked shirt, tattered charcoal American Graffiti-era sport coat and baggy gray pants, shows up backstage, having finished his warm-up activities in the parking lot. Pale and nervous, he tells Mailman: "Okay, let's get this travesty over so I can collect my check and get the hell outta here." Then be lumbers out, unannounced, onto the stage. Mailman turns to Bukowski's companion, Linda King, a spirited, full-figured 34-year-old poet and sculptor who has survived a stormy relationship with the poet for five years. "Is he all right?" Mailman asks. "Sure," she says. "He's only had a few beers and he's feeling pretty good. He wants to do well tonight." As the audience begins applauding, Bukowski takes a chair behind a small table on the stage. Hunched over close to the microphone, he announces, "I'm Charles Bukowski," then takes a long hit from a thermos bottle filled with vodka and orange juice, prompting cheers from several students. He grins a half-shy, halfway grin. "I just brought a little vitamin C along for my health . . . Well, here we are, on the poetry hustle again. Listen, I've decided to read all the serious poems first and get 'em outta the goddamn way so we can enjoy ourselves, okay?"

As he begins reading, a coed in the third row who's seeing the poet for the first time turns to a friend and asks, "Do you think he's as ugly as they say?" Her friend puts her finger tips to her lips in contemplation as she sizes him up. "Yeah, but he's impressive-looking somehow. That face . . . he looks like he's lived a hundred years. It's kind of tragic and dignified at the same time."

That face. By any conventional standards it *is* ugly, and for most of Bukowski's 55 years that's exactly what people called it. That's what they called it during all those years when he was working at bonecrushing, mind-stultifying jobs in slaughterhouses and factories, living on the underside of the American Dream. But things have changed. The crude, antisocial alcoholic is earning his living with his typewriter now, nailing the words to the page in intensely personal, rawly sensitive poems and wild, raunchy, anecdotal short stories that have earned him an international reputation with translations into other languages. He writes about what he has experienced: poverty, menial jobs, chronic hangovers, hard women, jails, fighting the system, failing, feeling bad. The impression created is of someone with his foot in a trap who's trying to gnaw himself free at the ankle. Which could make for a lot of drab reading if it weren't for the fact that there's frequent relief in a sardonic humor that sometimes gives one the feeling that W. C. Fields has been reincarnated as a writer.

Bukowski's appeal was summed up before the reading by Gerald Locklin, a burly, bearded poet who teaches literature at Cal State. Locklin, who has been following Bukowski's progress for many years and has known him for four years, was drinking beer with a couple students at the 49'rs and observing: "I think of him as a survival study. This guy has not only survived problems that would kill most men, he's survived with enough voice and talent left to write about it. You know, you're always running into people in bars who say that if they could only write about their lives, it would make such great reading. Well, they never do, of course. But Bukowski has."

Locklin also believes Bukowski "deserves credit for leading us in a new direction in American poetry with his direct, spontaneous, conversational free-form style. Many poets had been talking for a long time about getting more of a narrative quality into their work, but until Bukowski no one really succeeded. He just did it naturally, without really thinking very much about it. The more traditional poets hate him for it, but I think the trend he started was long overdue. His kind of style has its dangers: it can result in a lot of very ordinary poetry, and Bukowski has written his share. But at his best he's hard to beat, believe me."

Another view has been provided by poet Hal Norse, who had a falling out with Bukowski after being close to him for several years. Writing about their relationship in the *Small Press Review*, Norse said: "Hateful as he can be—and God, he can be so detestable you want to shove him up a camel's ass—somehow the warmth and snotty charm of the bastard come through so powerfully that he remains an attractive personality, ugliness and all."

So here the man is, making it at last. Sartre and Genet have volunteered compliments about his poetry. His position as an underground folk hero is secure. Colleges fly him around the country for readings. Some critics have gone so far as to compare his prose stories to those of Miller, Hemingway. The National Endowment for the Arts has blessed him with a grant. A university has established a literary archive in his name. His early out-of-print books are valuable collectors items. *The New York Review of Books*, for crying out loud, has reviewed him. Desirable young women keep knocking at his door. And now they call the face things like tragic . . . dignified . . . even beautiful. Bukowski appreciates the ironies of it.

The face, no bargain to begin with, has been abused terribly over the years. There was a blood disease that hospitalized him for months as a teenager with boils the size of small apples on his face and back ("It was my hatred for my father coming out through my skin—an emotional thing"), leaving a lifelong imprint of pockmarks. Later there were the cruel whores who gouged out pieces of flesh with their fingernails when he was too drunk to fight back, leaving more scars. In the middle of these facial road maps of past troubles is a bulbous nose, swollen and lumpy and red in futile protest against the exorbitant amounts of alcohol, and above the nose two small gray eyes set deep into the huge skull stare out warily at the world. An unexpected feature of the Bukowski body are the hands: two quite delicate hands at the ends of muscular arms, the hands of an artist or musician. Beautiful hands, really. ("I tell the women that the face is my experience and the hands are my soul—anything to get those panties down.") Those beautiful hands reach for his thermos bottle after each poem as he gathers momentum, reading about his women.

The vodka is working; the old man is rolling. Bukowski is in good form, just full enough of booze to bring out the showman in him, and the audience responds enthusiastically. On the humorous lines he reads drolly, stretching out certain syllables for emphasis in his mortician's voice and managing to get the same inflections into the spoken word as he has on paper. Despite his often professed dislike for readings, he seems to be enjoying himself now, and to cap off the performance he surprises his listeners by reading a section from a novel in progress. An uninhibited account of an encounter with a fat, sex-starved middle-aged woman ("I'm sorry to say this actually happened to me"), it keeps the audience roaring with its outrageous exaggeration: "She flung herself upon me, and I was crushed under 220 pounds of something less than an angel. Her mouth was upon mine and it dripped spittle and tasted of onions and stale wine and the sperm of 400 men. Suddenly it emitted saliva, and I gagged and pushed her off . . . Before I could move again she was upon me. She gripped my balls in both of her hands. Her mouth opened, her head lowered, she had me; her head bobbed, sucked, whirled. Although I was on the verge of vomiting, my penis kept growing. Then, giving my balls a tremendous yank while almost biting my pecker in half, she forced me to fall upon the floor. Huge sucking sounds fell upon the walls as my radio played Mahler. My pecker became larger, purple, covered with spittle. If I come, I thought, I'll never forgive myself . . ."

As he ends, most of the students rise to give him an ovation. He takes off his glasses and gives the crowd a little wave. "Now let's all go out and get smashed." He gathers his papers and gets up to leave. The applause continues as he walks away and, obviously pleased, he suddenly turns back and leans over the microphone. For just a moment his guard comes down. "You're full of love," he says "—ya mothers."

Henry Charles Bukowski Jr., novelist, short story writer, megalomaniac, lush, philanderer, living legend, classical music aficionado, scatologist, loving father, sexist, physical wreck, jailbird, pain in the ass, genius, finagling horse player, outcast, antitraditionalist, brawler and ex-civil servant, is sitting in the small living room of his three-room furnished bungalow, a tacky $105-a-month apartment with worn carpeting, scruffy furniture and frazzled curtains. It's his kind of place, one of eight bungalows in a small court just off Western Avenue in a section of Hollywood heavily populated with massage parlors, pornographic movie theaters and takeout joints. The lady in the bungalow next to his is a stripper and another tenant manages the massage parlor across the street. Bukowski feels at home here. For eight years he had lived in a similar cottage where his writing flourished, despite the fact that the place was, according to all who had been there, the filthiest dwelling they had ever seen (Bukowski personally, however, was, and is, immaculate; he's in the habit of taking four or five baths a day). Then he moved into a much more expensive apartment in a modern complex but he felt out of place and his typewriter fell increasingly silent. So he moved into this bungalow in the hope it would restore the right creative feelings, and so far it has. He hasn't been here long enough for the dust and beer bottles to collect in any appreciable quantities, but he's working on it. The only notable features of the place are two paintings that hang on the walls. They're by Bukowski and they're not bad.

He is guzzling from a 16-ounce can of beer, part of two six-packs I've brought along to help smooth the interview. He doesn't bother to put the six-packs in the refrigerator; it's apparent he figures we'll drink them before the evening is over. Barefooted and dressed in blue jeans and a faded yellow short-sleeved shirt with a button missing at the navel, he looks loose and relaxed. More relaxed, in fact, than I am. That Bukowski countenance is, after all, a little overwhelming in a face-to-face confrontation. Then, too, I've learned enough about the man in talks with people who know him well to know that nothing with Bukowski is predictable. His acquaintances have told me that he'll tolerate me and my questions, but won't go so far as to be cordial. So I'm surprised when he goes out of his way to put me at ease, shoving a beer in my hand and announcing: "I've been drinking beer most of the day, but don't worry, kid—I'm not gonna stick my fist through the window or bust up any furniture. I'm a pretty benign beer drinker . . . most of the time. It's the whiskey that gets me in trouble. When I'm drinking it around people, I tend to get silly or pugnacious or wild, which can cause problems. So when I drink it these days, I try to drink it alone. That's the sign of a good whiskey drinker anyway—drinking it by yourself shows a proper reverence for it. The stuff even makes the lampshades look different.

Norman Mailer has uttered a lotta shit, but he said one thing I thought was great. He said, 'Most Americans get their spiritual inspiration when they're intoxicated, and I'm one of those Americans.' A statement I'll back up 100%, *The Naked and the Dead* be damned. Only thing is, a man has to be careful how he mixes his alcohol and his sex. The best thing for a wise man is to have his sex before he gets drunk 'cause alcohol takes away from that old stem down there. I've been fairly successful at that so far." Grinning, he also informs me that a female friend had departed shortly before my arrival. "Yeah, I had her on that couch you're sitting on. She was pretty young, maybe 23 or 24. She was all right except she didn't know how to kiss. How come kissing the young ones is like kissing a garden hose? Christ, their mouths won't give, they don't know what to do. Ah, well, I shouldn't complain. That makes three different ladies in the last 36 hours. Man, I'll tell ya, women would rather screw poets than just about anything, even German shepherds. If I had only known about all this earlier, I wouldn't have waited till I was 35 to start writing poetry."

We start talking about his childhood, going over the details, most of which are still painful for him: his upbringing in Los Angeles after being born in Andernach, Germany; the terrible plague of boils over his face and back; the constant beatings by his father, a milkman who carried Prussian discipline to extremes, whipping his son almost daily with a razor strop for all sorts of imagined offenses; the feeling, even as a young child, of alienation and isolation, of not belonging, of being somehow inferior and superior to his peers at the same time. "The school idiot always gravitated to me," he recalls. "Ya know, the fucked up guy who was cross-eyed and wore the wrong kind of clothes and was always going around stepping in dog shit. If there was a pile of dog shit within ten miles, this guy would manage to step in it. So I sort of disdained him but somehow he'd wind up being my buddy. We'd sit around eating our pitiful peanut-butter sandwiches and watching the other kids play their games." Several other boys at school made a habit of beating up his hapless friend. For some reason, though, they left Bukowski alone. "They understood I was almost like him, almost as fucked up, but they were just a little wary of me," he says. "I seemed to have something extra, something in my demeanor that kept 'em from beating on me. Maybe it was a wild look in my eyes, I don't know, but they seemed to sense that if they tried it with me they might be in for some trouble. And I guess they would have been too." His tone is casual, unemotional, but traces of bitterness sneak through. "I got pretty hard from all those beatings from my father, ya know. The old man toughened me up, got me ready for the world."

When he was 16, he came home drunk one night, got sick and vomited on the living room rug. His father grabbed him by the neck and began pushing his nose, like a dog's, into the vomit. The son exploded, swinging from the heels and catching his father squarely on the jaw. Henry Charles Bukowski Sr. went down and stayed down a long time. He never tried to beat his son again.

At about the same time, young Charles started to frequent public libraries. He had decided that being a writer made good sense for a loner; the solitude of it appealed to him. At the libraries he was looking for literary heroes. Browsing through the aisles, he would flip through the books and when he found a page that interested him, he took the book home to read. "I'd find one writer and another," he says, "and after a while I found that I'd discovered the same ones who had pretty much stood up over the years. I liked the Russians, Chekhov and those boys. There were some others, most of 'em going a long way back. One day I noticed a book in the stacks called *Bow Down to Wood and Stone* by Josephine Lawrence. The title caught my eye, so I paged through it, but just the title was good. Then I picked up a book right next to it and when I looked through it I said, 'Hey, this bastard can write.' It was by D.H. Lawrence. There's a bit of color for ya."

He was badly disappointed in the contemporary American writers of the day. "I kept thinking, 'They're playing it too safe; they're holding back, not dealing with reality.' At least reality as I knew it. Hell, I'd see these people in the libraries with their heads down on the tables, asleep, with the books open in front of 'em and flies buzzing around their heads. That's a pretty good comment on the books, huh? Yeah, I guess that about summed up what I thought of most of the writing. And the poetry—Jesus! When I was growing up, poets were thought of as sissies. It's easy to see why. I mean, ya couldn't figure out what the hell they were up to. The poem could be about somebody getting punched in the mouth, but the poet never would come out and *say* that somebody got punched in the mouth. The reader was supposed to plod through the fucking thing 18 times to somehow puzzle this out. So when it came to both fiction and poetry, I thought I had a chance to make it 'cause what was being written was so pale and lifeless. It wasn't that I was so good, it was just that they were so goddamn bad."

As a young man, Bukowski wrote hundreds of short stories, sending them off to the wrong markets, magazines like *Harper's* and *Atlantic Monthly* where his style and subjects didn't have a chance. When the manuscripts kept coming back, he figured they weren't any good and threw them away. By the time he was 25 his efforts seemed so futile that he decided to abandon his writing ambitions completely. That's when he hit the road on what turned out to be a ten year drunk, a period when his life was measured out in six-packs and jugs of cheap wine. Along with the drinking bouts, there were countless odd jobs (he once guarded doors in a Texas whorehouse), a number of nights in jail and a few semiserious attempts at suicide.

There was also a woman named Jane. He met her in a bar and lived with her on and off for several years, They had two things in common: both were alcoholics and both were losers. Jane was bouncing off a shattered marriage to an affluent attorney. She was about ten years older than Bukowski, at the stage of life when, as he puts it, "a woman is still nicely put together, just dangling on the edge of falling apart, which is when they look the sexiest to me." Jane was the first woman who brought him any tenderness and he warmed to it. Up to the age of 22 or 23 he had never even tried to get laid because he was squeamish about his disfigurements, and after he did start pursuing women he found they were usually out to hustle him. As a result, he soaked up Jane's affection and stuck with her even after the occasional nights when she allowed herself to be picked up and taken home by other men.

Jane's drinking finally killed her, and a couple of years later, at the age of 35, Bukowski almost died himself from relentless boozing. Eleven pints of blood were pumped into him at L.A. County Hospital to save him from a bleeding ulcer. When he left the hospital, his doctors told him he would be a dead man if he touched alcohol again. It made him so nervous that he walked to the nearest bar and tossed down a few beers—a nice touch for the legend that was to follow. After a period of recuperation, he settled into a routine. At night he worked as a postal clerk at the dreary downtown post office. Then, in the early morning hours, he came home to a dingy apartment, turned the radio to a classical music station, sat down behind a battered old Royal and energized by a combination of whiskey, rage and desperation—wrote poems: direct, brutally honest poems tinged with his pain and hostility but stamped as well with a certain compassion and justification for life. He sent the poems out to little magazines and underground publications where, to his surprise, they began to be picked up regularly. Soon small independent publishers were bringing out collections of his work. He quickly earned a reputation as an underground poet of considerable talent and there were signs that it wouldn't end at that. In 1963, in an introduction to Bukowski's *It Catches My Heart in Its Hands,* writer and critic John William Corrington was moved to speculate that "critics at the end of our century may well claim that Charles Bukowski's work was the watershed that divided 20th-century American poetry between the Pound-Eliot-Auden period and the new time in which the human voice speaking came into its own. He has replaced the formal, frequently stilted diction of the Pound-Eliot-Auden days with a language devoid of the affectations, devices and mannerisms that have taken over academic verse and packed the university and commercial quarterlies with imitations of imitations of Pound and the others. What Wordsworth claimed to have in mind, what William Carlos Williams claimed to have done, what Rimbaud actually did do in French, Bukowski has accomplished for the English language."

Heady stuff. Meanwhile, this newly heralded genius continued to expend a sizable portion of his energies sorting mail. It wasn't until 1970, with the encouragement of his primary publisher, John Martin of Black Sparrow Press, that he finally summoned the nerve to quit the job. Panicked at giving up his security, he pounded out the first draft of his first novel, *Post Office*—a kind of *M*A*S*H* for civil servants—in three weeks, detailing in it the brain-deadening tedium and bureaucratic insanities that had gone with the job, along with descriptions of his brief, bizarre marriage to an heiress with a Texas fortune ("There went my only chance for millions") and his relationship with the woman who bore his daughter, Marina (whom he loves, visits weekly and helps to support).

Today he earns a comfortable though not gaudy income from royalties, readings and the column "Notes of a Dirty Old Man," which he writes for the *L.A. Free Press*. The big money may yet be on the way. There's a bit of wonderment in his eyes when he says: "I'll be sitting here trying to get some work done at the typer, and somebody will call about making a movie outta some of my stuff. Then I start talking about the author's cut and two-year options and how I gotta have net, not gross, and I think to myself, 'Good God, what's happening to me? What the hell's going on here?' Now that I've got a little bit of fame, people suddenly are coming to my door. I'm wary of it. I think I can handle it but I'm wary of it."

And what if a great deal of money does arrive?

"I would probably get the fat head and be utterly malicious and stinky. Test me. No, if you want the truth, I don't think it would get to me at this stage, I've been through too much, been toughened up for too long."

Taylor Hackford, producer of a documentary on the poet for KCET-TV, Los Angeles, and holder of the screen rights to *Post Office*, says Bukowski is filled with ambivalence about the late arrival of success. "Sometimes he feels the recognition he's finally getting is well deserved and long overdue," Hackford says. "Other times he feels like it's all a big joke someone's playing on him, like someone's going to take his typewriter away and tell him they were just kidding. There's a constant battle going on inside him between the feeling that he really is one of the best and a feeling of deep insecurity. I think he'll be all right as long as he doesn't get too far away from his typewriter. The one thing that could kill him is if he started doing a lot more readings, running around the country catching planes and staying in Holiday Inns. Readings make him nervous, so he tends to drink heavily before, during and after them, and it takes its toll. I think he recognizes this danger. In fact, he wrote a great story about it called 'This Is What Killed Dylan Thomas.' If he limits the readings and keeps the drinking under reasonable control, we're going to hear a lot more from the man in the future."

Bukowski, according to Bukowski, is at his "total peak. "I'm writing less but I'm writing much better. There's more care in each line. I have a lot of self-doubt, so I know I'm measuring these things right. Right now everything has come together. I'm on my way. I'm unbeatable. Tomorrow morning is something else. Who knows, it may all fall apart and I'll go mad or raving or rape a goat or something. There's always the chance that I'll end up back on skid row, drinking wine with the boys. I'd never mention that I was a poet or any of that silly-ass shit. I'd just sit there and drink with 'em and say, 'Well, fellas, I figured it might turn out like this.'"

The beer is disappearing rapidly and his eyes are badly bloodshot back in those deep sockets under the bushy brows. A light on a desk behind him creates a halo effect around the top of his head. The halo just doesn't fit. He looks a little liverish, but seems to be feeling fine.

I ask him how much he feels his physical appearance has affected his life.

"I don't know. I suppose it helped to make a loner out of me, and being a loner isn't a bad thing for a writer. I know the face is helping to sell books now. The shot of me they used on the cover of *Erections* has done a lot to sell that book. The face on that cover is so horrific and pasty and completely gone beyond the barrier that it makes people stop and wanna find out what the hell kinda madman this guy is. So it was good luck for me to go through a lot of the shit I went through 'cause now I have this mug that sells books."

And when it comes to women . . .

"That's a delicate question—does the face scare them?"

No, aren't there a lot of women who are attracted by it now?

"Yeah, I get all sorts of remarks about it. They say things like, 'You've got a face more beautiful than Christ's!' That sounds good at first, but when I think about it, Christ's face wasn't all that beautiful. But I find women like ugly faces. Yeah, I'll make that statement flatly. They wanna mother ya back to heaven. I have no complaints."

A phone call interrupts us, and from the conversation I can tell it's Linda King. "No," he tells her, "I can't come over tonight. I'm being interviewed." Glancing at me, he raises his voice to make sure I can hear him. "Yeah, this guy's here from this wild-ass, perverted publication, but he looks pretty goddamn respectable to me: ten-dollar haircut, tailored clothes, Florsheim boots. What am I telling him? A lotta lies, what the hell else? I think he believes 'em, too."

After he gets off the phone I suggest to him that his writing recently seems to reflect a softening in his stance toward women and ask if that has something to do with his essentially happy, if rather rocky, relationship with Linda.

He rubs his rat-colored beard. "Well, I guess I might admit to mellowing a little. I've been accused of hating women but it's not true at all. It's just that most of the women I ran into for a long time weren't exactly prizes. I'd sleep with 'em and when I woke up, they'd be gone with my money. If a man goes into a whorehouse, he's gonna get a whore, that's all there is to it. I met Jane when I was in my 20s and she was the first woman—the first person, for that matter—who brought me any love. It was the first time I discovered the stupid little things that people do that make them care about each other, like lying in bed together on a Sunday morning reading the paper or fixing a meal together. Gentle, corny things like that."

In an attempt to bait him a bit, I recall some contradictory statements he's made in the past about women. Like, on one hand, "women are the world's most marvelous inventions," and, on the other, "I wouldn't recommend getting involved with women to any man."

"Right. Both statements are absolutely true. No contradiction. Next question." He grins and drains his beer, knowing the evasion has succeeded. Then he decides to go on anyway. "Let me tell ya a little story, kid. Before I met Linda I went four years without a woman and I felt pretty good about it. Somehow I just reached a stage where I didn't wanna go through the strain of a relationship. I didn't wanna take the time. Women can be awfully time-consuming. And when you're a poet, they expect ya to go around spouting all this grand, glorious, profound stuff all the time about the meaning of life. Well, Jesus, I'm not like that. What can I tell 'em? I wanna fuck 'em, that's all. So after they're with ya four or five days and the most profound thing you've said is, 'Hey, baby, ya forgot to flush the toilet,' they think to themselves, 'What the hell kinda poet is this?' It takes a lot outta ya putting up with that stuff. During that four-year period I just decided not to join the chase for every cunt in a skirt. I'd come home from the job and I'd have the beer and my symphony music, a place to lay down and my typewriter. I masturbated a lot and got a lotta writing done, so I guess it turned out all right. Writing, after all, is more important than any woman. But I will make this concession: jerking off runs a distant second to the real thing. When you're with a woman ya like and the sex is good, there's something that takes place beyond the act itself, some sort of exchange of souls that makes all the trouble worthwhile—at least for the rest of the night. I mean, here ya are, masturbating, whacking away at this big ugly purple thing with the veins sticking out and fantasizing about how you're balling the daylights outta some woman, and then ya finish and go lay down on the bed and think, 'Well, that wasn't too bad—but something's missing. It's that exchange of souls."

It seems like an appropriate time to test out how seriously he takes the title of a great lover he has fostered in his stories. I inform him that Linda had volunteered the information that "he's a very creative lover. I've stayed with him five years, and if he wasn't good I could certainly find someone else."

"Well, I'll plead guilty to that," he says matter-of-factly. "I may as well admit it. I'm a good lover. At least I was the last time I did it. which wasn't long ago. But I think Linda's probably talking about sexual exploration, working down below there with the tongue and also getting in some creative movements ya haven't tried before. It's like writing a story or a poem—ya don't wanna do it the same way every time or it gets boring. It's hard to explain . . . It's just an instinctive thing to keep things fresh and exciting. Like maybe doing it standing up as a change of pace. I can do that with these goddamn legs of mine. Most of the rest of me is shit, but the legs are dynamite. And my balls. I have genuinely magnificent balls. No shit, if my dick was in direct proportion to my balls, I'd be one of the great all-time champion studs. But my balls aside. imagination is the key. It's a creative act."

Well, uh, Linda also said she had to teach you about oral sex.

"Huh?"

Linda said you had never practiced, uh, cunnilingus before you met her.

"Ummmmmm. Christ. she couldn't let it go at telling ya I'm a great lover, could she?" His fugitive's face registers either a scowl or a smirk. hard to tell which. "All right, that's true, when I met her, one of the first things she told me was that she could tell from my stories that I had never done that. Don't ask me how she figured that out. Anyway, she said it was a deficiency in my education. We set about to correct it and we did. I covered her with the reality of my tongue, how's that? Then she told me she said that I'd hafta try out my new techniques on another woman. Well, she was right about that, too. One thing it proves, though, it's never too late for an old man to learn new tricks. Another bit of Bukowski wisdom."

The beer is gone and Bukowski is hungry. He stands up and asks a question that comes out more as an order—"How about getting something to eat? I haven't eaten since I started drinking beer and that was quite some time ago." A few minutes later, we're weaving along Western Avenue in his blue '67 VW ("I'm gonna drive this sonuvabitch till it disintegrates"), headed, he declares, for nothing less than a Pioneer Chicken stand. "Been going there for years when I'm drunk and there's no food in the apartment. Main thing is, I hafta watch out for those red lights in the rear-view mirror. I can't afford to get picked up . . . might lose my license. Suppose they pull me over? What am I gonna tell 'em, that I'm Charles Bukowski, one of the world's greatest poets? That I have magnificent balls? Ya think the men in blue would buy that?"

A car ahead of us that had stopped for a red right fails to move when the light turns green. Bukowski unleashes a torrent out the window. "Come on, motherfuck! Move it! Get your ass moving!" The driver looks around nervously and finally takes off. "Did ya see that asshole? I'll bet he's a tourist, probably from Chicago . . . Yeah, I love this town. Well, I don't love it, but it's the only place I ever wanna live. I couldn't write anywhere else. I hope I die here. Not right away, maybe when I'm 80. That seems like a reasonable age to die. That gives me another 25 years. I can write a lot of shit in 25 years. Hey, I feel good tonight. Tonight I feel like I might make it to 80. I have some trouble with the stomach, my liver gets overloaded and my hemorrhoids are threatening to take over the world, but what the hell. I'll make it. I'm just ornery enough to make it."

We reach Pioneer Chicken and order two shrimp dinners. Sitting at an outdoor table, eating the shrimp and soggy french fries, Bukowski turns reflective, talking without prompting about his past, speculating about the effects of his father's beatings, reminiscing about the days on the road. Drunk, tired and disheveled, he stares at a young couple walking by and then, in a confessional tone, he says: "Ya know, I've felt kinda unreal and weird all my life. I've always had trouble getting along with people. I've always been the sonuvabitch—the guy who says the wrong thing and makes people feel bad. Sometimes I feel like I'm not really a part of this world." A pause. "I say I don't like people, but really

I get kinda charged up when I'm around 'em. I used to sit in my old apartment with the window open, typing and looking out at the sidewalk with people walking by. And I'd incorporate the people into my stuff. Maybe now that I've got a little success I can relax and say something nice to people once in a while instead of always being the prick." He stops, looks at me, starts to go on, then thinks better of it; perhaps he's thinking that he's already said too much. The moment of reflection passes. "Ah, hell, let's eat our shrimp and watch the broads go by."

We drive back and he parks on the street near his bungalow. Out on the sidewalk we shake hands. "Listen, kid," he says, "I don't have friends, but I do have acquaintances. So now you're an acquaintance."

"Bukowski," I say, "you're not a bad guy—for a prick.'

He laughs, shakes his head and walks off toward his apartment and his solitude.

Faulkner, Hemingway, Mailer . . . And Now Bukowski?!

RON BLUNDEN

1978

"Faulkner, Hemingway, Mailer . . . And Now, Bukowski?!," Ron Blunden, *The Paris Metro*, Oct. 11, 1978, pp. 15–16.

"One of those bizarre new saints of 20th century literature" (Philippe Sollers, *Le Nouvel Observateur*). "The best thing that happened to America since Faulkner and Hemingway" (Cavanna, *Charlie Hebdo*). "The best thing that happened to American literature since Norman Mailer" (Andre Berkoff, *Lui*). "A truculent martyr of the American dream" (Michel Braudeau, *L'Express*). "He goes further in sincerity, confusion, obscenity, in fierce and joyful provocation and in the mythification that transmutes them than Céline, Miller, Burroughs, and Kerouac" (Paul Morelle, *Le Monde*).

Last Friday night on the popular literary TV talk show *Apostrophes*, the man thus nailed for worship to the cross of celebrity writhed and moaned before bringing a painful week of public exposure in Paris to a very predictable anti-climax. Charles Bukowski, drunk to the point of inarticulateness and stoned out of his mind, having mumbled incoherently but with calculated rudeness through the other guests' vapid reminiscences, unhooked his mike, and staggered off stage with a little help from his friends 20 minutes before the end of the show—much to the delight of host Bernard Pivot, who kept suggesting with ill-concealed glee that "the great American writer wasn't much of a drinker after all." "Ladies and gentlemen," his prissy, patronizing grin seemed to say, "America sure is in bad shape, isn't it?"

And so, everybody seemed to have a reason to be satisfied. Bernard Pivot proved his point, or thought he did. (He later admitted that things had gotten a little out of hand.) The Paris left-wing intellectuals who have been lionizing "Buk" since they discovered him two years ago were

Bernard Pivot with poet Charles Bukowski on the French interview program Apostrophes *in September, 1978.*

delighted that he should play his dirty-old-man part so well. As for Bukowski himself—well, he might be the only loser. Not because he has been had by Pivot, or by anybody else—one might make a good case that he did what most people would only have dreamt of doing when trapped in such verbose mediocrity: walk away. (C'mon, Cavanna, admit the thought crossed your mind!). Bukowski might be a loser because the idea is dawning on him that no matter how thick the walls of indifference you surround yourself with, no matter how oblivious you are to feedback, there is no denying the simple, scary fact that success is like having your soul up for auction. You simply don't belong to yourself anymore—other people, the critics, the editors, the readers, have, in every sense, an interest in you.

161

Mailer, Faulkner, Hemingway . . . but Charles Bukowski? To Americans especially, most of whom have never heard of the obscure poet-writer enjoying such a vogue in Europe, the idea is particularly incomprehensible. A German immigrant who came to the States at age two, Bukowski gained some measure of local fame as a columnist for the Los Angeles counter-cultural magazine *Open City*. His column, "Notes of a Dirty Old Man," was later published as a collection of short stories. This was after a ten-year drinking bout had landed him in Los Angeles County General Hospital with a liver the size and color of a watermelon. Whether it was the booze or the 14 years he'd spent as a postman which proved more dangerous to his sanity remains open to discussion. Both, at any rate, contributed heavily to turning Bukowski into a writer of over 20 books of bitter, cynical, obscene, and often pathetic poetry and prose. He writes about the people he knows best: hobos, bums, whores, the suckers, and the hustlers—wasted people, wasted lives, orgies and drunken brawls. The title of one of his books, *Erections, Ejaculations, Exhibitions, and General Tales of Ordinary Madness*, gives a fairly accurate idea of his subject matter.

Bukowski himself went right back to drinking as soon as he got out of the hospital, and you can almost tell by the rhythm of his stories how many drinks he'd had when he wrote them. Some are stiff, aggressive, and a bit creaky. They were written too early in the evening. Others, the ones that were written too late, are runny, redolent with self-pity, and often incoherent. But a few are just perfect: funny and pathetic, raw and ribald, with a sense of purpose and pace that sets your juices flowing nicely, as Bukowski's were, no doubt, when he wrote them. At those moments, it takes somebody really frigid, like *Figaro* critic Jean Chalon, to deny Bukowski any kind of talent whatsoever.

Even so, Bukowski, whose writing in the States seldom leaked out of the underground newspaper circuit constituted by such publications as *Nola Express, the Evergreen Review, Knight,* and the *Berkeley Barb*, and who has remained virtually unknown to the East Coast literary establishment, was the first to be surprised by his sudden success in Europe. Last year, when the first of his books to be translated into French, *Notes of a Dirty Old Man,* was published, he became an overnight sensation (with a little help, it may be pointed out, from some unknown genius who used fake endorsements from Genet and Sartre to peddle his stuff to the intellectual community). Though his sales here are still modest, the critics have come down on him like locusts, comparing him to Céline, Miller, Artaud, Kerouac, Faulkner—you name it, they've got it. His slot is waiting for him in their manicured cultural cemeteries like an open grave. And the man I met last week in a small hotel in Saint Germain des Prés definitely sounded *scared*.

Bukowski had another word for it. He called it "disgust." Fair enough. After all, how honest can one afford to get with oneself? You see, it wasn't supposed to happen like this. Charles Bukowski was going to keep drinking, screwing, and writing obscurely in his seedy, low-rent neighborhood of Sunset Boulevard and Western, barely making it into the next day, till he dropped dead with a terminal case of cirrhosis, or with a heart attack while getting laid. But then Europe, that old whore, stepped in, with her crooked devices and old scores to settle. And the blessed little worries of day-to-day survival were obscured by something far more bothersome, as Bukowski realized he was in imminent danger of being praised to death.

As it happened, ours was his tenth interview of the day, and he wasn't exactly as fresh as morning dew. The drinking had apparently started early (too early, confided Linda King [*sic*], his current flame and all-purpose nurse) and the joint he kept relighting certainly wasn't his first. His eyes—or what I could see of them through slits in a face that looked like Dresden after the bombing ("Don't you think he has the most fantastic *gueule, chérie?*") were glazed and he spoke in a very low, rumbling slur. Yet beneath it all, you could feel something steely and lethal that would make you think twice about taking him for a ride. Bernard Pivot, who kept telling him to "shut up" during the show, will probably never know how close he came to having his televisual nose flattened.

Bukowski began our interview, predictably enough, complaining about his reception in France.

Bukowski: Intellectuals, they try to tie me in with all the literary figures of the past—Walt Whitman, Melville . . . God, it bores me so. They try to make a package out of me. I try to tell them no, you can't put a label on me. I'm a loner, I do my thing. But it's no use. They keep asking me about Kerouac, and didn't I meet Neal Cassady, and wasn't I with Ginsberg, and so on. And I have to tell them no, I was drunk during the whole beatnik thing; I was not writing then. And of course, they're disappointed. The French are particularly eager to associate me with the beatnik thing for some reason.

Metro: Well, the French feel guilty about the whole beat phenomenon. Nobody was even aware they existed when they were here in the Fifties, and when the French suddenly realized something had been going on at their very doorstep that was making literary history, it was too late. All the beats were dead or gone. But now they've got hold of Bukowski. He looks like a beatnik, he smells like a beatnik, and with a little luck he'll still be alive next week for interviews . . .

I see what you mean. I'm supposed to be the last surviving specimen of an extinct species. What a bummer. They also try to tie me in with the punk thing. I don't even know what a punk is—I wouldn't know one if he bit me. But even so, I guess I must be closer to the punks than to the beatniks. I'm not interested in this bohemian, Greenwich Village, Parisian bullshit. Algiers, Tangiers . . . that's all romantic clap-trap. I'm tired of labels. All I want to do is keep writing as I have been writing and not worry about labels, about what they say, about what they want.

Q: Success has made things more difficult for you?

I'd say it made things easier and more difficult at the same time. I guess I'm too old and I've lived through too much to be fooled by the praise and the fame and all that. I lived in a paper shack in Atlanta, Georgia, for $1.25 a day, without any water or electricity. I didn't even have a typewriter. I used to write on the edges of newspapers, and yet I already knew I was an outstanding writer, though nobody was there to tell me so except myself. It's all come too late for me not to be suspicious about it. And it does have some unpleasant side-effects. I get hate mail. I get hate phone calls. I get hate people who want to kill me. And people expect me to conform to my image all the time.

In America now, they expect me to be drunk in the gutter half the time, to be living with a sloppy whore with big tits and so on. But I've got a right to my own life. And even though I did live like that, I've got the right to change. I don't want to follow the image they've made of me.

It can get very tiresome to write about the same things over and over. How many times can I write about the whore who threw a bottle at my head? I like to change.

Q: But assuming that being published is an attempt to communicate, can you avoid getting an answer any more than you can avoid seeing your reflection when you look at yourself in a mirror?

I *don't* write to communicate. I just write, the same way I take a crap or scratch myself. Because I have to. Then if somebody is willing to give me money for it, fine. But basically, I write to save myself. It's a very selfish business. Now the Left comes along—they try to claim me. The punks come along—they try to claim me. . . . But I'm not there to be claimed. I'm just there to write the next page.

It's very difficult to explain to people that I write, and then I'm done with it. They keep going over what I wrote and saying: "You meant this, and you meant that." And I have to tell them no, I didn't mean that at all, though it probably would have made a greater story. I don't want to make claims for what *they* want to see. My idea of life is the next page, the next paragraph, the next sentence. Once you stop having that attitude, you stop behaving like a living molecule. You're dead. Once a story has rolled out of my typewriter, it's useless to me. It may be useful to someone else, but not to me. My editor told me one day that I could live off my royalties and that I should sit back and relax. He was only teasing, or course, but I said, "No, baby, no way! It has to be tomorrow, it has to be tonight!" That's my way of life.

Q: But whether you like it or not, aren't you committed in some way to what you have written?

Yes, I seem to be. I've found that out. I do feel disgust sometimes at the way my writing has been interpreted or used. Never anger, mind you, but disgust.

Q: Did you expect this kind of exposure when you came to France?

No, I was taken by surprise. I didn't suspect it was this good—or this bad—until I came here. I did expect a lot of exposure in Germany, because my sales there were high—like 100,000 copies sold over a five-month period. I couldn't go anywhere in Germany without people turning around and staring. At one point, I went into this shop to buy a raincoat and the clerk said: "Hey, you're Charles Bukowski!" And I had to give him an autograph. People kept recognizing me in the most improbable places. I wouldn't have believed it was possible, though I did know I was far more popular there than in the States. Here, in France, it appears to be mostly critical acceptance rather than word-of-mouth success.

But if my writing has to be based on anything, I'd rather it be based on the common man picking up my book and saying: "I like this," than on the critic saying: "This is very good." I hadn't expected so many interviews, so many people. I'd rather there hadn't been so many. People keep asking me how I find Paris. But you know, we haven't even walked around the block, we haven't seen Paris at all. I've been sitting here giving interviews all week long, interviews to the Communists, to the Leftists, to *Le Monde*, wherever they stand . . . . It's been a bit too much for me. I'm a very common, simple man. I do have genius, but with a very low common denominator. I'm simple, I'm not profound. My genius stems from an interest in whores, working men, street-car drivers—lonely, beaten-down people. And those are the people I'd like to see reading my stuff, and I don't want to see too many learned comments, too much criticism, or too much praise get between me and them.

Q: Did you already feel you were a genius back in that shack in Atlanta, or did that discovery come with success?

I've known it all along, ever since kindergarten, as a matter of fact. I remember thinking how weird the other children were. There was something wrong with them. They were the crowd. I hate crowds.

Q: Don't you think your having been born a foreigner might have had something to do with it?

Oh, sure. I was the outlaw. One of the worst things my parents ever did for me was buy me an Indian suit, complete with feathers, headband, and tomahawk. Here I was with my German accent, dressed up like a goddamn Indian while all the other little boys had cowboy outfits. That put me in a tough spot, believe me. But I got very good with that tomahawk. It did a lot more damage than their toy guns. Now I guess you could say my typewriter is my tomahawk.

Q: Do you hate people in general?

No. Quite the contrary. But as I said, I hate crowds. Crowds are shit, and the greater the crowd, the more the shit stinks. Take twelve men in a bar, drinking and kidding. They disgust me, they've got no identity, no life. But take each one of those men alone, listen to what he's got to say, see what's bothering him—and you've got a unique human being. That's what my writing is all about. And also that there's got to be something else. I'm a dreamer, I'd like a better world. But I don't know how to make it better. Politics is not the way. Government is not the way. I don't know the way. I'm just discouraged that men and women have to live their lives the way they do. It's painful to them, and it's painful to me, but I don't know the way out. So all I can do is write about the pain of it.

Q: The French must be giving you a rough time with their passion for purpose, for direction.

Yeah. You know, I wrote a poem once. In the poem I was sitting in a cafe in Paris, a recognized author, and they'd be asking me: "How do you do it? Why do you do it?" And I would just laugh and in the poem I had a cane—I guess I came here too early, I don't need one yet—and I would not answer the question. Instead, I would just slash the cane against the buttocks of a French waitress.

Shakespeare Never Did This

CHARLES BUKOWSKI

1979

Shakespeare Never Did This, Charles Bukowski, San Francisco: City Lights Books, 1979, Sections 4–6, 15.

4 To be awakened by Rodin who said there would be an interview at 11 a.m. in the patio. "A very important newspaper . . ." "All right," I said, not knowing that there would be 12 interviews in 4 days. The morning interviews were always the hardest, hungover, trying to get the beer down. No, I have no idea why I am a writer. No, my writing has no particular meaning that I know of. Céline? Oh sure. Why not? Do I like women? Well, I'd rather fuck most of them than live with them. What do I think is important? Good wine, good plumbing and to be able to sleep late in the mornings. Are you really disturbing me? Of course you are. Do you expect me to start lying at the age of 58? Buy me a drink. No, I'm not smoking dope. This is a *sher bidi* from Jabalpur, India.

One of the last interviewers was the head punk of Paris. He arrived in a leather suit with zippers all over it. He said he was down low, that he needed a bit of smack to get going. I told him I wasn't carrying. He had a tape machine. We drank beer with icecubes. I interviewed him while he ran his zippers up and down. I was tired of being interviewed. I asked him if his mother was still alive, various other things. One of the nicest things he said was that he liked pollution ...

5 On Friday night I was to appear on a well-known show, nationally televised. It was a talk show that lasted 90 minutes and it was literary. I demanded to be furnished 2 bottles of good white wine while on the tube. Between 50 and 60 million Frenchmen watched the program.

I started drinking late in the afternoon. The next I knew Rodin, Linda Lee and I were walking through security. Then they sat me down before the make-up man. He applied various powders which were immediately defeated by the grease on my face and the holes. He sighed and waved me off. They were sitting in a group waiting for the show to begin. I uncorked a bottle and had a hit. Not bad. There were 3 or 4 writers and the moderator. Also the shrink who had given Artaud his shock treatments. The moderator was supposed to be famous all through France but he didn't look like much to me. I sat next to him and he tapped his foot. "What's the matter?" I asked him. "You nervous?" He didn't answer. I poured a glass of wine and put it in front of his face. "Here, take a drink of this ... it'll settle your gizzard ..." He waved me off with some disdain.

Then we were on. I had an attachment to my ear into which the French was translated into the English. And I was to be translated into the French. I was the honored guest so the moderator started with me. My first statement was: "I know a great many American writers who would like to be on this program now. It doesn't mean so much to me ..." With that, the moderator quickly switched to another writer, an old time liberal who had been betrayed again and again but who had still kept the faith. I had no politics but I told the old boy that he had a good mug. He talked on and on. They always do.

Then a lady writer started talking. I was fairly into the wine and wasn't so sure what she wrote about but I think it was animals, the lady wrote animal stories. I told her that if she would show me more of her legs I might be able to tell if she were a good writer or not. She didn't do it. The shrink who had given the shock treatments to Artaud kept staring at me. Somebody else began talking. Some French writer with a handlebar moustache. He didn't say anything but he kept talking. The lights were getting brighter, a rather viscous yellow. I was getting hot under the lights. The next thing I remember I am in the streets of Paris and there is this startling and continuous roar and light everywhere. There are ten thousand motorcyclists in the street. I demand to see some cancan girls but I am taken back to the hotel upon the promise of more wine.

6 The next morning I am awakened by the ringing of the phone. It was a critic from *Le Monde*. "You were great, bastard," he said, "those others couldn't even masturbate . . ." "What did I do?" I asked. "You don't remember?" "No." "Well, let me tell you, there isn't one newspaper that wrote against you. It's about time French television saw something honest."

After the critic hung up I turned to Linda Lee. "What happened baby? What did I do?"

"Well, you grabbed the lady's leg. Then you started drinking out of the bottle. You said some things. They were pretty good, especially at the beginning. Then the guy who ran the program wouldn't let you speak. He put his hand over your mouth and said, 'Shut up! Shut up!'"

"He did *that?*"

"Rodin was sitting next to me. He kept telling me, 'Make him keep quiet! Make him keep quiet!' He just doesn't know you. Anyhow, you finally ripped your translation earphone off, took a last hit of wine and walked off the program."

"Just a drunken slob."

"Then when you reached security you grabbed one of the guards by his collar. Then you pulled your knife and threatened all of them. They weren't quite sure whether you were kidding or not. But they finally got to you and threw you out."

I walked into the bathroom and took a piss. Poor Linda Lee. In Germany and France, in both the newspapers and magazines she was always mentioned as Linda *King*, a former girl friend I hadn't been with for 3 years. It really hurt her. I wouldn't care to be called somebody else either, especially a former boy friend. And when I told the interviewers, "By the way, this is Linda Lee, *not* Linda King . . ." they never mentioned her. I say that any woman who is able to suffer living with me should be called by her right name.

When I got out of the bathroom the phone continued to ring. One was a call from Barbet Schroeder, my friend and the director of many strange and unusual films. "You were great, Hank," he said, "French television has never seen anything like it." "Thanks, Barbet, but I have very little recall of the evening." "You mean you did all that and you didn't know you were doing it?" "Yes, I get like that when I'm drinking."

Linda Lee and I had Eurail passes. It was time to get out of Paris. We had been invited some weeks before to visit her uncle in Nice. Linda's mother was there too. Why not?

15 We got the hotel room and I took out the poems wondering if I could fool them again. Then the phone rang. It was Carl. He said it might be a good idea if we went down to the Markthall for a check-out of the mike and so forth. I said all right and he came around with a car. Linda Lee and I got out at the Markthall and walked up the ramp. We were expected: there were tv cameras and questions from newsmen. I hadn't expected that. I felt like a politician. They followed me up the ramp with their tv cameras and flash bulbs and the reporters had little pads in their hands upon which they wrote answers to their questions. I answered some questions, then waved them off.

Inside they got me again. A girl from a news station in Austria. Tables, lights. I sat down. They always wanted more than the poem and that was senseless because the poem said it best. Too many writers became teachers, became gurus; they forgot their typewriters.

The girl looked at me: "I want to ask you some questions, Mr. Bukowski."

"Before I talk I need a bottle of wine."

She motioned to one of her crew and he ran off. Soon he was back with a bottle of red, a bad bottle of red. I took a sip at the glass, spit it out and said, "Well, all right, go ahead."

She got into women's lib and politics. She ran out little trap questions which I was supposed to stumble upon. There was nothing to stumble upon; the questions were dull and obvious. Perhaps the answers were too. I felt sleepy and indifferent. The wine was puke. Then the March to the Gallows played overhead. I felt as if I were at a high school graduation ceremony. I felt like unzipping and playing with my balls. The lights were hot. I didn't care, I didn't try. I said yes and I said no and I said maybe, and I said, "No I wouldn't fuck my mother, she's dead, you see, the bones would scrape my skin, but I had a dream once that I had intercourse with Mom. Best wet dream I ever had . . ." No. Yes. No. No. "I like Thomas Carlyle, *Madame Butterfly* and orange juice with the skins crushed in. I like red radios, car washes and crushed cigarette packages and Carson McCullers." No. NO! No. Yes, of course. "Mick Jagger? No, I don't like his mouth." "Bob Dylan? No, I don't like his chin."

The interview ended.

I got on up and went to check camera and lighting and mike and so forth. They were all right . . .

Quotes of a Dirty Old Man

Silvia Bizio
1981

"Quotes of A Dirty Old Man," Silvia Bizio, *High Times*, January 1982, pp. 33–36, 98, 100. [Incorporating four sections from "Bukowski: Rolling With Life's Punches," Silvia Bizio, *Los Angeles Times*, *Calendar Section*, January 4, 1981, pp. 6–7.]

Charles Bukowski knows whereof he writes. A marginal man, a heavy boozer, a denizen of the seamy L.A. nightlife, Bukowski drew on his rich experience to produce over 30 autobiographical books of poems, short stories, and novels.

And they sing. He possesses the hobo vitality of Kerouac, the blunt eroticism of Miller and the whimsical cut-to-the-bone philosophy of Cain. Bukowski came to writing late in life, after a 14-year-stint in the post office and a couple of extended stays in prisons and hospitals. But today, at 61, he is on the verge of mass acceptance. His stories are being produced as movies, he's a culture hero all over Europe and his last novel, *Women*, sold over 100,000 copies in the United States.

And Bukowski rolls on. Like the antihero of his novels, Hank Chinaski, he goes to the track every day and writes at night, with the radio pouring out classical music and the bottle pouring out red grape. Bukowski is currently at work on a novel on his early years, a section of which is excerpted in this issue. Silvia Bizio, an Italian journalist, caught up with Bukowski in his home in San Pedro, California, sometime between the ninth race and the fifth bottle.

HIGH TIMES: They like your stuff in Europe better than they do here. How do you explain that?

BUKOWSKI: Europe is one hundred years ahead in poetry, paintings, art—which is lucky for me. Here there aren't many who appreciate my work. The feminists especially hate me so much because they haven't read everything I've written; they only read parts of it. They get so infuriated they can't read the next page or the next story. That's not my fault; that's their fault. They get too ready to attack without going into the whole ball of shit that I have created.

HIGH TIMES: It's not only them. It seems you have a lot of problems in the Left in general.

BUKOWSKI: The Left doesn't like me? I am the working man, or at least I used to be.

HIGH TIMES: Well, at least from what I have seen in America.

BUKOWSKI: Oh, in America? I don't like the Left in America, because they are just well-fed Westwood Village little ninnies screaming slogans. They are too worried about getting a job or getting marijuana or tires for their cars or cocaine or going to a discotheque. So I don't think there is any underground radical movement here. Anything underground radical is media hype, just strict bullshit; and anybody who gets into it will quickly go into anything else that gathers them momentary gains. Abbie Hoffman, all those slickers. The whole Left in America is just glorious bullshit hype—nothing like the Wobblies in the '20s. The American Left are white-bellied shrieks of nowhere—they have always been. At least you could talk to those guys, the Wobblies. I would drink with them; I wouldn't go with them, though. But the Left . . . They don't know what struggle really means. The fight is in the streets. I come from the streets. I understand the streets. But the streets are the streets: There isn't much you can do with them. The streets are very beautiful, East Hollywood is very beautiful, Hollywood and Western, Big Sam the Whorehouse Man. The streets are good, they are full of people, marvelous people, and I don't like the rich any more than you do. You can put fifty thousand dollars in my bank, I still don't like the rich. I may eat dinner with them in the same cafes, the maître d' might know my name, but I still don't like them. Because they are dead. I don't like dead people, even if they have one million dollars. I take their million dollars but I don't take them.

HIGH TIMES: You think they are dead because of their money?

BUKOWSKI: I think it helps them. But the poor get dead for the same reason: lack of money. They get hateful, they lash out. So we'll go back to my original equation which I wrote fifty years ago: There are only two things wrong with money: too much or too little. Even when you have it just right, sometimes it doesn't quite work. It might be the climate, or the genes, or the person you are living with. Nothing ever works.

HIGH TIMES: You consider yourself apolitical?

BUKOWSKI: Sure, I don't have any politics. Why should I? It's like having gallstones: It costs money to have them removed, so why have them?

HIGH TIMES: I know you don't like political questions, but this has to do with your work. Do you think Reagan's election will bring about some changes in the American cultural world in general and your possibility of being published in particular?

BUKOWSKI: I am not a political person; I mean, I cannot foresee, I can only guess and say that the situation will become more repressive. The Moral Majority has voted Mr. Reagan in—many of them are Christian, many conservative—and naturally Mr. Reagan will see to it that most of their wishes are respected. But I don't give a fuck about it. It will not influence my writing, nor do I think it will influence my publications. My shit is not what you would call dirty in a physical sense; people tend to get nervous about what I write, they tend to hate me. Some poets of the "establishment" here—I know they hate me. I feel their hate, and I think it's good; it shows I am doing something. But, obviously, if everybody hated me, my books wouldn't sell. But many of the people who hate me buy my books. I can imagine what they are thinking: "Okay, I hate this guy so much I want to see what he is going to write next!" It's like at my poetry readings: Half of the people who come hate me. If I hated somebody, I wouldn't go to his reading; I would stay away.

There always has to be somebody who wants to kill you, run you over with his car, mutilate you, chop up your fingers—somebody who can't sleep at night thinking about you. Of course, with those who hate you come also the ones who love you, you know? "Oh, you are so great,

175

Bukowski! Oh, you saved my life! Oh, Bukowski! Oh, Bukowski!" It makes me sick.

HIGH TIMES: So you almost prefer people who hate you over the ones who love you?

BUKOWSKI: Not exactly that but . . . you know, many times I talk and I say things that I don't really think. I hate to say things that mean exactly what they are, unless it's something exceptionally important. Don't you think it's boring to always say things as they are? I don't just want to say, "Oh, yes, it's good, it's wonderful." It would make me feel too much like a politician. Often I say things that I don't really mean, but almost mean. Sometimes I even write this way. So don't take everything I say by the letter, because it isn't so.

HIGH TIMES: So sometimes you fooled us all with your writings. Is that what you are trying to say?

BUKOWSKI: Sometimes I even fool myself. And sometimes they reject my writing, and they say: "It isn't good at all, Bukowski!" And they are right: I write a lot of shit. Almost intentionally I write a lot of shit, to keep me going, and much of it is not good, but it keeps me exercising. But a lot of it is good. I'd say that seventy-five percent of what I write is good; forty, forty-five percent is excellent; ten percent is immortal, and twenty-five percent is shit. Does it add up to one hundred?

HIGH TIMES: Back to politics: Even though you say you're apolitical, some people see political themes in your work.

BUKOWSKI: They are entirely wrong. There is no political motivation in me. I don't want to save the world, I don't want to make it a better place. I just want to live in it and talk about what happens. I don't want the whales to be saved, I don't want the nuclear plants to be broken down and taken away: Whatever is here, I am with it. I may say I don't like it, but I don't want to change it. I am very selfish. What I mostly don't like is things like . . . I drive my car down the freeway, I get a flat tire, and I have to get out and change the goddamn thing. I have to change lanes and there isn't any lane on the right-hand side, and I have to get to the track. So you see, I have no profound feelings, I have no profound movement. I have nothing of this wanting anything at all. I just want to brush my teeth and hope my teeth don't fall off; I hope to get a hard-on next year: just simple little things. I am not looking for big things. I'll settle for small things, like the winner of the third race at the odds of three to one: That's all I want. Nothing very magic; I don't want to extend beyond my boundaries.

HIGH TIMES: Did you really work at the post office so many years?

BUKOWSKI: Oh yes! Eleven-and-a-half years at night and 2 and a half years during daytime. I could never sleep at night so I pretended it was some kind of night party. I would start writing late in the afternoon. I would come in already drunk and those people were so stupid they couldn't even tell whether I was drunk or not. And my friend Spencer would come in on drugs, and we were both out of it. I was telling Spencer "I am going to get out of here! I know how to bet horses!" So I still meet this guy 15 years later at the track. I meet him in the grandstand, and he is all screwed up, is sick, confuses my BMW with a Mercedes-Benz and thinks I am making it at the tracks. He called me one day and said, "I heard about you. You go around to these universities and you are conning people!" I said, "That's right, Spencer."

HIGH TIMES: You gave me the impression of being timid when I talked with you on the phone the other day.

BUKOWSKI: Well, I am worried about Linda [Beighle, Bukowski's girl friend]. She always senses when I talk to a woman that I am going to rape her. I care very much for Linda so I don't want to create any disturbances. So when I talk to a woman on the telephone I keep it very low tone: "Yes, no, okay." I don't say: "You want to come over for an interview? I'll have some wine, I'll have some logs on the fire, and I'll be all alone, autograph, anything you bring, with a big felt pen, full of writing material . . ." So I am always very careful to show that I am with somebody.

HIGH TIMES: A lot of women call you?

BUKOWSKI: Well, not now anymore: I am in hiding. Women come in, they are all full of life, and all of a sudden you say, well, when is the time that this thing comes out of the body and the whole face changes, and the smile stops, even sex gets bad. I don't know, I would say thirty-one days after the first meeting, a little devil jumps up and gives the fore-wording sound of things to come and then goes back and you think you are just imagining things. And six months later the devil really comes out and breaks windows and accuses you of all sorts of things you haven't done. It's a kind . . . I would call it a female nervous neurotic energy extending itself upon me, which is all right. One must suffer if one lives with somebody. One must pay for some temporary joy. So I know these things are coming, but each time I think, "I have seen this film before." But I'm sure the woman feels the same: "Oh, no, that happened with Ralph, I thought this one was okay!" So, we start spooking each other with what we are. And if I can't take it, we separate.

I have nothing to say about human relationships except they don't work. They never work: they pretend to work. It's a human truce. The best I heard is when I was working at the post office and this guy was telling me they had been married for fifty years. When he or she woke up he'd look at her and say in a very calm voice: "Now don't start anything and there won't be anything." To me that sums up the whole big thing. He just wanted a truce. Human relationships don't work, but we become together. At the beginning we are all charming. I remember a film with Woody Allen—he's good at this kind of thing—where the woman was saying: "But you are not like we were at the beginning; you were so charming!" And he said: "You know, I was just doing my mating thing, I was using up all my energies. I couldn't keep doing this, I'd go crazy!" So that's what people do at the beginning. You think they are so intelligent, so full of life the first few days. And then reality creeps in. "Jesus Christ, you leave your stockings all over the floor, you idiot asshole jerk! You flushed the toilet and there is still a turd in it!" So, human relationships don't work, they never did and they never will. They are not meant to. People were meant to live half alone and half together. With women I was all charming, but I felt like I was eating raw meat, that I couldn't quite chew too well. It became kind of a dirty trick. I am not religious, but I do have some damn morals of goodness. I don't like to just . . .

Well, it's okay, you fuck . . . I used to . . . after they'd go to work and I used to open their closets, look at their shoes, and I'd go to their bathroom, and see a picture of their boyfriend, and I'd say, "That jerk! She lives with this guy? I better get out of here!" And they'd say, "Phone me at work," "Hi, baby," but you don't give a shit; you lie in their bed, it's awful, and finally you realize and say, "What the hell am I doing? What am I trying to do?" A piece of ass is not that important! Because after you come, you have to live many hours without coming—at least I do: I am sixty. The whole thing is very confusing. You read the *Decameron*, Boccaccio. That is what influenced *Women* a great deal. I loved his idea that sex was so ridiculous, nobody could handle it. It was not so much love with him; it was sex. Love is funnier, more ridiculous. That guy! He could really laugh at it. He must have really gotten burnt about five thousand times to write that stuff. Or maybe he was just a fag; I don't know. So, love is ridiculous because it can't last, and sex is ridiculous because it doesn't last long enough.

HIGH TIMES: So what's not ridiculous?

BUKOWSKI: What's not ridiculous is the in-between time, waiting between sex and love and facing what is left over with a matter of goodness—not becoming bitter. I think we must become good with what is left in ourselves, with what is left over after it's not good anymore. In other words, to remain whole even though everything is not quite worked out. I think we need a little luck and a little glamour and a little strength and a little moxie just to carry it on. Hemingway would call it "grace in time of trouble," but he said it better than that. Moxie means carrying on when everything feels terrible. You park your car in the garage if you have a garage—if you have a car—you slam the door, you jack off and read a magazine instead of cutting your throat. It means carrying on when everything seems so terrible there is no use to go on, and you don't go to a god, you don't go to a church. You face the wall and just work it out alone. If you don't think that is tough, cookie . . . that is tough, cookie. To run somewhere, to grab something, a god, a woman, a drug, one evening of success, for the night, for the week, the year, for the lifetime; people don't hold still long enough to find out what the hell they are.

HIGH TIMES: I know you'll hate this question, but isn't alcohol an escape too?

BUKOWSKI: I knew you were going to say that. That's why I left it out! But you see, alcohol is such a pleasant god. It allows you to commit suicide and awaken again and kill yourself again. There is something

179

lengthy about an alcoholic's death. Drugs are fast; if you believe in a god, you are completely dead anyhow, because you have given away your whole brain process to somebody other than yourself. Alcohol is a slow process of dying. In other words, you are not quitting all at once. You are quitting inch by inch instead of quickly giving up. You are waiting around until maybe something might happen a little bit better. So I have been doing that since I was fourteen years old. And now I am driving a BMW, I live in a big house, the logs are on the fire, you are interviewing me, things seem better, but I know they are not. I know they are exactly the same: they change shape, but I know they are still very bad. They will always be.

HIGH TIMES: Are you talking only about yourself or the whole world in general?

BUKOWSKI: For me mainly, because I can't do the thinking or feeling for the others. But it seems I am, because often I get many letters in the mail about my writing, and they say: "Bukowski, you are so fucked up and you still survive. I decided not to kill myself," or, "you are such an asshole, man, you gave me the courage to live." So in a way I save people while taking a drink, and waiting. Not that I want to save them. I have no desire to save anybody. But it seems I have saved them. Being an asshole saves an asshole, okay? So these are my readers, you see? They buy my books—the defeated, the demented and the damned—and I am proud of it.

HIGH TIMES: Are you putting me on?

BUKOWSKI: A little bit, but not completely. Because the main man I attack in my writing is me, and basically I am almost everyone who is around. That's what the feminists seem to miss, the part of the stuff in between the written lines.

HIGH TIMES: Still, it was a group of women in Rome who put on the play called "Bukowski, We Love You." Did you know that?

BUKOWSKI: How am I supposed to go on writing when I hear all these good things about myself? I like the bad things better. We all thrive upon adversities. Dostoyevsky once said, "Adversity is the main-spring of self-realism." Well, it's one of them anyhow. Dostoyevsky . . . he always holds his time. The old test of time. Saroyan said, "The roar of Dostoyevsky!" He could write, I can write. He was S-K-Y and I am the Fleetwood Mac!

You can read Dostoevsky again, and John Fante . . . you should read a guy called John Fante. This guy was a tough mother who writes better than I do—almost better than I do. He's got more human soul than all the people who come to hear me. John Fante is my buddy out of nowhere, I love him, he's a magic person. Any of John Fante is immortal.

HIGH TIMES: Do you consider yourself an erotic writer?

BUKOWSKI: *Erotic!* I write about everything. The reason sex got into so much of my stories is because when I quit the post office, at the age of fifty, I had to make money. What I really wanted to do was write about something that interested me. But there were all those porno-graphic magazines on Melrose Avenue, and they had read my stuff in the *Free Press,* and started asking me to send them something. So what I would do was write a good story, and then in the middle I had to throw in some gross act of sex. And so I would write a story, and at a certain point I would say: "Well it's time to throw some sex into it." And I would throw some sex in it and kept writing the story. It was okay: I would mail the story and immediately get a three-hundred-dollar check.

HIGH TIMES: But do you see your stories as erotic? Do you think people get excited when they read them?

BUKOWSKI: I don't know. Some people have written me and told me that some of my stories have aroused them. Especially "The Fiend." Now, why the story of a man raping a little girl arouses people I don't know. Perhaps a lot of men want to do it and it is only the law and the fear that prevents them from doing it. Perhaps the fact that I described her clothing, slowly, what happened, has excited somebody. But I didn't get a hard-on while I was writing it.

HIGH TIMES: What about Henry Miller? Do you consider Miller an erotic writer?

BUKOWSKI: I can't read Henry Miller. He starts talking about reality but then he becomes esoteric, starts talking about something else. A couple of good pages, and then he goes off on a tangent, enters into abstract areas, and I can't read him anymore. I feel gypped.

HIGH TIMES: Gypped? What do you mean?

BUKOWSKI: He doesn't stay there. I want him to stay in the streets, not in the air.

HIGH TIMES: So good writing is writing that stays in reality, in the streets.

BUKOWSKI: I didn't say it has to be like that; I said that for me it is. So I try to stay in the streets, wherever I am; I try to stay with reality. I only describe things; I don't try to explain them. Only what I know worries me. What I don't know doesn't concern me. It's like at the post office: the boys used to say, "What I don't know doesn't hurt me. If my wife is fucking someone else, if I don't know it, it doesn't exist." All I know is what I see. I am in bed watching TV, all I know is Johnny Carson: that's reality!

I guess I am closer to the street people than I am to anybody, and when you get anybody who is a little higher, he becomes a mark. So that's why you have to lay low, do your work and just be quiet. Do your screaming in the pages but don't let them see you too often. Think about it: what is it that creates some kind of magic between somebody who creates and somebody who listens to creations? The magic I think often is the person who secludes himself from the masses; not deliberately, but it has to be done. Once the artist starts mixing with the masses, the artist becomes the masses.

HIGH TIMES: Is that why you didn't go to the International Poetry Festival of Castelporziano in Italy last summer? You were one of the "big absents" there.

BUKOWSKI: I didn't go because I didn't like the line of American poets I would be reading with. I would not read with them in Santa Monica, California; I wouldn't even be in the same room with them. So that's why I didn't go: I didn't like the company. I don't want to name anybody, but if it's true that they were bombarded with sand balls as you tell me, I am pleased. That's what I feel like doing when they read: I feel like vomiting and throwing my vomit at them.

HIGH TIMES: But those people wanted to hear Bukowski and Ginsberg . . .

BUKOWSKI: No, wait a minute, let's not confuse—

HIGH TIMES: All right, but Allen is a big idol in Italy, as you are.

BUKOWSKI: Who, Allen? [Sarcastically:] Allen is okay, Allen is all right, yes, they are all good poets: Gregory Corso, and Ginsberg's boyfriend, and Joan Baez, Timothy Leary, Frank Zappa, Bob Dylan . . . American culture is all right. American culture is . . . I think the whole thing has a big lag. It's like a body dragging a tail, but the tail is behind the body dragging in the dust.

HIGH TIMES: What about your screenplay, *Barfly?*

BUKOWSKI: I really have high hopes for "Barfly," not because Barbet (Schroeder) and I have struggled over it for so long, but because I think that we have a pretty good baby here. But how are we going to prove this? It's so difficult! You know what's happening now, inflation, interest rates going up 20% . . . I hate to say this, but I think that if *Barfly* is directed properly it's going to be better than *Cuckoo's Nest.* It will be more real because it talks about a madhouse which is not a madhouse and the inmates are not locked up.

HIGH TIMES: Is there a story in *Barfly?*

BUKOWSKI: There is some story; it's pepped up enough to keep everybody eating their popcorn. It's entertaining. I am trying to record what happened 30 years ago, with splendor. And it's an original story. I have never written anything about this. It's about three or four nights in my life, at the age of 24, 93% of what really happened.

HIGH TIMES: What is the best compliment that a male reader can give you? And what is the best compliment that a female reader can give you?

BUKOWSKI: The female readers are all the same. When I am at a poetry reading they come and say, "I am going to fuck you." The men don't say that; they say, "Hey, man you are great!" So the women readers excite me a little bit more. I think men like me more.

HIGH TIMES: In your books you always talk about your sexual pleasure, but we don't know much of how the women feel making love with you . . .

BUKOWSKI: Well, of course, I start with my pleasure; if there is something left, they can take it. When I am satisfied, it's all over. Ten seconds, it's finished. Sometimes it's only three or four seconds, and there is never any foreplay. It's all there: get over there, let's get it out of the way so I can watch TV. That's the way I do it.

HIGH TIMES: And so then Johnny Carson is a good conclusion?

BUKOWSKI: Johnny Carson after sex? Sometimes it's better than the sex that preceded it; sometimes not. We all have bad nights.

HIGH TIMES: Aren't you concerned about how women feel making love with you?

BUKOWSKI: Are you talking about that sex liberation bullshit? Well, okay, sometimes I tried to do all I could: a lot of foreplay; I know where the clitoris is, I know how to do all these things, I know, I know.

HIGH TIMES: Aren't you worried about your reputation?

BUKOWSKI: As a big lover? No, if they don't like what I am doing, they go to another man, which is what they usually do. Let them do all the foreplay.

HIGH TIMES: Is it true that you started writing *Women* after several years of celibacy?

BUKOWSKI: Several? It must have been ten, twelve, since the last time I had had sex. You need to recharge your sperm. Or perhaps I think that I have always known that women are trouble more than anything else.

HIGH TIMES: But you had to go through that experience, and start sleeping with women again . . .

BUKOWSKI: Because I thought that being a writer, and having been without women for twelve years . . . you can write a lot of things, but if you lack the other half of the human race, you are not a complete human being, you don't know what the hell is going on, right? I mean, you need a certain balance. If you want to write bad things about women, you have to live with them first. So I live with them in order to criticize them in my writings.

Do you think it was so terrible to be without sex in those twelve years? I was preparing for the tempest of women who would have arrived. Perhaps I knew it was going to happen. It's not a decision I made: things in life just happen. I didn't have my first fuck until I was twenty-three. Now I am sixty-one years old and I had my last one last year.

HIGH TIMES: Really? Why?

BUKOWSKI: It allows me to pick the winners better at the track. To me, sex is like a peanut butter sandwich.

What do you think happens when people arrive at a certain age when sex is not possible anymore? You can't love that person anymore? What's all this big deal about sex? Does everything have to be sex? Can't I ride a bicycle without thinking about sex? Am I an impure person because I don't think about sex? Is my mind wrong because I don't have a hard-on fifty percent of the times? I have nothing against fucking, but I think it can be overpriced.

People think that I am fixated with sex. I fucked, I fucked well and I wrote well about fucking, but this doesn't mean it's very important. I fucked a lot of women, I fucked and I drank, I drank and I *sexed*, and I discovered, drinking and *sexing*, that it is not that big of a deal.

People want to come here, and they say, "Hey, Bukowski, let's get drunk, I am bringing some whores over." I am not interested: "Hey, I don't want your whores." *They* think it's important. I didn't say it. It's just because I write good stuff about sex, but I could have written as well about frying eggs, except I didn't.

HIGH TIMES: What can you tell me about this book on childhood that you're writing now?

BUKOWSKI: Three-quarters finished; my editor says it's the best thing I have ever written. But it's not finished. It's a horror story, and it has been harder to write than the others. Because it's so serious, I have tried to make it a little funny, to cover the horror of my childhood.

HIGH TIMES: Was it a horror story?

BUKOWSKI: Oh, yes. Capital H. Why? Have you ever been beaten with a strap, three times a week, from the age of six to the age of eleven? Do you know how many beatings that is?

HIGH TIMES: Was it your father?

BUKOWSKI: Yes. But, see, this has been a good literary training. Beating me with that strap taught me something.

HIGH TIMES: What did it teach you?

BUKOWSKI: How to type.

HIGH TIMES: What's the link?

BUKOWSKI: The link is, when they beat you long enough and hard enough you have the tendency to say what you really mean; in other words, they take all the pretenses out of you. If you can get out of it, whatever is still there is usually something genuine. Anyone who gets severe punishment during childhood can get out of it quite strong, quite good, or can end up being a rapist, a killer, end up in a madhouse or lost in all kinds of different directions. So you see, my father was a great literary teacher: he taught me the meaning of pain—pain without reason . . .

HIGH TIMES: Is this perhaps the reason you write in isolation, without contacts with people? And is that why you write?

BUKOWSKI: Certainly nobody knows why they became writers. I am only saying that my father has taught me a lesson in life, taught me certain aspects of life, of people. And these people exist; I meet them every day as I am driving my car on the freeway.

HIGH TIMES: What kind of people?

BUKOWSKI: I am on the freeway, in the fast lane, behind somebody. He goes fifty miles an hour. I swing around him, I try to pass him, he goes sixty. I go sixty-five, and he pushes on the gas pedal. There is something in the human race which is very petty, very bitter. I see it from the way people drive on the freeway. When somebody wants to pass me, I put on the brakes, I let him go. The human race isn't very much.

HIGH TIMES: Did you always feel that way?

BUKOWSKI: It hasn't improved. I didn't notice any change. In one of my poems I wrote: "Humanity, you never had it from the beginning." I see no reason to alter that line.

HIGH TIMES: I assume you've done a lot of reading . . .

BUKOWSKI: Between the ages of fifteen and twenty-four I must have read a whole library. I ate books for dinner. My father used to say at eight o'clock in the evening: "Lights out!" He had the idea that we had to go to bed early, get up early and get ahead in the world by doing a good job at whatever you were doing—which is complete bullshit. I knew that, but these books were so much more interesting than my father. In fact, they were the opposite of my father: these books had some heart, had some gamble. So when he said, "Lights out," I would take a little light in my bed, put in under the covers and read, and it would get suffocating under that there and hot, but it made each page I turned all the more glorious, like I was taking dope: Sinclair Lewis, Dos Passos, these are my friends under the covers. You don't know what these guys meant to me; they were strange friends. I was finding under the apparent brutality people that were saying things to me quietly; they were magic people. And now when I read the same guys I think that they weren't so good.

HIGH TIMES: Do you ever see other writers?

BUKOWSKI: Why go see another writer? What's there to say? There is nothing to be said; there are only things to be done. Talking with another writer is like drinking water in the bathtub: you don't do it. Do you ever drink water in the bathtub? No, you see? I drink wine in the bathtub.

HIGH TIMES: Is there any living writer you respect?

BUKOWSKI: There are a couple, but it's better if I don't see them, when I am drinking. The majority of them would start talking about their work. They don't say, "My wife broke her arm yesterday." They say things like "I am working on a sonnet" or "I am going to New York." They talk shop.

HIGH TIMES: What about their books?

BUKOWSKI: I don't like the way they wear their clothes, I don't like their shoes and I don't like their books. I don't like their tone of voice. I don't like the way they puke after three drinks. Writers are very despicable people. Plumbers are better, used car salesmen are better; they are all more human than writers. Writers become human only when they sit at the typewriter; then they can become good or even exceptional. Take them away from their typewriter and they become pricks. [*Intensely*] I am a writer.

HIGH TIMES: Yet you don't think that of yourself.

BUKOWSKI: No. Because I worked in a factory, I became tame. I didn't become a writer until I was fifty, so I had the time to live in a different area of existence. That life helped me to maintain myself—can I use the word *sane? normal?* Somehow it doesn't seem the right word. I mean, it gave me a certain . . . *naturalness.* That's the word I am looking for: *naturalness.*

HIGH TIMES: When did things change in your life? When did the time of *Post Office* and *Women* stop?

BUKOWSKI: Nothing stopped. Another one worried about my soul! You know, at one time when people came by they used to see me in this tiny room full of beer cans, and getting up and going to the bathroom and vomiting, and I come out, light a cigarette, drink another beer— they thought I had a soul!

HIGH TIMES: And I bet they were very self-satisfied in seeing you feel horrible and sick. That's the image people have of Hank Chinaski.

BUKOWSKI: But I was having soul for them, and I was having it for me, too. It's okay, I understand. I was a tough guy. Now I am soft, mellow, I smile. I just want to live calmly with a decent woman, drinking together, watching TV, taking a walk . . .

HIGH TIMES: So no more of all these women in your life?

BUKOWSKI: I'm not saying that. Basically I have always been a loyal jerk. Every woman I lived with, even a whore, I have had a damn sense of loyalty and honesty with; and I wish everybody would have it, because it would make the world easier.

HIGH TIMES: What do you think this loyalty is based on?

BUKOWSKI: I guess it's based on other people's disloyalty—the ugliness of it. I don't want to be the first liar. I don't know where it comes from. I don't have any religion. To be good is better than being anything else if there is a choice. You don't have to be a Christian; it's not an obligation. Just to be good is an easy concept. It makes everybody feel better when I am being good. On the other hand, I admire evil people who can be original and strike out into new areas; but the kind of evil people I like are those who don't betray one person but those who cut through the beliefs of many people who are ignorant and just start new trends of thinking. There is a difference between two people fucking each other up and one person fucking the whole world with an original concept. Anybody strong like Hitler is going to be hated for centuries, but they are going to talk about him, make movies about him long after those who gathered together to conquer him subsided from human consciousness. Because it took some balls to crack through the morals of central understanding. I think this is okay if you can do it on a grand scale. If you can betray and kill all humanity, that is grand; but if you lie to the person you are living with, that's shit. Because it doesn't take any guts to do one, and it takes courage and originality to do the other.

HIGH TIMES: You said something before about not being religious, but weren't you raised as a Catholic?

BUKOWSKI: Yes, and I used to go to Catholic Masses, but not of my own will . . . When I was dying they called a priest to give me the last rites. He said, "You have down on your application you are a Catholic." You know, you can't talk when you are dying. I said, "Father, I just didn't want anybody to ask what I meant by agnostic. Just put down Catholic, it slides on in. I am not really a Catholic, I don't care." He leaned down on me and said, "My son, once a Catholic always a Catholic." I said, "Oh no, Father, that's not true! Please go away and let me die."

HIGH TIMES: Are you afraid of dying?

BUKOWSKI: Who me? Hell no! I came so close to it a couple of times, I'm not afraid of it. When you come so close I guess it feels good. You just go, "OK, OK." I guess especially if you don't believe in a god, you are not worried about going to hell or heaven, you are just going to relax from wherever you are at. There is going to be a change, they are going to show a new movie, so whatever it is, you say "OK." When I was 35 they had just about pronounced me dead at the General Hospital. I didn't die. I got out of the hospital—they had told me never to have a drink again or I was going to die—and the first place I went was to a bar and had a beer. No, two beers!

HIGH TIMES: What was that? A defiance to live?

BUKOWSKI: No, it was a defiance of all those who lie to you. Death is good, death is not good or bad. You know what they say, "the longest trip." Living with somebody you don't like to live with is worse than death; working eight hours at a job that you hate is worse than death.

HIGH TIMES: I heard that they are teaching you in some universities, that they are using your books as textbooks: the poems, *Factotum*. How do you feel about it?

BUKOWSKI: That doesn't make me feel good. It means you are safe enough to teach. If they say so I think maybe I must step on the gas pedal a little bit more. I don't want people to catch up with me: I want a big space between me and them.

HIGH TIMES: So you go around universities, occasionally, or you give a poetry reading once in a while. What do you do every day?

BUKOWSKI: I get up, I go to the track, I come back tired, I am too tired to type. Then Linda comes home from the store, and she is tired, we are sitting here. So I say, "Well, we might as well have a little drink!" Then after dinner she does her store figures, I go upstairs, I start writing, every day the same thing. If you are asking me if my writing is still good, yes, it's still good.

HIGH TIMES: So it seems that the racetrack is the only thing that stayed out of the world you described.

BUKOWSKI: In other words, you say I'm at the racetrack and I'm not in the streets anymore, so you are worried about my soul? What do you think is changed? Living in a big house, having a nice car?

HIGH TIMES: I think it's a big change. To wake up in the morning and know for once how to pay the rent.

BUKOWSKI: What's the difference? One who does not have it is going to give it away to luxuries; one who has it is going to continue. So when you look back at what I have written from 1979 on you'll see whether I failed or made it. My guess is that I've made it. But my good luck is that it happened too much, too late, and I think . . . if I am not wise enough to know that at the age of sixty, I know very little. If I know very little, I deserve to fail, so we'll see.

Charles Bukowski on Charles Bukowski as written to Gerald Locklin

1982–83

"Charles Bukowski on Charles Bukowski As Written to Gerald Locklin," *Home Planet News*, Vol. 3, No. 4, Issue 14, Winter 1982–1983, p. 9.

Gerald Locklin

Bukowski and I sometimes have occasion to correspond, usually over someone wanting to get in touch with him, and his letters are always good, so I got the idea of getting himself to pour himself a drink and write me a longer letter than usual, sort of a self-interview. I explained to him that I was trying to cook up some things on West Coast writing for you, described *Home Planet* to him, suggested a few topics to him, but left it open for him to go on about anything that was on his mind. I didn't want to do a formal interview, because I knew it would be distasteful to both of us and anyway there have been a number of such interviews done with him lately, most of them bad in one way or another. So here's the result. I like the way it turned out.

—Gerald Locklin

I like San Pedro. It's a good place to hide, close to Hollywood Park, Los Alamitos. You're not going to find a bevy of poets sipping expresso anywhere along Pacific and/or Gaffey. There are some drawbacks: not a decent eating place in town and the liquor stores often close at 9:30 p.m. But since I buy by the case and have 3 or 4 bottles hidden around, I'm always all right. There's a sense of relaxation and easiness around here that you don't find in too many places. I like it.

The films, yes, mainly the Ferreri I'd like to see. Gazzara can act and he's got good eyes. We'll see . . . I've met any number of movie people, mainly through Barbet Shroeder, cameramen, directors, mostly the European crowd, who I think get film down closer where actuality is, except now and then they come on with some so called avant-garde stuff which I remember seeing some 40 years ago in the Art Movies in New York City . . . .. On the Godard subtitles: I can't speak French and I was surprised that he gave me credit. What happened is that a Frenchman translated the script into English and then I took the English script and Americanized that. But, on the other hand, Godard used one of my poems for a movie scene and I don't get credit for that, except one night we were drinking and he handed me this batch of francs, so that's cash, not credit, o.k.

There have been some cameras around looking at me and I'm not exactly sure what this had to do with creation, except that they are poking at what is left of the Chinaski soul. It's not good stuff but when I get drunk enough I don't mind. Then I can talk, then I can say things. But too much exposure is death, so I knock off a good 50% of it, and soon may stop it all. Recently turned down $2,000 to give a poetry reading because my gut is turning from this hanging from a limb and being poked at. You put a piece of paper in the machine and you type something on it. That's the essence; all the other crap is the bleed, and when they bleed you long enough and sit down to that sheet of paper and nothing comes out, the old yea-sayers will be the first to leave. So it's best to leave them first and to get back to the mechanics of doing. Horses, booze and the typer. Anything that gets in the way of that is deathly, including women, and especially including women. The longer I manage to stay away from women the better I feel. Last night at the quarter horses I'm on the 2nd deck when I see this redhead with the ass and tits that I used to know, all that red hair in long fire, I see her walking up to a betting window alone. I run downstairs and bet the remainder of the night on the first floor. No more: that sticky web of madness is for the more hardy.

Besides, she was not a nice person.

Wormie? Well, to me it's the only lit mag. I mean, when I get a copy I can go right to the crapper and read it while I'm shitting and I can jump into the tub or into bed and read it. I don't have any trouble with most of the poems and when I'm finished I want more. I can't say that about any other mag. When I read them I get a headache, I get sleepy, I can't turn the pages, I can't believe the stuff they get off with, 19th century posing as the poet, stuff that is so terrible that it's unbelievable, it's like a joke that doesn't work, again and again, and they keep telling it over and over. Malone has the editor's eye, that's all there is to it . . . The *New York Quarterly* had a great format, and about 40 percent of the poems but they are in the process of folding even though they tell me it's not true. All I know is that it's been a couple of years since they've come out and that they're sitting on 25 or 30 of my accepted poems, but I'll live, I'll write some more.

New York City? I could only last 3 months there. It's a hard place to be without money and when you don't know the territory and you don't have a trade. That was 1944 or 1945, so maybe it's a nice place now, only I'm not going to try it.

Politics? Politics are just like women: get into them seriously and you're going to come out looking like a earthworm stepped on by a long-shoreman's boot.

Well, I've got an American Express card, a Visa and a BMW but I still write, and writing has always been a pleasure to me, a non-work item, it's as easy as drinking so I usually do them both together. I hear from other writers how HARD it is to write and if it were that god damned hard for me I'd try something different. I had my longest writer's block last month—7 days, and most of it was caused by *people* getting in between me and the machine. Martin of Black Sparrow told me, "I've got so many of your poems on backlog that if you died today I could bring out 5 or 6 more books and all of them would be good." Of course, he's a fan. Maybe only 3 of them would be good.

I've turned down several free trips to Italy, France, Spain. That's just more *interviews*, Gerald. I'm about on page 240 of HAM ON RYE (novel) which means it's just about done. Then a bit of re-write and then the 2 year wait for publication. That's all right. It was just 1970 that I quit the post office, and it's been a good fast glorious bang bang bang, and if I die right now I will have known that it was a real good cheap thrill.

There might be some new good writers around. I hope so. But I no longer read books. I read the newspaper, the race results, boxing matches. I've got on tv, pretty bad. I look forward to the Hearns-Leonard fight. Notice I've reversed the order of the names and also look for the fight to end that way. Duran was just a fat man. When Hearns hits Leonard, L. is going to get swatted by a lean thin man with a mule's hoof at the end of his glove. Leonard's got guts though and style. Whoever wins is really going to have to earn it.

Rivers of good wine to you,

Craft Interview
with Charles Bukowski

1985

"Craft Interview with Charles Bukowski," *The New York Quarterly*, No. 27, Summer 1985, pp. 19–25.

NYQ: *How do you write? In longhand, on the typewriter? Do you revise much? What do you do with worksheets? Your poems sometimes give the impression of coming off the top of your head. Is that only an impression? How much agony and sweat of the human spirit is involved in the writing of one of your poems?*

CB: I write right off the typer. I call it my "machinegun." I hit it hard, usually late at night while drinking wine and listening to classical music on the radio and smoking mangalore ganesh beedies. I revise but not much. The next day I retype the poem and automatically make a change or two, drop out a line, or make two lines into one or one line into two, that sort of thing—to make the poem have more balls, more balance. Yes, the poems come "off the top of my head," I seldom know what I'm going to write when I sit down. There isn't much agony and sweat of the human spirit involved in doing it. The writing's easy, it's the living that is sometimes difficult.

NYQ: *When you're away from your place do you carry a notebook with you? Do you jot down ideas as they come to you during the day or do you store them in your head for later?*

CB: I don't carry notebooks and I don't consciously store ideas. I try not to think that I am a writer and I am pretty good at doing that. I don't like writers, but then I don't like insurance salesmen either.

NYQ: *Do you ever go through dry periods, no writing at all? If so how often? What do you do during these periods? Anything to get you back on the track?*

CB: A dry period for me means perhaps going two or three nights without writing. I probably have dry periods but I'm not aware of them and I go on writing, only the writing probably isn't much good. But sometimes I do get aware that it isn't going too well. Then I go to the racetrack and bet more money than usual and scream at and abuse my woman. And it's best that I lose at the track without trying to. I can almost always write a damn near immortal poem if I have lost somewhere between 150 and 200 dollars.

NYQ: *Need for isolation? Do you work best alone? Most of your poems concern your going from a state of love/sex to a state of isolation. Does that tie in with the way to have things in order to write?*

CB: I love solitude but I don't need it to the exclusion of somebody I care for in order to get some words down. I figure if I can't write under all circumstances, then I'm just not good enough to do it. Some of my poems indicate that I am writing while living alone after a split with a woman, and I've had many splits with women. I need solitude more often when I'm not writing than when I am. I have written with children running about the room having at me with squirt guns. That often helps rather than hinders the writing: some of the laughter enters. One thing does bother me, though: to overhear somebody's loud tv, a comedy program with a laugh track.

NYQ: *When did you begin writing? How old? What writers did you admire?*

CB: The first thing I ever remembered writing was about a German aviator with a steel hand who shot hundreds of Americans out of the sky during World War II. It was in long hand in pen and it covered every page of a huge memo ringed notebook. I was about 13 at the time and I was in bed covered with the worst case of boils the medics ever remembered seeing. There weren't any writers to admire at the time. Since then there has been John Fante, Knut Hamsun, the Céline of *Journey*; Dostoyevsky, of course; Jeffers of the long poems only; Conrad Aiken, Catullus . . . not too many. I sucked mostly at the classical music boys. It was good to come home from the factories at night, take off my clothes, climb on the bed in the dark, get drunk on beer and listen to them.

NYQ: *Do you think there's too much poetry being written today? How would you characterize what you think is really bad poetry? What do you think is good poetry today?*

CB: There's too much bad poetry being written today. People just don't know how to write down a simple easy line. It's difficult for them; it's like trying to keep a hard-on while drowning—not many can do it. Bad poetry is caused by people who sit down and think, Now I am going to write a Poem. And it comes out the way they *think* a poem should be. Take a cat. He doesn't think, well, now I'm cat and I'm going to kill this bird. He just does it. Good poetry today? Well, it's being written by a couple of cats called Gerald Locklin and Ronald Koertge.

NYQ: *You've read most of the NYQ craft interviews we've published. What do you think of our approach, the interviews you've read. What interviews have told you something?*

CB: I'm sorry you asked that question. I haven't learned anything from the interviews except that the poets were studious, trained, self-assured and obnoxiously self-important. I don't think that I was ever able to finish an interview; the print began to blur and the trained seals vanished below the surface. These people lack joy, madness and gamble in their answers just as they do in their work (poems).

NYQ: *Although you write strong voice poems, that voice rarely extends beyond the circumference of your own psychosexual concerns. Are you interested in national, international affairs, do you consciously restrict yourself as to what you will and will not write about?*

CB: I photograph and record what I see and what happens to me. I am not a guru or leader of any sort. I am not a man who looks for solutions in God or politics. If somebody else wants to do the dirty work and create a better world for us and he can do it, I will accept it. In Europe where my work is having much luck, various groups have put claim on me, revolutionaries, anarchists, so forth, because I have written of the common man of the streets, but in interviews over there I have had to disclaim a conscious working relationship with them because there isn't any. I have compassion for almost all the individuals of the world; at the same time, they repulse me.

NYQ: *What do you think a young poet starting out today needs to learn the most?*

CB: He should realize that if he writes something and it bores him it's going to bore many other people also. There is nothing wrong with a poetry that is entertaining and easy to understand. Genius could be the ability to say a profound thing in a simple way. He should stay the hell out of writing classes and find out what's happening around the corner. And bad luck for the young poet would be a rich father, an early marriage, an early success or the ability to do anything very well.

NYQ: *Over the last few decades California has been the residence of many of our most independent voice poets—like Jeffers, Rexroth, Patchen, even Henry Miller. Why is this? What is your attitude towards the East, towards New York?*

CB: Well there was a little more space out here, the long run up the coast, all that water, a feeling of Mexico and China and Canada, Hollywood, sunburn, starlets turned to prostitutes. I don't know, really, I guess if your ass is freezing some of the time it's harder to be a "voice poet." Being a voice poet is the big gamble because you're putting your guts up for view and you're going to get a lot more reaction than if you're writing something like your mother's soul being like a daisy field.

New York, I don't know. I landed there with $7 and no job and no friends and no occupation except common laborer. I suppose if I had come in from the top instead of the bottom I might have laughed a little more. I stayed 3 months and the buildings scared the shit out of me and the people scared the shit out of me, and I had done a lot of bumming all over the country under the same conditions but New York City was the Inferno, all the way. The way Woody Allen's intellectuals suffer in N.Y.C. is a lot different than what happens to my type of people. I never got laid in New York, in fact, the women wouldn't even speak to me. The only way I ever got laid in New York was to come back 3 decades later and bring my own with me, a terrible wench, we stayed at the Chelsea, of course. The *New York Quarterly* is the only good thing that has happened to me out there.

NYQ: *You've written short stories, novels. Do they come from the same place your poems come from?*

CB: Yes, they do, there's not much difference—line and line length. The short story helped get the rent and the novel was a way of saying how many different things could happen to the same man on the way to suicide, madness, old age, natural and unnatural death.

NYQ: *You have a fairly distinct persona in most of your poems, and your strong voice seems to come out of that persona. It's the mask of a bored, dirty old man who's boozing it up in Li Po manner because the straight world isn't worth taking seriously. Usually there's an hysterical broad banging your door down while the poem is taking shape. First do you admit to this persona in your poems, and then to what extent do you think it reflects Bukowski the man? In other words are you the person you present to us in your poems?*

CB: Things change a bit: what once was is not quite what it is now. I began writing poetry at the age of 35 after coming out of the death ward of the L.A. County General Hospital and not as a visitor. To get somebody to read your poems you have to be noticed, so I got my act up. I wrote vile (but interesting) stuff that made people hate me, that made them curious about this Bukowski. I threw bodies off my court porch into the night. I pissed on police cars, sneered at hippies. After my second reading down at Venice, I grabbed the money, leaped into my car, intoxicated, and drove it about on the sidewalks at 60 m.p.h. I had parties at my place which were interrupted by police raids. A professor from U.C.L.A. invited me to his place for dinner. His wife cooked a nice meal which I ate and then I went over and broke up his China closet. I was in and out of drunktanks. A lady accused me of rape, the whore. Meanwhile, I wrote about most of this, it was my persona, it was me but it wasn't me. As time went on, trouble and action arrived by itself and I didn't have to force it and I wrote about that and this was closer to my real persona. Actually, I am not a tough person and sexually, most of the time, I am almost a prude, but I am often a nasty drunk and many strange things happen to me when I am drunk. I'm not saying this very well and I'm taking too long. What I am trying to say is that the longer I write the closer I am getting to what I am. I am one of those slow starters but I am all hell in the stretch run. I am 93 percent the person I present in my poems; the other 7 percent is where art improves upon life, call it background music.

NYQ: *You refer to Hemingway a lot, seem to have a love/hate thing for him, what he does in his work. Any comment?*

CB: I guess for me Hemingway is a lot like it is for others: he goes down well when we are young. Gertie taught him the line but I think he improved upon it. Hemingway and Saroyan had the line, the magic of it. The problem was that Hemingway didn't know how to laugh and Saroyan was filled with sugar. John

Fante had the line too and he was the first who knew how to let passion enter in, emotion in, without letting it destroy the concept. I speak here of moderns who write the *simple* line; I am aware that Blake was once around. So when I write about Hemingway it's sometimes a joke thing but I'm probably more in debt to him than I'd care to admit. His early work was screwed down tight, you couldn't get your fingers under it. But now I get more out of reading about his life and fuckups, it's almost as good as reading about D. H. Lawrence.

NYQ: *What do you think of this interview and what questions do you wish we'd asked you? Go ahead and ask it of yourself and then answer it.*

CB: I think the interview is all right. I suppose that some people will object that the answers lack polish and erudition, then they'll go out and buy my books. I can't think of any questions to ask myself. For me to get paid for writing is like going to bed with a beautiful woman and afterwards she gets up, goes to her purse and gives me a handful of money. I'll take it. Why don't we stop here?

The Charles Bukowski Tapes

DIRECTED BY BARBET SCHROEDER

JANUARY, 1985

"The Charles Bukowski Tapes," Produced and Directed by Barbet Schroeder, *Les Films du Losange*, Distributed by Lagoon Video, Volume 1, No. 2, "Starving for Art," and No. 4, "Nature." January, 1985.

CB: OK.

BS: You don't like Nature.

CB: Whores are natural.

BS: The trees, the countryside . . .

CB: They bore me. Carl Weissner took us through a trip through Germany showing us all the hills, the hills, and the greenness and I started nodding off. Shit, one time I was giving a poetry reading up in Oregon or Washington somewhere. Some guy was driving us. After the reading where I'm supposed to rape an English teacher, a female teacher . . . by the time I got there it was so dull I couldn't even get my dick up. Trees, greenness. It's OK, it's OK, but I mean it can finally be deadening (*Gesticulating to sky*). It's just like: green trees, green trees, green trees. OK. All right. What are you going to do with it?

Give me the cities. Give me smog. I like what the kid told me in Paris, the King of the . . . what, the King of the Punks, yeah. He said, people complain about smog. I love it. He zipped up and down. And you know there is a way of loving smog, it's not a non-truth. It feels good. You walk out and you go (*breathes in*). You're part of it, shit, you're walking through smog, you live through smog. You love the buildings, you love the inflation. There are creatures who adjust to conditions. There will be smog people, inflation people. The higher the price . . . you're gonna go into a place someday and the waitress will say: "Well, it's 365 dollars for a leg sandwich of mutton." And you'll say, "Is that all? I'm gonna pay you 565 dollars and here's a 365 dollar tip!" These are the people who are going to survive, don't you see? They're ready for inflation, they're ready for smog! They love it! What's the difference? It's only mental. Go with it! Here, have a 500 dollar tip! No, it's OK. It doesn't mean anything unless you want to make it mean something, hell! So you keep changing governments, you keep changing women, what's the difference? Here, we're back to women . . .

Starving for Art

BS: You said that starving doesn't create art, that it creates many things, but mainly it creates time.

CB: Oh, yeah. Well, hey, that's very basic. I hate to use up your film to say this. But you know, if you work an eight hour job and you're going to get 55 cents an hour . . . if you stay home you're not going to get any money but you're gonna have time to write things down on paper. I guess I was one of those rarities of our modern times who did starve for his art. I really starved you know to have a 24 hour day unintruded upon by other people. I gave up food, I gave up everything just to . . . I was a nut. I was dedicated. But you see, the problem is you can be a dedicated nut and not be able to do it. Dedication without talent is useless, you understand what I mean? Dedication alone is not enough. You can starve and want to do it . . . Hey, you know, I know. And how many do that? They starve in the gutters and they don't make it.

BS: But you knew you had talent.

CB: They all think they have! How do you know that you're the one? You don't know . . . it's a shot in the dark. You take it or you become a normal civilized person from 8 to 5. Get married, have children, Christmas together: "Here comes grandma! Hi grandma! . . . come on in, how are you?" You know, shit, I couldn't take that, I'd rather murder myself! I guess just in the blood of me, I couldn't stand the whole thing that's going on, the ordinariness of life. I couldn't stand family life, I couldn't stand job life, I couldn't stand anything I looked at. I just decided I either had to starve, make it, go mad, come through or do something. Even if I hadn't made it on writing I could not do the 8 to 5. I would have been a suicide, something. I'm sorry, I could not accept the snail's pace: Johnny Carson, Happy Birthday, Christmas, New Year's. To me this is the sickest of all sick things. So I just had luck, I held on, somebody took a poem or a short story somewhere. Now I just sit around and drink wine and I talk about myself because you guys ask the questions, not because I give answers, OK?

BS: OK.

Charles Bukowski:
The World's Greatest Fucker

ACE BACKWORDS
1987

"Charles Bukowski: The World's Greatest Fucker," Ace Backwords, *Twisted Image*, January 29, 1987, p. 1.

How are you doing? (boy, this is off to a great start, huh!)

About the same. I play the horses, come in at night, open the wine bottle and type. I don't type every night, maybe every 3rd night. And I never type when I don't want to type.

Are you happy with your new book?

I think the new book is on a level with all the others. I think the writing holds at a certain keel, the subject matter changes (sometimes) and that's about it.

How is your health holding up?

With all the drinking I've done and still do, I should be dead. Even had a complete check-up a couple of years ago. Doc could find nothing wrong. Liver OK and so forth . . . I told him of my manner of living and all the guy could tell me is, "I don't understand it." So I'm PLENTY LUCKY, you know. Although I have no desire to live a long time. 80 years will do me. That's 14 more. And like anybody else, I'd prefer to avoid any long and hampering illness.

What are you drinking at this moment?

Mirrassou 1984 Gamay Beaujolais.

You say "the madhouses, skidrows and graveyards are filled with the likes of me."
What do you think it was that saved you from that fate?

Well, I've made skidrow and the graveyard awaits. Staying out of the madhouse? Well, I suppose I never harmed anybody too badly, and the madness was released in the writing.

How did you come up with the brilliant idea to write poetry that actually had something to do with reality?

I was long discouraged with Poetry because I thought it was a con and slick and false and worked at by the snobs. Much of it (poetry) is still this way. I began to put down the word on paper as clearly as I could because doing it any other way made me sick at the gut. And when one speaks in simple terms one is more apt to speak of real things. But I had to write many many years to break through in this manner. The editors wanted the same old poetic stuff and stance and I couldn't, wouldn't do it. There was nothing brave about my refusal to write the same old tripe. It was closer to stubbornness.

If there was one piece of advice you could give to poets what would it be?

If you must work, try to get a job that is not related to writing, the Arts or anything of that manner . . . such occupations soften and protect one too much from the acts of daily living, from true occurrence.

John Lennon once said: "Art is life. The trouble with most up-and-coming artists is they're too busy with art to have time to live." Comment?

From what I know, John Lennon never produced anything real or worthwhile nor was the way he lived worth a twit either.

There is a rare feeling of clarity to your writing, a directness, a lack of artifice or false emotional posturing so prevalent in the arts (especially poetry!). Partly I think this clarity comes from the fact you seem to have so little to hide. Did it ever bother you that your writing was so personal and self-revealing?

When I sit down at the typewriter I never consider what will arrive or what the after-effect will be. Actually, it feels to me as if the typewriter were doing all of what it is and that I am just sitting there at a chair in front of it, drinking and listening to the radio and smoking. It's all free.

When I hear writers complaining about how PAINFUL it is to write, I don't know what they are talking about.

If you were gonna review your latest book, what would you say?

I'd say, "This fellow seems to write better all the time."

You write: "I always had this certain contentment—I wouldn't call it happiness—it was more of an inner balance that settled for whatever was occurring." This ability to take the madness in stride seems invaluable in this modern shit-stained world. At this very moment I imagine many of our TWISTED IMAGE readers dodging their fair share of shit. Any advice on maintaining that inner balance in the midst of this? (hey, you made it this far, that qualifies you as an advice-giver. And besides, who else are we gonna ask . . . Ann Landers???)

I don't know where this certain contentment comes from even in the face of severe adversity but, so far, it has been there. I get depressed, disgusted, have had a few flings at suicide, but all in all, over the long run I have been blessed with this certain inner easiness. It could come from the feeling that hardly anything is worth a shit, so why let it hack at you. Expect nothing and then when and if something comes along you'll feel like a winner. Endurance and patience can solve or at least diminish many agonies.

Will you ever give more poetry readings?

No. Unless I'm down to my last dime. I lose my mind.

You're a well-known Los Angeles writer. Yet when they made a film of your book it was made in Italy and not Hollywood. How the fuck did that come about? Wuddaya think of the film?

The film was a piece of wet shit flopping in the wind. Less said, the better. I've written a screenplay, BARFLY, to be directed by Barbet Schroeder. Acting leads: Mickey Rourke and Faye Dunaway. Cannon

Films. We begin shooting in Jan. 1987. If the actors can say their lines right, this could be a fair movie.

I recently met John Bryan the former publisher of "OPEN PUSSY", I mean "OPEN CITY" or whatever it was called. (In fact he's taken over writing the porn column "Sin Francisco" I used to write). What are your retrospective feelings about those underground hippy rags of the 60's?

Those were great days writing a column for the hippie newspapers. I had total freedom to say whatever I wanted. OPEN CITY was the best of them all. It was a sad and terrible day when John Bryan had to close it down.

How do you think they compare with the punk rags of the 80's?

Haven't read many punk rags so can't compare.

Have you ever tried LSD? How was it?

Yes, I tried LSD, didn't find it too enlightening, and didn't like the way it flashed back on me after the main trip was over. I mean, you'd be driving down the street and all of a sudden the car in front of you would split in half, become two cars and you didn't know which one to follow. (Best, of course, to drive just behind and in between them.) I prefer a trip on good mushrooms. There you remain *within* reality, only it becomes very funny or very frightening but always entertaining. I still prefer booze to anything. Grass sands you down too much, a rather inactive nothingness.

There's a spiritual quality to your writing—not in the religious sense—but just the fact that you get a helluva lot of your spirit onto paper. You're either a helluva spirited guy or a helluva talented writer or some insane combination of the two. I can't think of a question along these lines . . . I dunno, there's just something about your writing, this tremendous spiritual feeling going side by side with the general sordidness of life. "The impossibility of being human . . ." this unbreakable spirit of man surviving all this impossible madness. Do you know what I'm trying to say? Well, not to worry, neither do I.

Yes, there's something glorious about living in impossible situations and not going down. The human spirit can be an amazing god damned thing. It hasn't vanished yet.

Any other additional comments to win over the hearts and minds of our fab TWISTED IMAGE *readers?*

I hate giving any advice because each person and the situation of each person is different.

I hope you can keep on writing. I look forward to many more great Bukowski books, and I hope it is worth it to you to continue for many more years.

Would like to say, though, that TWISTED IMAGE has a lot of crazy energy and I hope you keep it going for some time.

Oh yes, Buk.

Tough Guys Write Poetry

CHARLES BUKOWSKI BY SEAN PENN

1987

"Tough Guys Write Poetry," Sean Penn, *Interview*, Vol. XV11, No. 19, September 1987, pp. 94–98.

Editor's note: Time magazine has called writer Charles Bukowski "the laureate of American lowlife." It is in Europe, however, that the author has found his greatest admirers. He is the most widely read living American writer in translation in the world today. More than 2.2 million copies of his works have been sold in Germany alone.

Now 66 years old, Bukowski has written 32 books of poetry, 5 collections of short stories and 4 novels. His best-known works are Ham on Rye, Women, Hot Water Music, South of No North, Post Office, The Tales of Ordinary Madness, War All the Time *and* Love Is a Dog From Hell. *His latest collection of poems is entitled* You Get So Alone at Times That It Just Makes Sense.

This fall a film made from his first screenplay, Barfly, *will open around the country. Starring Mickey Rourke and Faye Dunaway, directed by Barbet Schroeder and presented by Francis Ford Coppola, the film is an autobiographical account of Bukowski's early years as a writer.* Barfly's *two main characters, Henry and Wanda, are "immersed in an effort to escape the embalmed method of living which grips most of American society," according to Bukowski. "It is that fearful desire to continue to exist at any cost, their lives or anybody else's. Henry and Wanda refuse to accept the living death of acquiescence. This film is a focus on their brave madness."*

We asked actor and poet Sean Penn to visit Bukowski and focus on the brave madness of the great man himself.

Charles Bukowski was born in Andernach, Germany, in 1920. At the age of three he was brought to the United States and raised in Los Angeles. He currently resides in San Pedro, California, with his wife, Linda. A notorious boozer, brawler and womanizer, both Genet and Sartre called him "the best poet in America," but his friends call him Hank.

ON BARS:

Don't do too much bar stuff anymore. Got that out of my system. Now when I walk into a bar, I almost gag. I've seen so many of them, it's just too fuckin' much—that stuff's for when you're younger, you know, and you like to duke it with a guy, you know you play that macho shit—try to pick up broads—at my age, I don't need all that. Nowadays, I just go into bars to piss. Too many years in the bar. It just got so bad, that I'd walk into a bar, I'd walk through the door and I'd start to puke.

ON ALCOHOL:

Alcohol is probably one of the greatest things to arrive upon the earth— alongside of me. Yes . . . these are two of the greatest arrivals upon the surface of the earth. So . . . we get along. It is ultimately destructive to most people. I'm just one apart from that. I do all of my creative work while I'm intoxicated. Even with women, you know, I've always been reticent in the love-making act, so alcohol has allowed me, sexually, to be more free. It's a release, because basically I am a shy, withdrawn person, and alcohol allows me to be this hero, striding through space and time, doing all these daring things . . . So I like it . . . yeah.

ON SMOKING:

I like to smoke. Smoke and alcohol counterbalance each other. I used to wake up from drinking, you know, and you smoke so much, both your hands are yellow, see, like you've got gloves on . . . almost brown . . . and you say, "Oh, shit . . . what do my lungs look like? Oh Jesus!"

ON FIGHTING:

The best feeling is when you whip a guy you're not supposed to whip. I got into it with a guy one time, he was giving me a lot of lip. I said,

"Okay. Let's go." He was no problem at all—I whipped him easy. He was laying there on the ground. He's got a bloody nose, the whole works. He says, "Jesus, you move slow, man. I thought you'd be easy—the goddamn fight started—I couldn't see your hands anymore, you were so fucking fast. What happened?" I said, "I don't know, man. That's just the way it goes." You save it. You save it for the moment.

My cat, Beeker, is a fighter. He gets mauled up a bit sometimes, but he's always the winner. I taught him it all, you know . . . lead with the left, set up the right.

ON CATS:

Having a bunch of cats around is good. If you're feeling bad, you just look at the cats, you'll feel better, because they know that everything is, just as it is. There's nothing to get excited about. They just know. They're saviors. The more cats you have, the longer you live. If you have a hundred cats, you'll live ten times longer than if you have ten. Someday this will be discovered, and people will have a thousand cats and live forever. It's truly ridiculous.

ON WOMEN AND SEX:

I call 'em complaining machines. Things are never right with a guy to them. And man, when you throw that hysteria in there . . . forget it. I gotta get out, get in the car, and go. Anywhere. Get a cup of coffee somewhere. Anywhere. Anything but another woman. I guess they're just built different, right? (*He's on a roll now.*) The hysteria starts . . . they're gone. You go to leave, they don't understand. (*In a high woman's screech:*) "WHERE ARE YOU GOING?" "I'm getting the hell out of here, baby!" They think I'm a woman hater, but I'm not. A lot of it is word of mouth. They just hear "Bukowski's a male-chauvinist pig," but they don't check the source. Sure I make women look bad sometimes, but I make men look bad too. I make myself look bad. If I really think it's bad, I say it's bad—man, woman, child, dog. The women are so touchy, they think they're being singled out. That's their problem.

THE FIRST ONE:

Fuckin' the first one was the strangest—I didn't know—she taught me how to eat pussy and all these fucking things. I didn't know anything. She said, "You know, Hank, you're a great writer, but you don't know a damn thing about women!" "What do you mean? I've fucked a lot of women." "No, you don't know. Let me teach you some things." I said, "Okay." She said, "You're a good student, man. You catch on right away." That's all—(He got a little embarrassed. Not by the specifics, but rather by the sentimentality of the reminiscence.) But all that eatin' pussy shit can get kinda subservient. I like to please them, but . . . It's all overrated, man. Sex is only a great thing if you're not getting any.

ON SEX BEFORE AIDS (AND HIS MARRIAGE):

I just used to pop in and out of those sheets. I don't know, it was kind of a trance, a fuck trance. I'd just kinda fuck, and fuck (*laughs*) . . . I did! (*laughs*)

And the women, you know, you'd say a few words, and you just grab 'em by the wrist, "Come on, baby." Lead 'em in the bedroom and fuck 'em. And they'd go with it, man. Once you get in that rhythm, man, you'd just go. There are a lot of lonely women out there, man. They look good, they just don't connect. They're sitting there all alone, going to work, coming home . . . it's a big thing for 'em to have some guy pop 'em. And if he sits around, drinks and talks, you know, it's entertainment. It was all right . . . and I was lucky. Modern women . . . they don't sew your pockets . . . forget that.

ON WRITING:

I wrote a short story from the viewpoint of a rapist who raped a little girl. So people accused me. I was interviewed. They'd say, "You like to rape little girls?" I said, "Of course not. I'm photographing life." I've gotten in *trouble* with a lot of my shit. On the other hand, *trouble* sells some books. But, bottom line, when I write, it's for me. (*He draws a deep drag off his cigarette.*) It's like this. The "drag" is for me, the ash is for the tray . . . that's publication.

I never write in the daytime. It's like running through the shopping mall with your clothes off. Everybody can see you. At night . . . that's when you pull the tricks . . . magic.

ON POETRY:

I always remember the schoolyards in grammar school, when the word "poet" or "poetry" came up, all the little guys would laugh and mock it. I can see why, because it's a fake product. It's been fake and snobbish and inbred for centuries. It's over-delicate. It's over-precious. It's a bunch of trash. Poetry for the centuries is almost total trash. It's a con, a fake.

There have been a very few good poets, don't mistake me. There's a Chinese poet called Li Po. He could put more feeling, realism, and passion in four or five simple lines than most poets can in the twelve or fourteen pages of their shit. And he drank wine too. He used to set his poems on fire, sail down the river, and drink wine. The emperors loved him, because they could understand what he was saying . . . but, of course, he only burned his bad poems. (laughs)

What I've tried to do, if you'll pardon me, is bring in the factory-workers aspect of life . . . the screaming wife when he comes home from work. The basic realities of the everyman existence . . . something seldom mentioned in the poetry of the centuries. Just put me down as saying that the poetry of the centuries is shit. It's shameful.

ON CELINE:

The first time I read Céline, I went to bed with a big box of Ritz crackers. I started reading him and eating these Ritz crackers, and laughing, and eating the Ritz crackers. I read the whole novel straight through. And the box of Ritz was empty, man. And I got up and drank water, man. You should've seen me. I couldn't move. That's what a good writer will do to you. He'll damn near kill you . . . a bad writer will too.

ON SHAKESPEARE:

He's unreadable and overrated. But people don't want to hear that. You see, you cannot attack shrines. Shakespeare is embedded through the centuries. You can say "So-and-so is a lousy actor!" But you can't say Shakespeare is shit. The longer something is around, snobs begin to attach themselves to it, like suckerfish. When snobs feel something is safe . . . they attach. The moment you tell them the truth, they go wild. They can't handle it. It's attacking their own thought process. They disgust me.

ON HIS FAVORITE READING MATERIAL:

I read in *The National Enquirer*, "Is your husband homosexual?" Linda had said to me, "You have a voice like a fag!" I said, "Oh, yeah. I always wondered." (*laughs*) This article says, "Does he pull his eyebrows out?" I thought, shit! I do that all the time. Now I know what I am. I pull my eyebrows out . . . I'm a fag! Okay. It's nice for *The National Enquirer* to tell me what I am.

ON HUMOR AND DEATH:

There's very little. About the last best humorist was a guy called James Thurber. But his humor was so great, they had to overlook it. Now, this guy was what you call a psychologist/psychiatrist of the ages. He had the man/woman thing—you know, people seeing things. He was a cure-all. His humor was so real, you almost have to scream out your laughter in a frantic release. Outside of Thurber, I can't think of anybody . . . I've got a little touch of it . . . but not like he did. What I've got I don't really call humor. I'd call it . . . "a comic edge." I'm almost hooked on the comic edge. No matter what happens . . . it's ludicrous. Almost everything is ludicrous. You know, we shit every day. That's ludicrous. Don't you think? We have to keep pissing, putting food in our mouths, wax comes in our ears, hair? We have to scratch ourselves. Really ugly and dumb, you know? Tits are useless, unless . . .

You know, we're monstrosities. If we could really see this, we could love ourselves . . . realize how ridiculous we are, with our intestines wound around, shit slowly running through as we look each other in the eyes and say "I love you," our stuff is carbonizing, turning into shit, and we never fart near each other. It all has a comic edge . . .

And then we die. But, death has not earned us. It hasn't shown any credentials—we've shown all the credentials. With birth, have we earned life? Not really, but we're sure caught with the fucker . . . I resent it. I resent death. I resent life. I resent being caught between the two. You know how many times I've tried suicide? (Linda asks, "Tried?") Give me time, I'm only 66 years old. Still working at it.

When you have a suicide complex, nothing bothers you . . . except losing at the track. Somehow that bothers you. Why is that? . . . Because you're using your mind [at the track] not your heart.

I never rode a horse.

I'm not so interested in the horse, as in the process of being right and wrong . . . selectively.

ON THE TRACK:

I tried to make my living at the track for a while. It's painful. It's exhilarating. Everything is on the line—the rent—everything. But, you tend to be too cautious . . . it's not the same.

One time I was sitting way down at the curve. There were twelve horses in the race and they all got bunched together. It looked like a big charge. All I saw were these big horses' asses going up and down. They looked wild. I looked at those horse asses and I thought, "This is madness, this is total madness!" But then you have other days where you win four or five hundred dollars, you've won eight or nine races in a row, you feel like God, you know everything. It all fits together.
(*Then to me:*)
CB: All your days aren't good, are they?
SP: No.
CB: Some of them good?
SP: Yeah.
CB: Many of them?
SP: Yeah.
(*After a pause, the laughter of surprise*)
CB: I thought you were going to say "Just a few . . ." How disappointing!

ON PEOPLE:

I don't look too much at people. It's disturbing. They say if you look too much at someone, you start to look like them. Poor Linda.

People, mostly, I can do without. They don't fill me, they empty me. I respect no man. I have a problem that way . . . I'm lying, but believe me, it's true.

The valet at the track is okay. Sometimes, I'm leaving the track and he'll say, "Well, how you doing, man?" I'll say, "Shit, I'm ready to go for the jugular . . . throw up the white flag, man. I've had it." He'll say, "Oh no! Come on, man! I'll tell you what. Let's go out tonight, get drunk. We'll kick some ass, and suck pussy." I'll say, "Frank, let me consider that." He'll say, "You know, the worse it gets, the wiser I get." I'll say, "You must be a pretty wise man, Frank." He'll say, "You know it's a good thing you and I didn't meet when we were younger." I'll say, "Yeah, I know what you're going to say, Frank. We'd both be in San Quentin." "Right!" he says.

ON BEING RECOGNIZED AT THE TRACK:

The other day I'm sitting there and I feel them staring at me. I know what's coming, so I get up to move, you know? And he says, "Excuse me?" And I say, "Yes, what is it!" He says, "Are you Bukowski?" I say, "No!" He says, "I guess people ask you that all the time, don't they?" And I say, "Yes!" and I walked away. You know, we've discussed this before. There's nothing like privacy. You know, I like people. It's nice that they might like my books and all that . . . but I'm not the book, see? I'm the guy who wrote it, but I don't want them to come up and throw roses on me or anything. I want them to let me breathe. They wanna hang out with me. They figure I'll bring some whores, wild music, and I'm gonna slug somebody . . . you know? They read the stories! Shit, these things happened 20 to 30 years ago, baby!

ON FAME:

It's a destructor. It's the whore, the bitch, the destructor of all time. I've got it the sweetest because I'm famous in Europe and unknown here. I'm one of the most fortunate men around. I'm a lucky dog. Fame is really terrible. It is a measure on a scale of the common denominator, minds working on a low level. It's worthless. A select audience is much better.

ON LONELINESS:

I've never been lonely. I've been in a room—I've felt suicidal. I've been depressed. I've felt awful—awful beyond all—but I never felt that one other person could enter that room and cure what was bothering me . . . or that any number of people could enter that room. In other words, loneliness is something I've never been bothered with because I've always had this terrible itch for solitude. It's being at a party, or at a stadium full of people cheering for something, that I might feel loneliness. I'll quote Ibsen, "The strongest men are the most alone." I've never thought, "Well, some beautiful blonde will come in here and give me a fuck-job, rub my balls, and I'll feel good." No, that won't help. You know the typical crowd, "Wow, it's Friday night, what are you going to do? Just sit there?" Well, yeah. Because there's nothing out there. It's stupidity. Stupid people mingling with stupid people. Let them stupidify themselves. I've never been bothered with the need to rush out into the night. I hid in bars, because I didn't want to hide in factories. That's all. Sorry for all the millions, but I've never been lonely. I like myself. I'm the best form of entertainment I have. Let's drink more wine!

ON LEISURE:

This is very important—to take leisure time. Pace is the essence. Without stopping entirely and doing nothing at all for great periods, you're gonna lose everything. Whether you're an actor, anything, a housewife . . . there has to be great pauses between highs, where you do nothing at all. You just lay on a bed and stare at the ceiling. This is very, very important . . . just to do nothing at all, very, very important. And how many people do this in modern society? Very few. That's why they're all totally mad, frustrated, angry and hateful. In the old days, before I was married, or knew a lot of women, I would just pull down all the shades and go to bed for three or four days. I'd get up to shit. I'd eat a can of beans, go back to bed, just stay there for three or four days. Then I'd put on my clothes and I'd walk outside, and the sunlight was brilliant, and the sounds were great. I felt powerful, like a recharged battery. But you know the first bring-down? The first human face I saw on the sidewalk, I lost half my charge right there. This monstrous, blank, dumb, unfeeling face, charged up with capitalism—the "grind." And you went "Oooh! That took half away." But it was still worth it, I had half left. So, yeah, leisure. And I don't mean having profound thoughts. I mean having no thoughts at all. Without thoughts of progress, without any self-thoughts of trying to further yourself. Just . . . like a slug. It's beautiful.

ON BEAUTY:

There is no such thing as beauty, especially in the human face . . . what we call the physiognomy. It's all a mathematical and imagined alignment of features. Like, if the nose doesn't stick out too much, the sides are in fashion, if the earlobes aren't too large, if the hair is long . . . It's kind of a mirage of generalization. People think of certain faces as beautiful, but, truly, in the final measure, they are not. It's a mathematical equation of zero. "True beauty" comes, of course, of character. Not through how the eyebrows are shaped. So many women that I'm told are beautiful . . . hell, it's like looking into a soup bowl.

ON UGLINESS:

There's no such thing as ugliness. There is a thing called deformity, but outward "ugliness" does not exist . . . I have spoken.

ONCE UPON A TIME:

It was wintertime. I was starving to death trying to be a writer in New York. I hadn't eaten for three or four days. So, I finally said, "I'm gonna have a big bag of popcorn." And God, I hadn't tasted food for so long, it was so good. Each kernel, you know, each one was like a steak! I chewed and it would just drop into my poor stomach. My stomach would say, "THANK YOU THANK YOU THANK YOU!" I was in heaven, just walking along, and two guys happened by, and one said to the other, "Jesus Christ!" The other one said, "What was it?" "Did you see that guy eating popcorn? God, it was awful!" And so I couldn't enjoy the rest of the popcorn. I thought; what do you mean, "it was awful?" I'm in heaven here. I guess I was kinda dirty. They can always tell a fucked-up guy.

ON THE PRESS:

I kind of like being attacked. "Bukowski's disgusting!" That makes me smile, you know, I like it. "Oh, he's a horrible writer!" I smile some more.

I kind of feed on that. It's when a guy tells me, "Hey, you know, they're teaching you at such and such a university," my mouth drops. I don't know . . . to be too much accepted is terrifying. You feel you've done something wrong.

I enjoy the bad things that are said about me. It enhances [book] sales and makes me feel evil. I don't like to feel good 'cause I am good. But evil? Yes. It gives me another dimension. (*Bringing up the pinky finger of his left hand . . .*) Did you ever see this finger? (*The finger seems paralyzed in a downward "L" configuration.*) I broke it, drunk one night. Don't know how, but . . . I guess it just didn't set right. But, it works just fine for the "a" key (on his typewriter) and . . . what the hell . . . it adds to my character. See, now I've got character and dimension. (*He laughs.*)

ON BRAVERY:

Most so-called brave people lack imagination. As though they can't conceive of what would happen if something went wrong. The truly brave overcome their imagination and do what they have to do.

ON FEAR:

I don't know a thing about it. (*He laughs*)

ON VIOLENCE:

I think violence is often misinterpreted. Certain violence is needed. There is, in all of us, an energy that demands an outlet. I think that if the energy is constrained, we go mad. The ultimate peacefulness we all desire is not a desirable area. Somehow in our construction, it is not meant to be. This is why I like to see boxing matches, and why, in my younger days, I'd like to duke it in back alleys. "Expulsion of energy with honor," is sometimes called violence. There is "interesting madness" and "disgusting madness." There are good and bad forms of violence. So, in fact . . . it's a loose term. Let it not be too much at the expense of others, and it's okay.

ON PHYSICAL PAIN:

When I was a kid, they used to drill me. I had these big boils. You toughen up to physical pain. When I was in General Hospital they were drilling away, and a guy walked in, and he said, "I never saw anyone go under the needle that cool." That's not bravery—if you get enough physical pain, you relent—it's a process, an adjustment.

Mental pain can't be adjusted to. Keep me away from it.

ON PSYCHIATRY:

What do psychiatric patients get? They get a bill.

I think the problem between the psychiatrist and the patient is that the psychiatrist goes by the book, while the patient arrives because of what life has done to him or her. And even though the book may have certain insights, the pages are always the same in the book, and, each patient is a little bit different. There are many more individual problems than pages. Get it? There are too many mad people to do it by saying, "dollars per hour, when this bell rings, you're finished." That alone will drive any near-mad person to madness. They've just started to open up and feel good, when the shrink says, "Nurse, make the next appointment," and they've lost track of the price, which is also abnormal. It's all too stinking worldly. The guy is out to take your ass. He's not out to cure you. He wants his money. When the bell rings, bring in the next "nut." Now the sensitive "nut" will realize when that bell rings, he's being fucked. There's no time limit to curing madness, and there's no bills for it either. Most psychiatrists I've seen look a little close to the edge themselves. But they're too comfortable . . . I think they're all too comfortable. I think a patient wants to see a little madness, not too much. Ahhhh! (*bored*) PSYCHIATRISTS ARE TOTALLY USELESS! Next question?

ON FAITH:

Faith is all right for those who have it. Just don't load it on me. I have more faith in my plumber than I do in the eternal being. Plumbers do a good job. They keep the shit flowing.

ON CYNICISM:

I've always been accused of being a cynic. I think cynicism is sour grapes. I think cynicism is a weakness. It's saying "everything is wrong! EVERYTHING IS WRONG!" You know? "This is not right! That is not right!" Cynicism is the weakness that keeps one from being able to adjust to what is occurring at the moment. Yes, cynicism is definitely a weakness, just as optimism is. "The sun is shining, the birds are singing—so smile." That's bullshit too. The truth lies somewhere in between. What is, just is. So you're not ready to handle it . . . too bad.

ON CONVENTIONAL MORALITY:

There may not be a hell, but those who judge may create one. I think people are over-taught. They are over-taught everything. You have to find out by what happens to you, how you will react. I'll have to use a strange term here . . . "good." I don't know where it comes from, but I feel that there's an ultimate strain of goodness born in each of us. I don't believe in God, but I believe in this "goodness" like a tube running through our bodies. It can be nurtured. It's always magic, when on a freeway packed with traffic, a stranger makes room for you to change lanes . . . it gives you hope.

ON BEING INTERVIEWED:

It's almost like being caught in the corner. It's embarrassing. So, I don't always tell the total truth. I like to play around and jest a bit, so I do give out some misinformation just for the sake of entertainment and bull-shit. So if you want to know about me, never read an interview. Ignore this one.

Boozehound Poet Charles Bukowski Writes a Hymn to Himself in *Barfly*, and Hollywood Starts Singing Too

Margot Dougherty and Todd Gold
1987

"Boozehound Poet Charles Bukowski Writes a Hymn to Himself in *Barfly* and Hollywood Starts Singing Too," Margot Dougherty and Todd Gold, *People*, November 16, 1987, pp. 79–80.

Beer in hand, the potbellied old boozer shuffles around his living room. His face is a topographic road map of pockmarks and warts. A tiny self-portrait hangs near the front door. He jeers at it. "Tough guy," he says with a W.C. Fields rasp. "I think I'm Bogart."

Others have thought worse of Charles Bukowski. At 67, he has misspent most of his life with cheap booze and cheaper broads, brawling in sleazy bars. His joy was in his writing, especially since he didn't have to stop guzzling to do it. The bottle has to be there. "*Has to*," he confirms. "Unless I'm entertained, nobody's going to be entertained." Four novels, five books of short stories and more than 1,000 poems have won Bukowski a small but devoted following in the U.S. Hank, as he's called, likes being an acquired taste. To the liquor-laced laureate of the gutter, celebrity is a curse. And now this had to happen.

His name is popping up in gossip columns. He dines with Norman Mailer, takes Sean Penn to the racetrack and gets visits from Madonna. "Why," his next-door neighbor asks, "would Madonna come to see you, Hank?"

Because, as it happens, Hank is the notorious character behind *Barfly*, the critical and box office hit that has turned Bukowski into a hot Hollywood ticket. "It makes me feel suspicious of my own abilities," says Bukowski, who had previously seen his novel *Tales of Ordinary Madness* turned into a flop 1983 movie that made him "scream at the screen." Bukowski based his *Barfly* screenplay on a blurred recollection of himself around age 25. It's the story of an unabashedly drunken writer (Mickey Rourke) and his loves: Wanda (Faye Dunaway) and Mr. McCleary (cheap whiskey). The *New York Times* called it a "classic." Bukowski sees it as a simple slice of life: his. Regardless, he says, "It's a damn good movie."

And a success that almost never happened. After French director Barbet Schroeder commissioned the script from Bukowski in 1979 for $20,000, it took six years to find a producer. "Nicely done," read the rejections, "but who cares what happens to a drunk?"

When Sean Penn read the script he cared. Penn offered to play the lead for a dollar. "Then we had a hot item," says Bukowski. But Penn wanted his buddy Dennis Hopper, another renowned Hollywood ex-derelict, to direct. Bukowski wouldn't desert Barbet. Enter Mickey Rourke and Cannon Films with a budget of about $4 million.

Rourke gets rave reviews from his real-life prototype. "He really puts out," says Bukowski. Surprisingly, Rourke has admitted that he's not a Bukowski devotee. Drink may be Bukowski's choice, says Rourke, the son of an alcoholic father, "but I don't have to respect him for it." Bukowski laments such feelings. "Even drug addicts get public sympathy," he says. "Drunks just aren't recognized as human beings."

Bukowski was born in Andernach, W. Germany and moved to L.A. when he was 4. He was terrified of his father, a Prussian milkman who beat him regularly. He was 13 when he took his first drink; he says it eased the pain. After two years of journalism courses at Los Angeles City College, he dropped out at the start of World War II. For the next 10 years he wrote and drifted around the country. At 36, his regimen of constant and indiscriminate drinking landed him in an L.A. hospital with a bleeding ulcer. Thirteen pints of blood later he was released and told never to drink again. He went straight to a bar.

Bukowski continued to scrape by with jobs as a janitor, truck driver, shipping clerk and postal worker. Through it all—or because of it all—he churned out poems, pornography and stories for underground magazines. "If you're going to write, you have to have something to write about," he says. "The gods were good to me. They kept me on the streets. If you're a genius at 25, you burn out."

Only moderately well-known at home, Bukowski has long been a celebrity overseas. Prisoners and the insane worldwide flood the author with letters, which he answers. "Those are the interesting people," he says. "And the hardest to fool." When an inmate in New Zealand wrote that Bukowski's work was passed from cell to cell, the author says, "It was the first time I was proud of my writing."

Women, he admits, are another addiction. In 1956 he married Barbara Frye, who published a small poetry magazine. It wasn't until he visited her estate in Texas that he discovered she was wealthy. "Baby, it will spoil everything," he told her. He was right. They divorced in less than a year.

His only child, Marina Louise, now 23 and a recent engineering graduate of California State University at Long Beach, is the daughter of ex-girlfriend Frances Dean Smith. "Marina is cool," says Bukowski. "She knows if she said, 'God, I love the way you write,' it would offend me. We're alike. We don't come out and say things that should be understood."

Marina Bukowski

Bukowski's wild days are long gone. "Fights, drink, picking up women—I think that came with youth," he says. In 1976 he met Linda Lee Beighle, now 36, a former health store owner who has recently taken up acting. "He was drunk when we met," she says. An ardent fan of Bukowski's work, Beighle doses her husband with upwards of 35 vitamins a day and forbids him red meat and hard liquor. "I don't know whether I do Linda any good," says Bukowski, "but without her I wouldn't be here." Two years ago they married and settled into a comfortable, one-bedroom house with a garden in the dockside community of San Pedro, Calif. Bukowski's *Barfly* success already has

Hollywood sniffing for more. "I've never wanted to be rich," says Bukowski. "I just want a place to live, food to eat, so I can continue typing."

The old reprobate may be domesticated, but he still spends nearly every day at the nearby racetracks. His wife isn't worried. Most nights by 10 p.m., she says, her Hank climbs the stairs to his ramshackle writing room. "He closes his door," says Linda, "opens his wine bottle, turns on his classical music, then pushes the keys. It just erupts." His work in progress, *Hollywood*, based on the making of *Barfly*, flows easily. "I'm up there alone," says Bukowski, beaming, "having a party."

Charles Bukowski: Poetry, Short Stories, and now . . . Screenplays!

CHRISTIAN GORE

1987

"Charles Bukowski: Poetry, Short Stories, and Now . . . Screenplays!", Christian Gore, *Film Threat*, Issue 13, 1987, pp. 17–20.

Questions

How were you involved in the making of Tales of Ordinary Madness?
(Now a cult classic at video stores across the country)
These people purchased the rights for a few stories from the book of same title. I had nothing to do with the way it was put together.

How did you like handsome Ben Gazzarra playing you?
Didn't. Ben is too much the standard macho man, relaxed in his view of life, satisfied with self.

If you didn't like Ben, who would you have rather had play you?
Jack Nicholson.

What was your initial reaction upon seeing the film?
Lo, it was to puke. I was in the audience and I was drinking and I screamed at the screen. Alas, nothing changed.

Which of your short stories would you think best make a film?
("6 inches" would be my choice)
Many of them. I've forgotten most of what I have written, so I really can't choose. But most of my stuff is dramatic with a comic edge, so there's a chance it's entertaining.

What are you drinking now?

Tonight I'm *not* drinking but generally I stay on a good red wine. That's when I'm drinking here. Outside, at a bar or wherever I am, I prefer a vodka 7.

What are your favorite kinds of films?
Don't have.

Which TV evangelists would you most like to see in a porno film?
None. I see enough of those fuckers as I flip through the tube.

I read that you wrote a screenplay, Barfly. *What's the scoop, I heard it will star Mickey Rourke and Faye Dunaway and be produced through Walt Disney?*
It has already been shot and should see a Fall release. Cannon Films.

Do you hate movies as much as you hate poetry?
Yes. They are equally bad, totally wasted forms populated by one-tenth talents with sickening egos.

Do you want to direct?
No. Do you?

Now that you've enjoyed some kind of monetary success and can't really write articles complaining about being poor do you write articles about getting your stereo ripped off from your BMW?
I have done that. But I'm hardly rich, but if I ever get rich I'd like to believe that I'm old enough and have waded through enough crap not to have it completely dilute me. I'm lucky now, at 66, that each day brings me nearer to death, which thought tends, I hope, to keep some of the bullshit out of my efforts at the typer. There's a danger in everything, there's a danger of being poor too long, of starving too long. I'd prefer a touch of almost everything in this merry-go-round and I've gotten plenty. What happens to any individual in any circumstance depends much upon the guts or lack of with some luck tossed in.

If these four jockeys were in a horse race: Charles Manson, Jesus Christ, Ronald Reagan and Allen Ginsberg, who would you bet on?
Christ, Ginsberg, Manson and Reagan, in that order.

Do you have a VCR? If so, what do you watch?
Yes. Nothing. The fucking thing has sat there for months and months. Last thing I watched were *The Bukowski Tapes.* Not bad.

Do you find TV news entertaining?
No. They are formally fake and false, I mean the newscasters. Where do they find these people?

How is it working within the Hollywood system, did you get screwed? (Literally or figuratively)
I got a little bit screwed, not too bad. Now I am getting out.

Did you meet Mickey Rourke and Faye Dunaway? What are they like?
Yes. Mickey Rourke is a real human guy, on and off the set. And in *Barfly* he really came through with the acting. I felt his enjoyment and inventiveness. Faye Dunaway just can't match his talent or his humanness but she filled her role.

When working on the film, were you offered coke?
No. Or at the few parties. I liked that. But I was offered many drinks and I took full advantage of that.

What do you think of Film Threat *magazine?*
I don't read it. My wife, at times, does. I've got a problem: I can't read anything. It just falls from my hands.

If paid, would you consider writing for it?
No, because film doesn't interest me.

Any last comments?
Somewhere I think I've lost a page of your questions. But I recall your asking, what movies do I like?

Well, I liked *Eraserhead, One Flew Over the Cuckoo's Nest, The Elephant Man* and *Who's Afraid of Virginia Woolf.*

Thank you anyhow for asking. I have to be careful with my life now. Ate at Musso and Frank's today and the waiter knew my name.

All right, Gore, keep it going . . .

Thanks for taking the time to do this (that is if you've done it)
ho, well, shit, you're welcome . . .

Buk

Charles Bukowski and the Outlaw Spirit

Jay Dougherty

1988

"Charles Bukowski and the Outlaw Spirit," Jay Dougherty, *Gargoyle* 35, 1988, pp. 98–103.

On West German Success
Letters to Carl Weissner and Letter-Writing

GARGOYLE: Your books have sold over 2.5 million copies in West Germany. They're in every department store, every train station, and of course every book store. As Carl Weissner, your German translator, has said, at this point they sell by themselves; they need no advertising. To what do you attribute your phenomenal success there?

CHARLES BUKOWSKI: I believe that the German public is more open to gamble and new ways of presentation. Why this is, I don't know. Here in the U.S. a more staid and safe literature seems preferred. Here people don't want to be shaken or awakened. They prefer to sleep through their lives. To them, what is safe and old seems good.

G: But what do you feel the German reading public sees in your work? Do you really feel that, as you say in some of your poems, the success is solely attributable to the work of your translators?

BUK: With the German public, I do believe it does help that I was born there. It doesn't help in the sale of millions of copies. Maybe 100,000. I am a curiosity. My translators? Well, they are probably pretty damned good. The books seem to go well in France, Italy and Spain. England, no. Who knows why? I don't know why. You know, I try to keep my wordage and my line structure simple and bare. This doesn't mean that I say nothing. It means that I say it directly without a smokescreen. The English and the Americans are used to the old literary bullshit—that is, being lulled to sleep by the same old crap. If they read something and find that it isn't interesting or that they can't understand it, they often-times presume it to be profound. Or so I tend to believe.

G: Why do you think Americans have not embraced you so wholly? Is it a matter of circulation, that John Martin, your publisher, doesn't have the means of, say, a New York publisher to advertise your books and get them out to the most possible outlets.

BUK: Yes, Black Sparrow Press has a limited circulation and this tends to hold down being known widely in the U.S. Yet they have published book after book of mine throughout the years, and most of the books are still *in print* and *available*. Black Sparrow and I almost began together and it is my hope that we will end together. It would be fitting.

If I had gone to a large New York publisher, I might have larger U.S. sales and I might be rich, but I doubt that I would continue writing in a workmanlike and joyful fashion. Also, I doubt that I would have the same uncensored acceptability that I have at Black Sparrow. As a writer I consider myself in the best of worlds: famous elsewhere and working here. The gods have spared me many of the pitfalls of the average American writer. Black Sparrow came to me when nobody else would. This after working as a common laborer and a starving writer, being largely ignored by the large presses and most of the major magazines. It would be ungrateful of me to see a large New York publisher now. In fact, I don't have the slightest desire to do so.

G: Your early letters to Carl Weissner, letters which began about 1961, are characterized by incredible energy and anger and insight. They are some of the most substantive letters by you that I've seen. And yet Weissner, at the time the correspondence began, was then but a student, one you had never met or heard of before the correspondence started. What were your motivations at the time for writing him these letters? What was your living situation like, your outlook on life?

BUK: I have no idea how it all started with Carl Weissner; that was almost three decades ago. But somehow we got in contact. I believe he saw some of my work in the U.S. little magazines. We began corresponding. His letters were quite incisive, entertaining (lively as hell), and he bucked up my struggle in the darkness, no end. A letter from Carl always was and still is an *infusion* of life and hope and easy wisdom. I was in the post office at the time and living with a crazy alcoholic woman and writing anyhow. All our money went for booze. We lived in rags and a rage of despair. I remember I didn't even have money for shoes. The nails from my old shoes dug into my feet as I walked my routes hungover and mad. We drank all night and I had to get up at 5 a.m. When I wrote, the poems came out of this and the letters from Carl were the only good magic about it.

G: How did you picture Carl?

BUK: How did I picture him? Exactly as he looked and acted when I met him. One hell of a hell of an amazing human.

G: What would you say has been the most important and substantial correspondence that you've been engaged in?

BUK: Letters to Carl Weissner. I felt that with Carl I could say anything I wanted to, and I often did.

G: Is there anyone today to whom you write letters of comparable length or energy?

BUK: No.

G: Did you see the letters that you wrote to Weissner or anyone else as a kind of practice ground, a testing ground for your writing or ideas?

BUK: No, I never tested my writing abilities in letter writing. For instance, I read that Hemingway often wrote letters when he couldn't write anything else. To me, this would be a betrayal of the person you were writing to. I wrote letters because they just came out. They were a need. A scream. A laugh. Something. I don't keep carbons.

G: Did poems or stories ever evolve out of your letters?

BUK: Few stories or poems came out of the letters. If they did, it was afterwards. A small thought: shit, maybe I ought to use that line or that idea elsewhere. But not too often, hardly at all. The letter came first. The letter was the letter as the letter.

Carl Weissner with Buk in 1978,
(Courtesy of Linda Bukowski)

G: Carl Weissner has characterized your early letters to him as "soul food." Whom have you most enjoyed receiving letters from and why?

BUK: As I said, Carl's letters were the best. They kept me going for weeks. I even wrote him at times to say something like, "God damn, man, you've saved my life." And it was true. Without Carl I would be dead or near dead or mad or near mad, or driveling into a slop pail somewhere, mouthing gibberish.

G: You've always been fairly meticulous about dating your letters, and a lot of energy has gone into at least the Weissner letters. Did you ever at any point—before, that is, you sold the letters to Santa Barbara— sense an audience outside of the person to whom you were writing? That is, do you think you wrote, consciously or unconsciously, with posterity in mind?

BUK: Carl's letters were sold to Santa Barbara along with other things because that was survival. I didn't even have the letters. I asked Carl for them and he popped them over. Like that. No, I never thought of an audience outside of Carl in the letters. If I had, they would have been shitty letters. I was writing to Carl because I felt he knew what I was saying and that his answers would be joyous, crazy, brave and on the mark. I've read too many *literary* letters, published, that the famed writers have written. They do seem to write to more than one person, and that's their business unless they write to me.

G: What do you enjoy most about writing letters? When do you write them?
BUK: Writing letters, like writing poems, stories, novels, helps to keep me from going crazy or from quitting. I write letters at night when I am drinking, just as I write my other stuff.

On Poetry and Craft

G: In your poems, you sometimes write about enjoying your time at the typewriter, how easy it is to be a writer, and so on. What are your feelings about the nine-to-five, workaday world and the goals after which most strive?
BUK: The nine-to-five is one of the greatest atrocities sprung upon mankind. You give your life away to a function that doesn't interest you. This situation so repelled me that I was driven to drink, starvation, and mad females, simply as an alternative. The ideal, for one like me, of course, is to make it off your writing, your creativity. I found that I was unable to do this until the age of fifty, when I began to make just enough income to survive without the nine-to-five. Luckily, for me, of course, because at that time I was working for the United States Post Office, and most of the nights were eleven-and-a-half hours long, and most of the days off were canceled. I was near insanity, and my whole body was such a mass of nerves that almost any place I was touched could make me scream, and I had great trouble lifting my arms and turning my neck. I quit the job at fifty, and the writing seemed to arrive in better form.

G: How do you feel that writing poetry—or writing in general—helps you cope with the mindlessness you perceive around you?
BUK: Writing keeps you alive because it eases the monsters in the brain by moving them to paper. The listing of horrors seems regenerative, and often comes out in the writing as a form of joy or humor. The typewriter often sings soothing songs to the sadness in the heart. It's wondrous.

G: You have consistently refused to become political within the literary arena, refused to be associated with literary "schools" or trends. But in a recent poem directed against "Academics" and the generally conservative poetry they profess, you say:

> we don't care how they
> write the poem
>
> but we insist that there are
>> other voices
>> other ways of creating
>
>> other ways of living the
>> life
>
> In this battle against the
>> Centuries of the Inbred
>> Dead
>
> let it be known that
>> we have arrived and
>> intend to
>> stay

Do you see yourself as in the center of a kind of unheralded proletarian poetry that is finding more and more outlet within the small presses and little magazines?

BUK: Regarding the poem in general, I don't see myself as the center of anything but myself. I travel alone. That particular poem you note was written for others than myself. That is, I feel that a more human, accessible yet true and vibrant poetry is gradually coming forth. I note it especially in some of the littles; there is a movement toward more clarity, reality . . . while the academics are still standing still, playing secret and staid games, snob and inbred games which are finally anti-life and anti-truth.

G: Your work continues to be ignored by most anthologies in the U.S., with the notable exceptions of your appearing in *The Norton Anthology of Poetry* and *A Geography of Poets* (Bantam). Why do you think this is, and how do you feel about being in *Norton,* probably the most widely-used college-level anthology?

BUK: I didn't know that I was in the Norton. If I am, alright, I don't think it will kill anybody off. I am not an expert on anthologies. I suppose they are mostly the choice of one man. And my guess is that most of these men are university-connected, hence conservative, careful, and worried about their jobs. What they choose could hardly shock a nun or a bus driver, but it might put them to sleep.

G: Outside of your books with Black Sparrow, you continue to publish your poetry mostly in little magazines. What do you think is the state of literary and little magazines? The established quarterlies versus the Xeroxed occasionals?

BUK: I don't read many established quarterlies except *The New York Quarterly,* and I am prejudiced toward them because I have appeared in every one of their issues from No. 7 through No. 34. I find that they are not afraid of newness or warmth, but like I say, since they have been so good to me, I may not be the perfect judge here.

On the littles, I'd say that the greatest weakness is that they publish their own editors too often. Most of the poems are not really fully evolved: an off-hand "so-what" attitude prevails. Yet, within many issues, there are poems that are really there, fully. Now and then, astonishing talents will appear. Most of them don't last too long; something in life swallows them up. But life renews: when you've just bout given up on everybody, here comes another slashing through. The hope that's always there makes the littles worthwhile.

G: To you, what characterizes the best and worst poetry being written today?

BUK: The worst poetry copies the best and the worst of the past. Most poets come too much from protective environments. A poet must live before a poet can write, and sometimes the living must be almost enough to kill. I am not suggesting that poets seek dangerous situations, and neither am I suggesting that they avoid them.

G: What contemporary or new writers do you see as holding promise? And what qualities of their work attract you?

BUK: John Thomas. Gerald Locklin. What qualities? Read them.

G: A few commentators have criticized your poetry, especially your recent poetry, as being little more than prose cut up into lines. Do you feel the same way? What qualities do you feel distinguish your poetry from your prose?

BUK: The critics might be right. I'm not sure what the difference is between my poetry and my prose. Perhaps the styles are similar. The mood probably isn't. I mean, the mood is different in the poetry and the prose. That is, I can only write prose when I am feeling good. Poetry I can write when I am feeling bad, and I write most of it when I am feeling bad, even if the poem comes out in a humorous fashion.

G: I personally disagree with those who say that even the recent poetry is prose cut up into lines, for I see either conscious or unconscious decisions being made with regard to, for example, line breaks— very often you seem to break a line either to force the poem to be read or stressed in a certain way or to push the reader into a temporary expectation that is then in the next line disappointed. How *do* you decide on line breaks in your poems?

BUK: Subconsciously, I guess, I am trying to make my poetry more and more bare, essential. That is, to hand a lot on a little. This might give those critics vent to holler their dirty word "prose." That's what the critics are there for: to complain. I don't write for the critics; I write for that little thing that sits just in and behind my forehead (ah, cancer?).

Line breaks? The lines break themselves and I don't know how.

G: From what I understand, *Dangling in the Tournefortia* was one of the few books, if not the only book, *not* edited heavily or "selected" by John Martin. Did you insist on the continuity of the poems there?

BUK: John Martin selects all the poems for all the books. I'm not sure a writer knows which of his work is best. If I were to get precious and fuck around with selecting my own poems, then there I would lose time which I could put to better use writing or being at the racetrack or taking a bath or doing nothing. John has a great eye in lining the poems up in order. He loves to have one lead rather into the other, more or less, and if you will check the books of poems you will find that there is almost a little story told, even though the poems are often about separate things. John loves to do this, in spite of all the work involved, and I am glad that somebody is noticing.

G: You seem to be experimenting more in your poetry with a kind of fragmentary poem, composed solely of images, like "Lost in San Pedro." What changes do you sense or see occurring in your poetry, concerning either technique or subject?

BUK: If the poems are changing in their way, it could be because I am getting closer to death. Poems about whores showing their panties and spilling beer on my fly no longer seem quite apt. I don't mind nearing death; in fact, it almost feels good. But different paints are needed for the damned canvas. Of course, many of the things that bothered me when I was seven years old still bother me now. On the other hand, when things were going the worst, I never felt cheated out of anything or wronged. I might have thought that I was a better writer than many famous writers living or dead, but I considered that a natural course of events—oftentimes those on top show very little. The public creates its own gods and it often chooses badly because the public reflects its own image.

As I go on, I write as I please and as I must. I don't worry about critics or style or fame or lack of fame. All I want is the next line as it truly comes to me.

G: What are your plans for future writing projects? What are you working on now?

BUK: I am into a novel, Hollywood. Now, that's prose and I have to feel good and I haven't felt good lately, so I am only up to page fifty. But it's all there inside of my head, and I hope to feel good enough long enough to write it. I can only hope so because it's a real laugher. Hollywood is at least 400 times worse than anybody has ever written about it. Of course, if I ever finish it, then I'll probably get sued, even though it's true. Then I can write another novel about the court system.

Charles Bukowski

ALDEN MILLS
JULY/AUGUST, 1989

"Charles Bukowski," Alden Mills, *Arete*, July/August 1989, pp. 66-69, 73, 76–77.

If I were to introduce myself, I'd be kind, I'd say,
"Here's a guy who won't spit it out."

What started you writing?

Well, you know, to come out of the factory or the warehouse, the wasted day, all those hours mutilated, what better way to attempt to erect a balance? It helped me keep the knife from the throat, no matter that the stuff came back. I read the books and the magazines and noted the milk-white deadliness of the writing. If I had to write only for myself, then that would be it. True, I did take ten years off to concentrate on drinking only, but this gave me a backlog of experience to reach into for later typing.

What goes on in your mind before you write? Is your writing planned and carefully crafted?

When I sit down to the machine I have no idea what I am going to write. I never liked hard work. Planning is hard work. I'd rather it came out of the air or some place behind my left ear. I have found that I'm in a trance-like state when I write. Sometimes my wife will walk into the room and ask me something while I am typing and I will SCREAM!

Not because the work is so precious or because I am precious but because I have been shocked awake. Writing, to me, well, I could say it's like going to a good movie, it just unfolds, it feels good, there is no work involved. And, of course, I set the stage: radio on to classical music, and the wine bottle there. It is a good time. If I don't feel good about writing, it's not going to work. I mean, I can be feeling like hell, but I can still be feeling good about the writing. The hell transfers into a positive area. Or so it feels to me.

The reader never has to wade through anything extraneous in your work. Do you rewrite?

Not prose. I just finished the novel *Hollywood.* Wrote it straight through, without a word change. With a poem, I will tend to drop a line or two out of each poem as I rewrite it. So I do rewrite the poem, but not the novel or short story. Why? I don't know.

In one of your poems, you said you would drink heavily and then type all night. Your goal was to write ten pages before going to sleep, but you'd often write as many as twenty-three. Can you tell me about this?

I had just quit the post office and was attempting to be a professional writer at the age of fifty. Maybe I was scared. The chips were on the table. I was writing the novel *Post Office* and felt that my time was limited. At the post office, my starting time had been 6:18 p.m. So each night I sat down at 6:18 p.m. with my pint of Scotch, some cheap cigars and plenty of beers, radio on, of course. I typed each night away. The novel was finished in nineteen nights. I never remembered going to bed. But each morning, or near noon, I found all these pages spread across the couch. It was the good fight, at last. My whole body, my whole spirit, was wild with the battle.

For you, is there a difference between writing done while drunk and writing done while sober? Does one state lend itself better to writing?

I used to always write while drinking and/or drunk. I never thought I could write without the bottle. But the last five or six months I have had an illness that has limited my drinking. So I sat down and wrote without the bottle, and it all came out just the same. So it doesn't matter. Or maybe I write like I'm drunk when I'm sober.

Was Whitey a real-life friend of yours?

"Whitey" was an off and on drinking partner in this hotel on Vermont Avenue. I went there now and then to see a girlfriend and often stayed two or three days and nights. Everybody in the place drank. Mostly cheap wine. There was one gentleman, a "Mr. Adams," a very tall chap who took a fall down the long stairway two or three nights a week, usually around 1:30 a.m., when he was making a last attempt at a run of the liquor store around the corner. He would go tumbling down this long, long hard stairway, you could hear the sound of him banging along, and my girlfriend would say, "There goes Mr. Adams." All of us always waited to see if he would go through the glass doorway, which he sometimes did. I think he got the glass doorway about fifty percent of the time. The manager just had somebody come and replace the doorway the next day, and Mr. Adams went on with his life. He was never injured, not badly. That fall would have killed a sober man. But when you're drunk, you fall loose and soft like a cat, and there's no fear inside of you, you're either a bit bored or a bit laughing inside of yourself. Whitey just let it go one night, blood roaring from the mouth. I had done the same thing a few times, so I related. Blood is purple and a bit of stomach comes out and the blood *stinks*. I came out of it after a dozen pints of blood and a dozen pints of glucose. But we never saw "Whitey" again.

Your work is sometimes dark, but I would never describe it as "negative." Your mother once said to you, "People like to read things that make them happy." How do you feel about this?

When my mother said [that] to me it was the result of my father and my mother finding and reading some of my writings I had hidden in my bedroom when I was a young fellow. They found and read my works, and my father went into a rage: "NOBODY WILL EVER READ SHIT LIKE THIS!" That's when my mother chimed in with her "People like to . . ." I didn't answer either of these critics.

Well, of course, people like to read things that make them happy. I haven't read too many things like this myself. But I have read things that have allowed me to go on one more day or one more week or one more month, when otherwise I might not have possibly made it. All my work has not been attacked, I've lucked onto some good reviews, the *New York Times*, elsewhere, but to me the finest praise I have ever received was from somebody doing time in Australia who wrote me, "Your books are the only books that pass from cell to cell . . . ." I allowed myself to feel good about this one for a couple of days.

What inspires you? Mozart and Mahler? The racetrack?

I'm not sure what inspires me. Rushes of desperation. Death in the left shoe. Or even long hours of soothing calm. Classical music lifts me. The track gives me a view of the masses. Dante would know about

these. I have been influenced by quite a few writers: Dostoyevsky, Gorky, Turgenev, the *very early* Saroyan, Hemingway, Sherwood Anderson, John Fante, Knut Hamsun, Céline and Carson McCullers. Oh yes, James Thurber. And in poetry, Robinson Jeffers, e.e. cummings, some of Ezra Pound.

Your works intimate a reclusiveness. What draws you away from others? Is it the "I just seem to feel better when they're not around" syndrome?

Yes, at the worst of times, in the worst of cities, if I could have a small room, if I could close the door of that small room and be alone in it with the old dresser, the bed, the torn window shade, I would begin to fill with something good: the unmolested tone of the singular self. I had no problems with myself, it was those places out there, those faces out there, the wasted, ruined lives—people settling for the cheapest and

243

easiest way out. Between church and state, the family structure; between our educational and entertainment systems; between the eight-hour job and the credit system, they were burned alive. Closing the door to a small room or sitting in a bar night and day was my way of saying no to all that.

In one of your poems ("hey Ezra: listen to this"), you say, "Literary fame can be the consequence of knowing when to go wild and how."

Of course, you can only go wild with style, style being your own true way. If one attempts to get famous, one will not get famous. Writing is partly a way to keep from going mad. You write because it's all that you can do. It's either that or jump off the bridge. Fame comes as an aftermath, and it has nothing to do with anything, and if you believe in it, you are finished as a writer and a human being.

Your poem "friendly advice to a lot of young men" says that one is better off living in a barrel than he is writing poetry. Would you give this same advice today?

I guess what I meant is that you are better off doing nothing than doing something badly. But the problem is that bad writers tend to have the self-confidence, while the good ones tend to have self-doubt. So the bad writers tend to go on and on writing crap and giving as many readings as possible to sparse audiences. These sparse audiences consist mostly of other bad writers waiting their turn to go on, to get up there and let it out in the next hour, the next week, the next month, the next sometime. The feeling at these readings is murderous, airless, anti-life. When failures gather together in an attempt at self-congratulation, it only leads to a deeper and more abiding failure. The crowd is the gathering place of the weakest; true creation is a solitary act.

Your poems and fiction deal with similar themes and settings, yet we, as readers, never grow tired of them, and they never seem redundant.

Life doesn't change very much and so I am stuck in that. When there are changes they are so violent and sudden that we hardly know about it, or we are altered to such an extent that we are never the same again. I write about what occurs, and it has an almost deadening similarity. In my writing, my people sometimes work their way out of this, at least temporarily—which is the theme. It's no good quitting; there is always the smallest bit of light in the darkest of hells.

Hollywood

CHARLES BUKOWSKI
1989

Hollywood, Charles Bukowski, Santa Rosa: Black Sparrow Press, 1989, pp. 172–174.

Then I got an ego boost. A television crew came from Italy and one came from Germany. They both wanted interviews with me. The directors were both ladies.

"He promised us first," said the Italian lady.

"But you'll take all his juice away," said the German lady.

"I hope so," said the Italian lady.

I sat down before the Italian lights. We were on camera.

"What do you think of film?"

"Movies?"

"Yes."

"I stay away from them."

"What do you do when you're not writing?"

"Horses. Bet them."

"Do they help your writing?"

"Yes. They help me forget about it."

"Are you drunk in this movie?"

"Yes."

"Do you think drinking is brave?"

"No, but nothing else is either."

"What does your movie mean?"

"Nothing."

"Nothing?"

"Nothing. Peeking up the ass of death, maybe."

"Maybe?"

"Maybe means not sure."

"What do you see when you look up the 'ass of death'?"

"Rhythm, Dance, Quickness." *The New York Times Book Review,* June 11, 1989.
—Pamela Cytrynbaum

When Charles Bukowski gets angry, he writes books—and Hollywood, he says, is a novel of outrage.

"I guess I never believed Hollywood—I heard it's a horrible place—but when I went there, I found out how really horrible, horrible, horrible, horrible it was, black and cutthroat," Mr. Bukowski said in a telephone interview from his home in San Pedro, Calif.

"Somehow when you get it on paper, tell it, it gets it out of your mind. It keeps you from jumping out a window or slitting your throat."

The hardest part about writing, Mr. Bukowski said, "is sitting down in that chair in front of the typer. Once you do that, the movie begins, the show starts. Once I sit there, there's no planning, there's no effort, there's no labor. It's almost like the typer does it by itself. You get in a kind of a trancelike state.

The words "come out sometimes like blood and sometimes like wine," he said.

The 68-year-old writer believes that words and paragraphs should be short and to the point.

"Pace, rhythm, dance, quickness," he said, explaining his staccato style. "This is the modern age. Atom bombs are hanging on trees like grapefruits. I like to say what I have to say and get out."

Mr. Bukowski's first story was published when he was 24 years old, but most of his 45 books of poetry and prose were written after he was 40. For that, he said, he is thankful.

Writers who reach success early in their lives, the author said, "live as writers, they don't live as creatures of the street, and soon they miss the point of what's going on in the factories and with people working 16-hour days. I'm a late bloomer. I was lucky. It allowed me to live with all these bad ladies, have all these horrible jobs and all of these nightmarish adventures."

"The same thing you do."

"What is your philosophy of life."

"Think as little as possible."

"Anything else?"

"When you can't think of anything else to do, be kind."

"That's nice."

"Nice is not necessarily kind."

"All right, Mr. Chinaski. What word do you have for the Italian people?"

"Don't shout so much. And read Céline."

The lights went out on that one.

The German interview was even less interesting.

The lady kept wanting to know how much I drank.

"He drinks but not as much as he used to," Sarah told her.

"I need another drink right now or I'm not going to talk anymore."

It came immediately. It was in a large white paper cup and I drank it down. Ah, it was good. It suddenly seemed foolish to me that anybody wanted to know what I thought. The best part of a writer is on paper. The other part was usually nonsense.

The German lady was right. The Italian lady had used up all my juice.

I was now a spoiled star. And I was worried about the cornfield shoot.

I needed to talk to Jon, to tell him to make Francine drunker, madder, with one foot in hell, one hand yanking corn from the stalk as death approached, with the nearby buildings having faces out of dreams, looking down on the sadness of existence for us all: the rich, the poor, the beautiful and the ugly, the talented and useless.

"You don't like movies?" the German lady asked.

"No."

The lights went out. The interview was over.

And the cornfield scene got reshot. Maybe not exactly the way it could have been, but almost.

Charles Bukowski

DAVID ANDREONE AND DAVID BRIDSON
1990

"Charles Bukowski," *Portfolio*, David Andreone and David Bridson, October/November 1990, pp. 16–19.

How would you introduce yourself?
If I were to introduce myself, I'd be kind, I'd say, "Here's an old guy who won't spit it out."

What is your favorite form of escapism?
Writing, drinking, playing the horses.

What is the trait you most deplore in yourself?
Hesitation.

What is the trait you most deplore in others?
Nightmare faces and the tribal instinct.

Who are your favorite painters?
I have no favorite painters. I will sometimes see a painting, like it in a sense and then forget it.

How do you go about your writing?
If I really knew then I could no longer do it.

What is your writing attempting to explain?
I am not sure that I explain anything in my writing but I do feel better for having written it. To me, creation is just a reaction to existence. It's almost, in a sense, a second look at life. Something happens, then there is a space, then often, if you are a writer, you rework that happening out

in words. It doesn't change or explain anything but in the trance of writing it down a rather elated feeling occurs, or a warmth, or a healing process, or all three and maybe some more things, depending. Mostly when I write something that works for me, I get a very high feeling of good luck. And even in purely inventive work, ultra fiction, it is all taken from basic factuality: something you saw, dreamt, thought or should have thought. Creation is one hell of a marvelous miracle, as long as it lasts.

Your writing is sometimes dark but I would never describe it as negative. How do you feel about what your mother once said, "People like to read things that make them happy?"

Well, if there is a darkness in my writing it is a darkness that is trying to work into the light or if it can't make it into the light it is a darkness that lives somehow and anyhow within and against all odds. Just for the hell of it. About my mother, well, she never had much of a chance, she believed everything she had been told or taught and she never stumbled upon any counter-sources to pull her out of that. Of course, maybe she didn't have the will or the spirit to escape the obvious. She might have been simple-minded. I remember hearing throughout my childhood: "Smile, Henry, be happy." I mean, she actually thought that if I smiled I would be happy. And that I should write big smiling stories. All caused by the fact that as a young man I had written some things and hidden them in a dresser drawer. My father found them and the shit flew. "NOBODY IS EVER GOING TO WANT TO READ CRAP LIKE THIS!" And he was almost right: I didn't have very much luck until I was fifty years old. His only memory of me was of a guy who lived in cheap rooms and drank with crazy women.

What is your opinion of the "famous" contemporary writers that fill today's book-stores?

Most writers start with a bit of flare and daring-do, then get famous and start playing it careful. From wild gamblers they go to being straight practitioners. End up as university profs. They write because they are now writers, not because they feel like writing, not because it's the only thing they want to do, ever and always, hooked, nailed. Gloriously.

Some well-known writers and others claim that writers can't write when they drink.

I write as well either way. It's just more entertaining to *me* to write while drinking. What they are saying is that *they* can't write drunk.

Those same people also say incessant drinking is a slow form of suicide. How do you react to this?
For many people who are caught out of place and time in our society, drink is not a slow form of suicide but a deterrent to it. Drink is the only music and dance they are allowed. The last cheap and available miracle. When I came in from the slaughterhouse or the parts factory, that bottle of wine was my god in the sky. These fancy Dan writers are too immersed in their own assholes to know anything of the real populace and what they are attempting to endure. I only chippied with drugs but I can see where a man at total bottom will take two or three hours of blazing light and or peace or dream in exchange for the life he must face forever, doomed like a pig waiting for the blade. He will take those two or three hours in exchange for anything else offered. Damn the price. There is no price.

photo by Jean-François Duval

What is the greatest love of your life?
Linda Bukowski.

Which person(s) do you most despise?
I don't despise anybody. I have dislikes. Any number. If you insist upon the personal: Bob Hope, Bill Cosby, Paul McCartney, Meryl Streep, Bing Crosby, the whole Fonda family except Peter. Cary Grant, Kissinger. Hell, I don't know. John Wayne. I am beginning to despise myself for even listing these. The dead and the living. The living dead. Katherine Hepburn. My face in a hangover mirror.

Have you ever been to Disneyland?
Disneyland? I would never pay admission to go to hell.

You once said, "You've got to be large. . . . You've got to be able to make some mistakes while you play in a game you can never win anyhow." If you take this out of the context of writers and apply it to the masses, what does it mean?
If you apply it to the masses you are going to have chaos. It means that they aren't going to accept the eight hour job, the payments on the car, the t.v. programs, the movies, saving to send Jimmy to college, all the sundry dumb things they do, you are going to have bank holdups galore, the whitehouse on fire, empty churches, streets full of drunks and on and on . . . . The masses can't be large. They make mistakes but they are all mistakes. The masses can't get out, they don't want to, just paying off a credit card bill is one of their greatest victories. You can't blame the masses too much, they have few alternatives. It takes a truly daring, inventive soul to break free.

Another question like the previous one . . .. "This is our time on earth. Why pull up and play it short?" Could you explain what you mean?
When a man plays it short, he doesn't look so good, act so good, he doesn't even walk right. Most people are dead long before they are buried, that's why funerals are so sad. Most people quit too easy, they accept the short end, they compete for small prizes and become small. I don't expect everybody to be a genius but I never guessed that so many would rush to idiocy with such aplomb.

What do you consider the most overrated virtue?
Bravery.

What circumstances justify a lie of conscience?
None at all.

What is your greatest regret?
I have no regrets.

When and where were you happiest?
Here and now.

What other talent would you like to possess?
The ability to become invisible.

Does being alive bring you happiness?
Being alive brings me an admixture just like the dentist or the trash collector.

Is there something or somebody out there that most people have missed? For those who don't believe in god life can be a horrific experience. Do you still have hope, or have you given up, cashed in your chips? If there's nothing out there to take away the crap, how do we achieve some sense of meaning or happiness in life?
Most people have missed everything, the fine paintings, the good books, the great classical symphonies. They believe that survival consists of commercial success. And those who believe in a standard god are the ones who are having the horrific experience. Their minds are filled with thousands of years of garbage. They buy the standard. We face the factors of life as they are. If we get kicked in the ass we don't figure that it's God's will. Or if we do something exceptional we don't give credit to the Above. We use our minds which are free of standard concepts and beliefs. We are fortunate ones. As for death, I am ready for death, I will face it on my terms as I have attempted to live my life. Happiness and meaning in life are not constants but I do believe at times we can have both if we can arrange to sometimes do what we want to do, what we truly feel like doing instead of following pre-set rules. It's all quite simple and worth fighting for. Those who bow before false ways and false gods garner the confusion and the horror of wasted lives.

How would you like to be remembered?
Would not like to be. After death vanity has no place and before, it is an illness of the spirit.

Outsider Looking Out

KEVIN RING

1990

"Outsider Looking Out," Kevin Ring, *Beat Scene 11*, Autumn 1990, pp. 9–11.

(Courtesy of Linda Bukowski)

Can you recall the first thing you had published and how you felt about it?

No, I can't recall. Can remember my first major publication, a short story in Whit Burnett's and Martha Foley's *Story* magazine, 1944. I had been sending them a couple of short stories a week for maybe a year and a half. The story they finally accepted was mild in comparison to the others. I mean in terms of content and style and gamble and exploration and all that. Got another story accepted about that time in Carese Crosby's *Portfolio* and after that, I packed it in. I threw away all the stories and concentrated upon drinking. I didn't feel that the publishers were ready and that although I was ready, I could be readier and I was also disgusted with what I read as accepted front-line literature. So I drank and became one of the best drinkers anywhere, which takes some talent also.

Why did you leave it so long to go into writing full time, I guess there are a few reasons?

Yes, the drinking. And in between, the bumming between cities, the low-level jobs. I saw little meaning in anything and still have a problem with that. I lived a rather suicidal life, a half-assed life and I met some hard and crazy women. Some of this became material for my later writings. I mean, I *drank*. There was a bit of a death scene in a hospital, charity ward. I was spewing blood out of my mouth and my ass but didn't go. Came out and drank some more. Sometimes if you don't care whether you die or not, it can be hard work going. Then two and one half years as a letter carrier and eleven and a half years as a postal clerk didn't exactly give me a zest for life either. At the age of 50, twenty years ago, I quit my job and decided to become a professional writer, that is, one who gets paid for his scribblings. I figured either that or skidrow. I got lucky. I still am.

Tell us a little about your friendship with John Fante, you love his books and you became his friend . . .

As a young man, I hung around the libraries during the day and the bars at night. I read and I read and I read. Then I ran out of things to read. I kept pulling the books out of the shelves again and again. I could only read a few lines and I felt the fakeness and I put them back. It was a real horror show. Nothing related to life, at least not to mine and the streets and the people I saw in the streets and what they were forced to do and what they became. And one day I happened to pull out a book by somebody named Fante. The lines leaped at me. Fire. No bullshit. But I'd never heard of Fante, nobody spoke of Fante. He was just in there. A book. It was called *Ask The Dust*. I didn't like the title but the words were simple and honest and full of passion. Holy shit, I thought, this man can write! Well, I read all of his books that I could get hold of and I knew that there were still some magic people on the earth. It was decades later in my writings that I mentioned a "Fante". Now all of my writings are not published but they are all sent to John Martin, Black Sparrow Press, and he asked me once, I believe it was over the telephone, "You keep mentioning a 'Fante'? Is this a real writer?" I told him that it was and that he should read this fellow.

Soon I heard from Martin, he was very excited, "Fante is great, great! I can't believe it! I am going to republish his works!" And then came the stream of Black Sparrow Fante books. Fante was still alive. My wife suggested that since he was such a hero to me that I go visit him. He was in a hospital, dying, blind and amputated; diabetes. We made visits to the hospital and once to his home where he was briefly released for a short time. He was a little bulldog, just brave without trying. But he was going. Still he wrote a book in that state, dictating it to his wife. Black Sparrow published it. He was a writer to the end. He even told me about his idea for his next novel: a woman baseball player who made it to the big leagues. "Go ahead, John, do it," I told him. But soon it was over . . .

Do you know anything about this film being made from one of his books, is it "Bandini" that they've filmed?

I'm not sure about the movies. I think at least five of his books are being made into movies. A strange turn. He worked for Hollywood, you know. That's where he vanished to. That's where his other writing stopped. "Why the hell did you go to Hollywood, that slime pit of nowhere?" I asked him. "Mencken told me to," he said, "go ahead and take them." Mencken, that son of a bitch. He sent Fante to hell. H. L. had published many of Fante's stories in the old *American Mercury*. Fante met Faulkner there. Faulkner would enter his cottage in the morning sober and come out dead drunk each evening. They had to pour him into a taxi cab.

We heard reports that you were moved by the Dominic Deruddere film *Crazy Love* based upon your writing. What are you feelings about this film?

I liked *Crazy Love*. As I told Deruddere, "You made me look better than I am." He oversensitized me. But it came out nicely and much of it was actually me.

How is the biography of you by Neeli Cherkovski progressing? Have you had much contact with him over it? How do you feel about someone writing about your life?

The biography is just about finished. Well, I've known Cherkovski since he was 14 years old or maybe it was 16. He's got me on tape drunk, many times, babbling away. Photos, all that. He seems to have been around me a long time, has seen many of my women, has seen me vicious, kind, foolish and all that. He wrote a book about some poets called *Whitman's Wild Children* and it contained such humor and easy writing that when he approached me about writing one on me, I said, "Go ahead." I asked not to see it. I also told him not to go easy on me. It should be worth some laughs. Really can't do much harm. If it does, I'll write my way out of it.

Neeli Cherkovski

You are very popular in Europe, France, Germany, Switzerland and other places, some of your stories even being translated into comic book form, why is this do you think? Is it Carl Weissner's influence?

Carl Weissner's influence on my work, getting it translated, getting it around, getting it seen, well, it just can't be discounted. The comic book things are really rather well done. I don't know what causes this comic book stuff. Maybe it's a sickness.

City Lights put out *Shakespeare Never Did This*, did you enjoy that trip to Germany?

Actually *Shakespeare Never Did This* is about two trips to Europe and I put it together as one. I do get them mixed up because of all the heavy drinking. I really gave some hotels over there a very rough time but they never called the police which, I think, is real class.

How important has Black Sparrow Press been to you? You seem to have been very loyal to each other.

Black Sparrow Press promised me $100 a month for life if I quit my job and tried to be a writer. Nobody else even knew I was alive. Why shouldn't I be loyal forever. And now the royalties from Sparrow match or surpass all other royalties. What a flashing heaven of luck

You show tremendous kindness and loyalty to small presses. Why is this?

The small presses always published things of mine that the larger presses were afraid of. They still do.

Do you have a favourite book of your own?

Each last book that I write is my favorite book.

It's well known that you like classical music, who is your favourite, any particular reasons?

Sibelius. The long deep tonality. And a passion that knocks your lights out.

Do you still go to the races much? Is that something that you've done for a long time?

I went to the racetrack in an attempt to find a substitute for drinking. It didn't work. Then I had drinking and the track. Nobody bothers me at the track. And planning your plays, placing your bets, you find out a great deal about yourself and also about the other people. For instance, knowledge without follow-through is worse than no knowledge at all. It's a good school, although sometimes a boring one, but it keeps you from thinking that you are a writer or whatever you are trying to be.

Do you have ideal conditions under which you write? Do you write most days?

The ideal conditions are between 10 p.m. and 2 a.m. Bottle of wine, smokes, radio on to classical music. I write 2 or 3 nights a week. It's the best show in town.

Will you ever come to Europe again. A few years ago you were billed as coming to the London Book Fair!

I don't think I'll travel anymore. Travel is nothing but an inconvenience. There is always enough trouble where you are.

Can you give us any clues on your next book?

Usually one book a year. I know that it sounds awful to say so but I think that I am writing better than I ever have.

What lies in the future for you? Will you keep writing?

If I stop writing I am dead. And that's the only way I'll stop: dead.

Bukowski Reflects: The Street Smart Sage Discusses Skid Row, Women, and Life at 70

Mary Ann Swisler

1990

"Bukowski Reflects: The Street Smart Sage Discusses Skid Row, Women, and Life at 70," Mary Ann Swisler, *Village View: The Westside Weekly*, Vol 5., No. 17, November 30–December 6 1990, pp. 20–21.

He has a face like a Tom Waits song about bitterness and of fistfights waged and lost. His sparkling eyes are the color of nothing and set deep in his forehead. The nose that has ballooned from more than a half century of hard drinking is a trademark of a lifestyle that poet and novelist Charles Bukowski has chronicled in 45 books of poetry and fiction, as well as the 1987 movie *Barfly*.

His complexion is smooth and flushed from daily treks to Los Angeles racetracks. Only a few tiny boils are left from a case of pubescent acne that his doctor called the worst he'd ever seen. The memories still prompt him to comment, "When I see certain movies like *The Elephant Man* and *The Hunchback of Notre Dame*, I kind of identify to a certain extent with those poor creatures."

Poet and novelist Charles Bukowski (and Henry Chinaski, his literary alter ego) has done nothing to change his image of chronicler of alcoholism and Skid Row, or as the poet from hell in this year's *Septuagenarian Stew: Stories and Poems*, taking his customary swings at recovering alcoholics, feminists, and the middle class. To further aid his reputation, "Hank" recently lent his slow, bluesy voice to the narration of a documentary about the plight of Skid Row regulars in the upcoming HBO special *The Best Hotel on Skid Row*, premiering on December 4, at 9:30 p.m. The brainchild of filmmakers Renee Tajima and Christine Choy (*Who Killed Vincent Chin?*), *Hotel* has been accepted for a third screening by Cannes Film Festival. Peter Davis, of *Hearts and Minds*, co-produced the one-hour film.

Compared to the bums of today, Bukowski considers himself lucky, upon recalling his own days of "low-down slumming." He explains: "I wasn't on the streets too much. I was in flophouses and I did a little park bench time in different cities so I wasn't a Skid Row type. I was just on the edges . . . I was about as close as I could get to it without being it."

Rather than becoming like the lost souls he writes about, Bukowski has cultivated an international reputation since the publication of his first work in 1960, the book *Flower, Fist and Bestial Wail*. Bukowski's greatest following can be found not in this country, but in Germany, the country of his birth.

An evening with the 70-year-old Bukowski reveals a man largely shedding his tyrannical image, exposing a stately old lion underneath. Yet, he's as hellbent as ever on bashing recovering alcoholics—not for quitting but because they've never drunk enough to actually mourn their years of drinking. "I've drunken more alcohol than most men have drunk water," he boasts.

Signs that Bukowski has shades of likability included framed birthday and Valentine's Day Cards he made for his wife that are hung in his living room. Like many male writers with a notorious reputation, one of the most fascinating aspects of Bukowski's life is his marriage to his wife Linda, a longtime resident of the South Bay who rebelled against an old money family in Philadelphia early in life. The former Linda Beighle went on to run one of the many health food restaurants that dotted L.A. in the 1970s. Although she closed up the Redondo Beach eatery in 1978, two months before "Hank" proposed marriage, Linda says she still passes on nutritional advice to her husband. She's managed to get him to stop eating red meat and largely to limit the liquid portion of his diet to wine and beer. "He'll stay healthy for years," she says.

Village View: Why did you narrate *The Best Hotel on Skid Row?*

Charles Bukowski: I did it for the money. Especially when I found out the subject matter. You know, being and ex-bum and having lived on Skid Row, I just fell into it. They said they needed a narrator and I said okay. We had a little struggle since I speak so slowly, to fit in with the

Dew Drop Inn

Salads

All topped with Dew Drops Lelicious, Uniece Dressing

Healthy Greens and Sprouts - Lettuce, Spinach, Celery, Cucumber, Bell Pepper, Alfalfa and Mung Sprouts. — Sm. 1.25 / Lg. 1.75

Mixed Vegetable Garden - Tomato, Carrots, Onion, Cucumber, Celery, Green Pepper, Sprouts, Lettuce, Ect, Ect. — Sm. 1.65 / Lg. 2.50

Dew Drop Delight - A Super Salad with a Dynamite Combo of Mixed Vegetables, including, Greens, Celery, Carrots, Onion, Tomato, Cucumber, Mushrooms, Guacamole, Cheese, Hard Boiled Egg, topped with Sprouts and Seeds!! Whew......... — Sm. 2.50 / Lg. 3.25

Tuna - White Albacore, Tomato, Cucumber on a Bed of Lettuce, Topped with Alfalfa Sprouts and Seeds. — Sm. 2.25 / Lg. 3.25

Tunacado - Same as Above, with Guacamole. — Sm. 2.45 / Lg. 3.25

Dream Salad - Design your own, Choosing from any, or all of our possible ingredients

Fresh Fruit Combination - Papaya, Banana, Orange Slices, Peaches, Grapes, and/or other fruits in season, topped with Seeds. Yogurt, Honey, Pollen — 30¢ 15¢ 20¢ — Sm. 1.50 / Lg. 2.95

Drinks

Fresh Made to Order - Carrot, Orange, Grapefruit — Sm. 70¢ 85-carrot / Lg. .85¢ 1.00-carrot

Also - Strawberry-Apple or Strawberry Orange-Apple — Sm. b¢ / Lg. 85¢

Roger Rooter - Carrot, Beet, Celery, Cucumber, Spinach

Smoothies - A Smoothee is a groovy combination of Apple or Orange juice, Banana, Strawberries, blended with a dab of Honey, to fill you with Energy + Happiness. — 95¢

Yogurt Smoothie - Same as Above with a scoop of Yogurt. 1.20

Charles Bukowski designed this menu for the Dew Drop Inn, Linda Lee Bukowski's health food restaurant in Redondo Beach.

time frame. So I drank and Peter Davis worked me and bossed me a bit in a nice manner. And we got it done. Like handling a scruffy, mangy old lion. Making him do a few tricks and he did it well.

VW: What's different on Skid Row now compared to your days down there?

CB: It's much harder now with the drugs and more unemployment and less sympathy for the homeless than there used to be, and less of a way out. So it's much sadder. When I used to go down there it was a lark. You know, go down to Skid Row for a couple of weeks. You could bounce back. There are women down there now and families and drugs and they kill each other and it's pretty damned gruesome and pretty damned horrible.

In my time it used to be just guys drinking wine, you know. And some of them had a good time; they thought it was adventuresome. There's no feeling of adventure down there now. You're just there because there isn't anyplace else. I don't know. It's a damn shame that it has to be that way and I don't know what to do about it.

Before, there were more jobs for a guy who didn't have a trade. If he wanted to work, he could mostly work at some factory or doing some low-labor jobs. Now those jobs no longer exist. All the auto plants have shut down. Everything just shut down. We have McDonald's and fast food. We have what we call service jobs which don't handle the population [downtown].

When you're on the row now, you're on there to stay. That's it.

VW: Would you have any kind of advice to give to someone on Skid Row?

CB: No, I would just say, "For your warmth go to the wine instead of the drugs and try to last it out."

VW: Are you trying to make a statement with this documentary?

CB: I'm a small part of the whole thing. I'm just the narrator of *Best Hotel on Skid Row*. I'm just the voice. I wasn't trying to make a statement, I'm just a hired hand. I make my statements at the typewriter.

VW: Does it help to live on the outskirts of Los Angeles?

CB: And how! Maybe I shouldn't publicize what a great place this is to hide out in, they'll all come running. This is a place where there are very few poets, very few painters, very few moviemakers, very few anything but common sort of average human beings. And this is very refreshing, just to meet someone who isn't a so-called *artiste*. So-called *artistes* are great pains in the asses, you know. Even when they're good, they're only good artists for a short period of time, a year, a year and a half, two years, three years. Fame gets to them or money gets to them or women get to them or drugs or any number of things. So, usually someone who calls themselves an artist is usually someone who was an artist in the past and had a little luck and now they're being held up by their publicity agents. I always said you can go to bed being a writer and wake up being nothing at all. This is because you haven't lived properly, acted properly or drank enough. I think I've endured because I started so late that I'm still making up ground. It's like when you get famous when you're 23, it's pretty darn hard to last even until you're 32. If you get a little minor splash of fame when you're 53, you're more apt to handle it. So now I'm 70 and I don't think my head has been turned too damn much. And the typewriter's still humming and I think it's turning out good crap.

VW: Do you think women have changed much since you wrote the novel *Women?*

CB: I've been with the same woman for twelve years now and being a good boy and haven't cheated [so] I'd have to go back a ways. I doubt very much if women have changed very much at all. They're very difficult, whimsical creatures. Very changeable. Men are hardly as changeable as women and I think that's the main difference.

VW: Would you say it's because they're adaptable?

CB: They're not adaptable. (*laughs*) Hell no. They're more frantic.

VW: In what way?

CB: To begin with they're trapped by the American way of admiring a woman—for her so-called beauty. You know, facial features, the breasts, the eyes, the buttocks. And women have these things in abundance at their best time, in their prime of life. And they get used to flattery, gifts, and all eyes upon them. And when this stops, as it will as women age, they rather miss this overadulation. When it's taken away, I think I've found that women become quite bitter about it. This is a very sad thing to me because they suck to the bait.

VW: Would you say that feminists are right, then, that a woman should develop her mind?

CB: That's a very good point, but there are all kinds of feminists. Some women become feminists after the happening. If you could become a feminist before the catastrophe I'd say you have a very wise woman. There are good feminists and bad feminists, and good Communists and bad Communists, and good white guys and bad black guys. It depends upon the individual.

VW: How are you different from your macho, misogynist image?

CB: That image is done by word-of-mouth by people who haven't read the totality, all the pages. It's more or less a word-of-mouth, gossipy thing. It's almost, I'm sorry to say, without foundation. Except I will say that in my life when I've met a woman who you could call a bad woman, a bitch, I've written her up as a bitch. Also when I was a bastard, I wrote myself up as a bastard. So I think I'm pretty fair.

VW: Where does Henry Chinaski end (the protagonist most closely resembling the author) and Charles Bukowski begin?

CB: They're about the same except for a minor embellishment to keep me from getting too bored with him.

VW: I just read *Hollywood* (the author's novel about the making of the movie *Barfly*). This could've been a bitter experience, and here was this nice guy having the time of his life.

CB: I am sometimes a good guy.

VW: Are you a nice guy?

CB: Sometimes.

VW: What's worse—an overzealous fan who appreciates your work or a fan who thinks he or she knows the real Bukowski?

CB: They're equally obnoxious.

VW: Are they any different from the ones you'd end up fighting with in bars?

CB: I prefer the people in bars because that's just common, jive ass bullshit. A guy says, "You want to step outside?" That's clear, open language. He's not worried about your literary credits or anything else.

VW: Have you ever been approached to do a beer commercial?

CB: No.

VW: Would you?

CB: It would have to have some humor and it would have to be different from the ones they have now with the dancing girls and all that dumb crap. I'd have to examine it first.

VW: Do you think colleges ruin writers?

CB: Of course.

VW: How?

CB: If you're weak enough to seek instruction, you're generally not strong enough to do anything else.

VW: Are creative writing teachers worse than people who call themselves artists?

CB: Oh, Christ. I don't know which is more disgusting. Just about everything's disgusting except this bottle of beer.

VW: You don't do many interviews. Even when your book came out this year, didn't you want to plug it through the media?

CB: That's one of the grand things about not being put out by a New York publisher. Those poor fuckers, they gotta go around to book signings, parties and [their publicists] say, "Oh you're on TV in the morning and on the Carson show at night." It's living, fucking hell. It has nothing to do with writing. You're just a salesman pushing a product. And a writer should never have to do that. Their writing should be strong enough that it sells itself.

VW: How would you feel about the title "poet from hell?"

CB: I think it's ridiculous. It's too glamorous because even when I was in so-called "hell," I enjoyed it. All the small rooms I lived in, you know, the cheap tiny room when I starved trying to write, I adored being fucked up and half mad. I adored being in hell, I adored not being able to get the rent up and waiting for a return response from a short story I sent out to *The New Yorker*. I felt I was really living high and good. I really wasn't in hell. To another person it might've seemed like hell. To me it was a necessary and great and glowing thing, the gamble of it. I loved it.

Pen & Drink

ROBERT GUMPERT

1991

"Pen and Drink," Robert Gumpert, *Weekend Guardian*, December 14–15, 1991. (Reprinted in *Sure, The Charles Bukowski Newsletter*, No. 4, 1992, pp. 22-32).

"Beautiful, baby, beautiful . . ." The words slide from Charles Bukowski's 71-year old concrete-mixer face like thick slurries of newly-spun cement. For Bukowski, the beautiful sound is the rich glug of wine splashing down into his glass. Moments later, after he has swilled his first taste from our fifth bottle of vintage red, he says it again: "Beautiful, baby, beautiful . . ."

He settles back into the sofa and laughs, for he's on his way again, drinking through another night. Yet he also lets slip an ironic, performer's wheeze for few other literary legacies are as set in concrete as this one—the hazed-over image of "Hank" Bukowski and his beautiful bottle of drink.

This peculiarly American linkage between writing and drinking may have been defined by Faulkner, Fitzgerald, Hemingway and Lowry but, more than anyone else, Bukowski has sustained the iconic myth of literary drunkenness.

Despite their handful of great books, his loaded predecessors died as "victims of the bottle." Bukowski though just grinds on relentlessly at 71, writing and drinking, drinking and writing.

This has always been the Bukowski way, even during his bleakest days as "the ovenman" in a dog-biscuit factory or during the 11 hung-over years he worked for the US Post Office or the longer stretch he spent as a skid row bum.

Whether in his 50 books of ceaselessly autobiographical poetry, short stories and novels or in his screenplay for Barbet Schroeder's *Barfly*, Bukowski has written about himself and drink for 47 straight years, always with a bottle close at hand.

The first 35 of these "literary" years were filled working for foremen with "rodent eyes and small foreheads" and desperate night-time writing in broken-down hotel rooms. While writing, Bukowski would listen to Mahler, Rossini, Sibelius and Shostakovich and drink anything as long as it made him fly from the day's grind. When he wasn't writing or drinking or falling in and out of love with alcoholic women and prostitutes, he was reading Céline, Dostoevsky, Kierkegaard, Lawrence, Nietzsche, Pound, Thurber and more lifted from the Los Angeles public library.

Although his consuming need to write and his taste for dead writers and music remains unchanged, the last ten of Bukowski's years have been fundamentally different.

He now lives in a big house with a pool and a Jacuzzi in the garden, albeit in the blue-collar harbour town of San Pedro, near Los Angeles. He writes on a computer, pays cash when he swaps his black BMW for a more expensive model and only drinks the finest red wine.

These changes have not come about only because he was pulled out of the gutter 12 years ago by his dependably witty wife, Linda, 30 years his junior. They have also not just been brought about by the homage paid to him by among others Sean Penn, Madonna, Dennis Hopper, Mickey Rourke, Harry Dean Stanton, David Lynch and Jean-Luc Godard. Nor has Bukowski's comparatively serene septuagenarian escape from impoverishment emerged merely in the wake of the three feature films already made about him—*Tales of Ordinary Madness*, *Crazy Love* and *Barfly*—and the three others set for production, including Paul Verhoeven's diversion from *Robocop* and *Total Recall* to direct a screen version of Bukowski's novel, *Women*.

More compelling and constant than any of this has been the writing itself. Beneath the "emptying of hundreds and hundreds of bottles down the rivers of nowhere," there has been much brutally lucid writing; writing which, despite its inexorable inconsistencies, allowed both Sartre and Genet to hail Bukowski as America's "greatest poet" as he careered down "this mad river, this gouging, plundering madness that I would wish upon nobody but myself."

There are various ways in which the best American writers deal with public scrutiny. Celebrity, more than alcohol these days, is a persistent backdrop to the higher echelons of American writing.

Auster, Doctorow, DeLillo and Pynchon have been able to conceal themselves behind often labyrinthine writing and shifting shields of privacy. But where they have remained elusive, the literary personalities of the older guard of Bellow, Roth and Updike are entrenched in American writing as "real presences." Then there is "Hank" Bukowski whose work and life is apparently one and the same thing.

Yet Bukowski's inexhaustibly auto-biographical writing still solicits uncertainty amongst American literary juries. They continue to regard him warily as the country's terminally un-cool dirty old man of writing. Instead, Bukowski's more fervent followers tend to be either European poetry professors or else imaginative Californian women who have a penchant for lying naked on photocopying machines so that they can send Xeroxed copies of their private parts to their poetically drunken San Pedro saviour. This ambiguous Bukowski charisma is bound up in his almost mythological shit-sniffing, vomit-spewing and punch-taking immersion in the more vicious remnants of human existence.

Imagination in much of Bukowski's writing is literally redundant for supposedly everything has already happened to him and all he needs to do is to remember and never to invent.

The traditional American dilemma of separating the real from the fictional "I" hits a dead-end with Charles Bukowski. There is no writerly fear of public scrutiny here. Everything he writes comes from within himself for there is nothing private, nothing that needs to be obscured, nothing that should be excluded.

This means that Bukowski is much more a writer of feelings than ideas, which partly explains the reductive strain to his work. Yet, Bukowski writes about confused excess and seething melodrama with remarkable clarity.

This undiminished sense of control distinguishes Bukowski from the hapless Beat writers with whom he was so wrongly lined; and the restrained rhythm of his writing enables him to invest both grace and humour into an otherwise tortuous past. That, perhaps more than anything else, is the reason why Bukowski writes; for his stark words exude a curiously affirmative resonance of all he has endured in 71 long years.

Charles Bukowski was born in Germany in 1920 and traveled to the US with his parents three years later. They settled in East Hollywood, Los Angeles, hoping they had landed in the promised land. Ten years later he abandoned this typical American dream. Just as he is still an outsider to the literary establishment, Bukowski then was a derided teenage outcast.

The trouble started with his father, "a cruel, shiny bastard with bad breath." "Yeah, I've written about him a lot over the years," sighs Bukowski, "for I guess that's where it all started—the disgusted realization that it takes something extraordinary, like drinking or writing or classical music, to move beyond such people. That's why I took to Dostoevsky so quickly because you remember what he says in *The Brothers Karamazov*—"who doesn't want to kill the father?" Who exactly?

"He gave me terrible beatings which only stopped the day I fought back. At 16 and one half I knocked him out with one punch. He never touched me again. But the disgust he made me feel for life never left. But disgust is better than anger. When you're angry you just wanna get even, when you're disgusted you just wanna get away; and with disgust you can laugh. I'm still laughing, remembering him telling me that I was gonna be nothing but a bum. Hey, he was right, but he never knew that I'd turn out to be such a stylish bum . . ."

Bukowski's life outside his irredeemably bruised family was hardly any happier. As the second world war loomed, his German descent consigned him even further to the sidelines of flag-waving Hollywood life. But as his best and most painfully funny novel, *Ham on Rye*, reveals, his adolescent alienation had as much to do with a sulphurous outbreak of acne as with his lack of patriotic purity.

"Man," he murmurs amidst that cementy life, "I was covered with these boils. But that's when I started acting tough and writing. I'd take on anyone. I'd lose mostly but, boy could I take a helluva punch. My record was something like five won, 14 lost, two drawn.

"Yeah, I wanted to be a tough guy but, more than that, I wanted to write. I lived amidst dirt and starvation and to survive, to make sense of the senseless, I wrote . . ."

By then Bukowski had hit skid row. Those years of bumming and writing were only replaced by a more strangulated version of "living hell" in the form of unyielding conveyor-belt work in the notorious dog biscuit factory.

After two years as a postman and a further nine in the postal sorting room, Bukowski was promised $100 a month for life by Black Sparrow Press and with this shred of guaranteed income he decided never to work, outside of writing, again. He already had a reputation as being America's most influential renegade poet and from then on the books just flooded from him—beginning with his nightmarishly bureaucratic novel *Post Office*, which took him only 20 straight nights and another 20 accompanying bottles of whiskey to write. His first two great collections of short stories, *Tales of Ordinary Madness* and *The Most Beautiful Woman In Town* soon followed.

These were dark, strange stories which both prefigured and eclipsed the wave of "dirty realism" that engulfed American short story writing a decade later with the breakthrough of Raymond Carver and Richard Ford. Bukowski wrote about small-time desperation and hopelessly faded dreams, in yellowing bar rooms and stinking race tracks, with his stories being underpinned by the drunken certainty that "we will all end up in the crud-pot of defeat." But he had also begun to write with deceptive precision and with a tenderness which touched on the lyrical.

Significantly, these are the Bukowski stories where fact and fiction no longer blur and the writing shines with almost diseased imagination—in the "Copulating Mermaid of Venice, California," two muscatel-swigging bums steal the body of a just-dead young woman and fuck and fall in love with her before taking her down to Venice Beach where they walk with her into the waves and then, finally, lingeringly, let her drift out to "where the pelicans dive amongst glittering, guitar-shaped fish"; in "The Fiend" the malignant desire of a Mahler-listening paedophile splits open with awful consequences; in "The Murder of Ramon Vazquez" an ageing, homosexual Hollywood star is whipped to death by two nihilistic teenage brothers; in "The Most Beautiful Woman in Town," a 20-year-old called Cass slits her own throat while "the night kept coming on in and there was nothing I could do."

As always, Bukowski was still writing poetry. To supplement his meager monthly allowance and the unreliable arrival of royalty cheques, he began to accept paid invitations to read his poetry at campuses. And the Bukowski mythology was etched in concrete for then he was deranged, debauched and, always, drunk.

Raymond Carver, perhaps the most missed American writer in recent memory, celebrated the Bukowski of this time with his boozily enamored poem "You Don't Know What Love is (An Evening with Charles Bukowski)." He was also then a writing drunk but, in his last 11 "gravy years" with Tess Gallagher, Carver finally found sober serenity in writing.

Bukowski, now in his own "gravy years," remembers Carver fondly: "Yeah, Raymond Carver, I liked him a lot more than someone as over-rated as Fitzgerald," Bukowski mumbles. "Man, that night he wrote about me I was drunk, naturally, and screaming at all these professors and college kids—'babies, I look around this room and I see plenty typers but I see no writers for you guys don't know what love is'—oh boy, I was singing that night and Carver caught that.

"I remember we escaped to a bar, me and Carver and him saying 'Hank?' And me saying 'Yeah, Ray?' He said, 'I'm gonna be a famous writer, Hank!' And I say, 'Is that so Ray?' He laughed, 'Yeah Hank, my friend's just become literary editor of *Esquire* and he says he's going to publish every goddamn short story I sent him!' So I say 'beautiful, baby, beautiful.'

"We drank all night. The next morning Carver's banging on my door. He wants breakfast. Big mistake. Greasy eggs and bacon come swimming in their plates and Carver needs just one look. When he comes back from the toilet I say, 'That's ok Ray, I finished my plate and now I'm gonna eat yours an' then we're gonna go out and find us another bottle.' An' we did. But Ray gave up drinking an' that was fine by me 'cos he really started to write then. I'm different. I drink and I write, I write and I drink, an' there's a rhythm to it, so it's worked all right for me . . ."

Bukowski would certainly not be "all right" or able to maintain any kind of writing rhythm if he had not met Linda in 1977. He readily acknowl-edges the certainty of his own death years ago if Linda, ironically then a health food restaurant owner in Redondo Beach, had not forced him to face the damage he was doing to himself. "When Linda met me I was a broke dead-arse living in a hole in the wall. I was near the big burn-out but she's looked after me real well."

"Oh Man!" Bukowski groans. "I'm way too old now. Before Linda came along I'd take them in. Those were the days when the more screwed-up critics started to call me 'Genius Bukowski.' So you'd get those women sending me nude photographs and saying they want to come clean house. Hell yeah! But I'd meet them at the airport and I was always lucky. I'd be thinking 'Oh no, I bet that's her, the one with the not-so-nice face, like mine' but then this fresh young 25-year old would bounce up and say 'Hi Hank!' And I'd say 'Well hi there—yeah beautiful baby, beautiful!'

"I remember once three young women were sitting on my porch drinking beer and giggling when the postman walks up the drive. I know how the guy feels so I give him a big smile. He says 'Hey bud, mind if I ask you something?' I say, 'go ahead, friend.' 'Well,' he says, 'I wondered why all these beautiful young women are drinking beer with you 'cos you ain't exactly what I'd call a pretty boy.' I laugh with him—'Go ahead baby, it's all right, I know I'm ugly—the secret is availability.'

"The availability's gone now but they keep sending their Xeroxes. It's strange, lying butt-naked on a Xerox machine so you can send the copy to some 71-year-old guy. But to them I'm 'Bukowski—the poetic genius.' Men too! Guys write telling me how I saved their lives. And remember, Linda, all those young German boys we've had flying to LA just so that they can knock on the door and ask to get drunk with me. Man, I just kick their butts and then they scream all the way down the driveway,

'Bukowski you're nothing, you're a sick old bum.' I can deal with those guys—it's just when you get people like that one couple. They camped outside the house for days in their big Winnebago. They used to barbecue all day long—just so that they could say 'Yeah man we barbecued steaks outside Bukowski's house.' Big deal! Sartre got it all down in a few crisp words—'hell is other people'—on the nose, baby!"

Bukowski's infamy in America is nothing compared to the mysterious heights of adulation he is subjected to in Europe—especially in Germany and France where a book of his can sell 100,000 copies and over-blown critics suggest that his writing "possesses all the passionate excess of Rabelais's *Gargantua*, the verbal virtuosity of Joyce, the demonic cruelty of Céline's best work." Bukowski takes none of this seriously which, certainly on the Joycean semantic angle, is the wise thing to do, especially when he has a tendency to go for these kinds of titles: *Politics Is Like Trying To Screw A Cat In The Ass, Erections, Ejaculations, and General Tales of Madness, Ten Jack-Offs, My Big-Assed Mother, Sometimes You Go A Bit Crazy, Great Poets Die in Steaming Pots Of Shit, Ruin, Nowhere* and *All the Pussy You Want*. But then Bukowski is similarly blase about the East Coast intelligentsia's dismissal of him as "a mere reprobate."

"It's best to listen to none of them," he says, "especially in Europe where I'm like Mick Jagger. I walk down the street and they're all these people going 'Bukowski, Bukowski.' It's tedious but I did have one of the finer moments in my life when I was last in Paris. I was sitting at this café and one of the waiters came over from this ultra-chic restaurant across the road and he said, 'excuse me, are you the great writer, Bukowski?' I said 'you bet.' He clicks his fingers and these five guys appear from nowhere.

"They're dressed in fancy waiter gear and they stand in line in front of me and then, cool as anything, they bow. Then they turn on their heels—no need for words. Beautiful!

"I think of that moment when I curse myself about Sartre. You know he really wanted to meet me but I said 'no way baby!' I wasn't into Sartre one little bit, I just had my bottle to take care of. But I've been reading some of his better writing lately and it's damn fine. I regret turning him down but then I think 'what the hell we'd probably just've ended up boring each other' and I remember my bowing Paris waiters instead . . ."

Fame finally settled across Charles Bukowski's blasted face when Barbet Schroeder celebrated the writer's early years in *Barfly*. That it ended up being a merely adequate Bukowski film perhaps rests on the fact that Mickey Rourke rather than Sean Penn ended up playing the title role. Penn was desperate to make the film, but with Dennis Hopper directing instead of Barbet Schroeder. Bukowski emphasizes that he had little moral choice in backing anyone but Schroeder.

"I didn't care for all those goddamn chains Hopper had around his neck. But Sean was all right! I knew he had wildness to do it, much more than Mickey Rourke who doesn't touch a drink anyway! I got to like Sean, especially when he came over with Madonna. She's talking about Swinburne! I'm making my usual cracks about Madonna trying to be hip. Sean gets angry. He stands up but I say quietly, 'Sit down Sean, you know I can take you baby.' When he sits down I think, 'I like this guy.'

"But Barbet fought so hard to get the money for this movie. When Hollywood studios were screwing him around he bought a chainsaw. Then he walks into the film studio, right into the executive office, and starts up his chainsaw. He says to these fat bastards, 'Right, I'm going to cut off one of my fingers for every ten minutes you don't give me the money for my Bukowski movie.' I think they guessed he meant it 'cos they gave him the money!"

Bukowski, of course, went on to write about these *Barfly* experiences in his novel, *Hollywood*. Although the backdrop had shifted from the post office to the movie business Bukowski's technique of recording every detail of his own life remained the same. Even the names of the novel's characters hardly differ from their real-life counterparts, running along only slightly adapted Jean-Luc Modard, David Cynch and Wenner Zergog tracks. Hollywood, like much of Bukowski's writing, is uneven but, as always, there is an unerring accuracy to his insight and no other book gets close to the corrupt heart of American movie-making.

Yet it is the book after *Hollywood*—*Septuagenarian Stew*, a staggering 375 page collection of poetry and short stories—which marks out the inevitable reappraisal of Bukowski's work.

Although its effect induces a shudder in Bukowski, *Septuagenarian Stew* has been embraced by everyone from the *New York Times* to the *TLS*. The book charts the familiar Bukowski legacy of bums and whores, manual workers and losing racetrack gamblers; his primary themes are still loss and drinking through to the other side of despair. But what gives the book its blackly ironic edge is that Bukowski also writes about the new things in his life—the pool, the house, the cars, the computer and the closeness of death—and he does so with the same romanticized, even nonchalant sense of loss used in his earlier work.

"The writing's not bad for an old guy I guess and, yeah, maybe now I fear the loss of my soul. When I wrote my first computer poem I was anxious that I would be suffocated by these layers of consumerist suffering. Would old Dostoevsky have ever used one of these babies? I wondered, and then I said—'hell, yeah!'

"Inside I feel the same—only stronger with the writing getting better as I get older. Right now I'm trying something new. I call it *Pulp* and it's easily the dirtiest, weirdest thing I've written. It's about this private detective, Nicky Ballaine (!)—and, for a change, he's not me. The publishers are getting anxious, for this one's way over the edge. Maybe they're starting to like me too much out there so I'm gonna test them a little with *Pulp*. They're either gonna crucify me or else everyone's gonna start writing like me. That's worth a drink!

"But, hell, I'm just gonna keep going. Every day I'll wake up around noon, Linda and I'll have some breakfast, then I'll go to the track and I'll play the horses while avoiding the people saying 'hi, Bukowski, the original barfly!' Then I'll come back and I'll swim and we'll have dinner and I'll go upstairs and I'll sit at the computer and I'll crack me a bottle and I'll listen to some Mahler or Sibelius and I'll write, with this rhythm, like always. So now, while we open another bottle, tell me, how'm I doing baby?"

Purity and Survival:
John Martin and Black Sparrow Press

NEIL GORDON

1992

"Purity and Survival: John Martin and Black Sparrow Press," Neil Gordon, *Boston Review*, November–December, 1992, pp. 26–27.

John Martin

Charles Bukowski doesn't give interviews. He doesn't have to—and if he did, he still wouldn't: there is probably no literary figure in America who has done less to promote himself, or more to make himself unacceptable to the literary establishment. Since John Martin found him working in the L.A. post office in the late 60s and became his regular publisher, his fortunes have changed considerably. The man who was portrayed by a violent, drunken, sexy and uncontrollable Mickey Rourke in the movie *Barfly* has now published over three dozen works of poetry and prose and is included in the *Norton Anthology of American Poetry*. Even without his royalties from Germany and France, where he is a great bestseller, Bukowski is in my guess a wealthy man. He does not give interviews, not to the famous, not to the powerful; and yet, in response to my request to talk to him—not about himself but about his publisher—he telephoned me immediately and invited me to his home.

I drove to Mr. Bukowski's house south of Los Angeles early in the evening, filled with trepidation. Bukowski's temper is famous, as is his impatience with so-called Eastern intellectuals. But what frightened me most was the fact that I was about to meet the person I had long considered one of the greatest writers of our century—it was Bukowski's work, in fact, that first introduced me to Black Sparrow. His writing documents a life of tremendous struggle with booze and the degradation of menial work, certainly, but on a more profound level with an utter refusal to bring himself into line with a world of falsity with which we all, in some way or another, reach an accommodation. His voice, whose toughness, simplicity, and direct honesty often hide the breadth of style and intellectual acuity he commands, is in my experience unique, and when he turns lyrical, his writing is of an entirely original, powerful poetic beauty.

I arrived at his house late, for I stopped in a nearby bar to fortify myself with a quick drink, and then, out of a form of procrastination, had some trouble tearing myself away from the Forman-Stewart championship bout that was playing on the bar's TV. As it turned out, I needn't have bothered, for Charles and Linda Bukowski were watching the same match when I arrived, and a good deal more fortification than I required was offered during the evening. And in the face of the Bukowskis' kindness and acceptance, my nervousness evaporated instantly. While we watched the end of the fight, I had time to observe Bukowski's legendary face: now in his early seventies, he's craggy and scarred—like W.H. Auden's as a wildcat fighter; the casual comfort of his house, the many, many cats—all strays taken in by the Bukowskis— lolling around the living room. Centrally displayed, to my surprise, was a first edition of James Thurber's *The Last Flower* inscribed to Cecil B. DeMille. After the fight ended, the Bukowskis insisted on taking me to dinner at a portside restaurant, after which we returned to the house and drinking ice-cold Heinekens and smoking Bidis, we talked far into the next morning.

———

NG: I was wondering how John Martin first got in touch with you.

Charles Bukowski: OK. Take 1966 as the year. I'd say it's the midafternoon, I'm about on my ninth or tenth beer. I don't think I'm typing, I'm just sitting on the couch. There's a knock on the door, I open it, and there's this well scrubbed, conservative looking gentleman, with a necktie and a suit. I'm not used to these types coming to my door, you know. "Yes, what is it?" He says something like this: "I've always been a great admirer of your work. I'd like to come in." "Oh, well, come on in. You want a beer?" He says, "No." So that kind of put me off right there: this guy's inhuman, he doesn't drink beer. So, he kind of sat down.

And he said, "Have you got any writing around?" And I said, "Open that closet door." He walked over and opened it. Big pile of paper came out. He says, "What's this?" I said "Writing." He says, "No kidding?" I said, "Yeah." He says, "How long did it take you to write this?" I said, "Oh, I don't know. Half a year, three or four months, a year and a half." And he says, "Oh, this is astonishing. You mind if I read it?" I said, "No, go ahead."

So I sat there drinking beer and he sat down on the floor there and started reading these pages. It was mostly poetry. He'd pick up one of the poems, and he'd say: "Oh, this is *very* good." "Oh, yeah?" "This is great. This is an immortal poem." I said, "Oh yeah?" "This one's not so good here, this one's not so good. Oh, Hey!" And he got all excited, and he sat there a long time going through all this material, and then he said, "You know, I'm starting a press." I said, "Oh yeah?" He said, "I wonder if you'd mind if I took three or four of these poems, you know, with me, and, you know, kind of looked them over. And I think we'd like to put out a broadside or two of these poems here." And I said, "Suit yourself. Sure." He said, "There'll probably be some money in it for you, I don't know how much, we'll have to see." I said, "That's OK, just, you know, whatever."

I kept writing, and I'd hear from him off and on, "Send me some of the stuff you're writing, let me look at it." So you know, I'd mail him a little bit. Finally, he said, "I'll tell you what, Hank." I said, "What is it, John." He said—I'd been in the post office then for eleven and a half years—he said, "I'll tell you what. If you quit the post office, I'll give you a hundred dollars a month for life." I said, "What?" He said, "Yeah. Even if you don't write anything, even if you never send me anything, if you never write anything ever again, I'll give you a hundred dollars a month for life." I said, "Well it sounds pretty good. Can you give me a little time to think it over?" He said, "Sure." I don't know how long I thought, I think I had two more beers, I called him back, I said, "It's a deal."

NG: So when John Martin showed up at your door, was that like a big . . .

CB: Indeed. It opened all the doors. I didn't take it for granted. When John sent the hundred, it was like the whole sky opened up and brightened and the sun came through. It was like he sent me five million.

So time went on and he published this book, and then another book would come out, and the checks slowly got a little larger. He became Black Sparrow Press and he was publishing other writers. And the checks kept growing just a little bit, very encouraging.

He was always very encouraging, like he bought me a typewriter after he gave me the hundred a month. He says, "What kind of typewriter do you want?" "A big one I can beat the shit outa." So he drove over in his car, brought the typewriter. And then he used to send me stamps in the mail. You know, just a whole bunch of stamps. And it's very encouraging. I mean, what beginning writer gets a little boost like that? And so as the years went on, it just grew and grew and grew and he grew.

You know, John's published all these tons of great literature, and there's just kind of this silence from those critical people, I don't know why. Like you know, H.L Mencken, they call him a great editor. There's just silence for Martin. It's inexcusable.

NG: Well one reason is he keeps his distance . . .

CB: Yeah. (*Laughs*) You won't see John at a party. He's too busy doing his actual work. So he doesn't make the contacts. Yeah, too bad. And too good.

What the Hell: Last Words

GUNDOLF S. FREYERMUTH

1993

"What the Hell: Last Words," Gundolf S. Freyermuth, *That's It: A Final Visit with Charles Bukowski*, Xlibris Corporation, 2000. pp. 82–84.

Bukowski and Freyermuth at last interview, 1993

© Michael Montfort

"If you want to sell a script to a Hollywood producer," I said to Charles Bukowski that Sunday afternoon in August, 1993, "you must sum up the content in one sentence, that says everything and gives away nothing . . ."

"I can't do it." Bukowski shook his head.

"Then you don't sell."

"Okay, that's all right." Bukowski reached slowly for his water glass and took a sip. Then he said: "I can't do it in one sentence. But I can do it in one word. Fun. F-U-N, baby." He curved the corner of his mouth upward without smiling: "Speaking of fun, that's it?"

"Do you really want me to stop?"

"Ah, no," Charles Bukowski now grinned. "It doesn't matter too much. Whatever you want."

"What are you writing right now?" I asked.

"Just poems. Poems are easy. You can write poems when you're feeling good, when you're feeling bad. See, prose I can only write when I'm feeling good, for some reason. But a poem I can write when I'm not feeling anything. So a poem is very handy doing it, I can always write it. And then I feel better. That's about it. "Nothing profound."

"The writing's easy, it's the living that is sometimes difficult," Bukowski admitted in his 1985 interview for the *New York Quarterly*. If you don't find a reason to live, they say, you will die.

Charles Bukowski, however, would have had more than one reason not to miss the Nineties. Gaining his reputation in the sloppy Seventies, he belonged as much to the snug Eighties as a bum in a bistro. The ruthless hustle of stock-jobbing and jogging, being pushy and working out, the empty circles of career and consumption, this ragout of restlessness was not his idea of the pursuit of happiness. "In a time when everyone has just a certain life style," a reporter commented after meeting with Bukowski in 1985, "there is one man who lives." Against the zeitgeist.

"He was a writer who insisted on being out-of-step with his times," publisher John Martin said about his best author. "The most important thing to realize about him is that he didn't want to go with any trends or join groups. Charles Bukowski stood alone."

Today, however, the trends catch up with his life and vision.

"Charles Bukowski was politically incorrect, before some thinly talented radio personality made it the rage," Suzanne Lummis writes. "He sported the grunge look before a Seattle band set the fashion. He predated the new appreciation of older women; he declared women are the most desirable at the age when they're just starting to fall apart, which is good news for some of us."

In the early Nineties, the hour of downgrading had come; and that, of course, favored Bukowski. "Radical cheap" described the need of the moment for private and public budgets. Looking for new substance in a a way of life that had been exhausted by luxury, leading trend stylists were seized by a deep "nostalgie de la boue," a nostalgic longing for the gutter—at least that's what the *New York Times* maintained. Today "hip" means, the newspaper reported: "in a Charles Bukowski kind of way."

281

"Oh, well, I like that," Bukowski said.

"So what are your feelings about the Nineties?"

"Well, you know . . . ." The old man was hesitating. "I'm getting near the end . . . ah, of existence. The writing is taking on a little different tone. Not deliberately, it's doing it by itself . . ." For a moment, his eyes looked directly into the red sun that was setting behind the house next door. "What the hell . . . We can't write the same stuff over and over again. There is variance. I hope there is some variance."

"You said you're getting near the end of existence . . ."

"Well . . . we all are, aren't we?"

"If that's what you meant, it's not really news . . ."

"I didn't mean it as news," he said in a husky voice and reached for his glass of water. "Just as a general statement."

"Some people spend their lives closer to nature, and that is to say, to death." While Charles Bukowski drank, I wrote down this sentence. Along with a second: "However, nothing prepares those who live such a life for their own death."

In a letter Charles Bukowski typed on New Years Eve, 1978, he predicted: "I've got to do another fifteen years of good, hard writing— let's see: fifty-eight and fifteen equals . . . well, best not to think about that . . ."

Tomorrow was August 16, 1993, and Charles Bukowski turned seventy-three.

"You once wrote," I asked, "that you plan to live and work another fifteen years . . ."

"Oh. Well, ah . . . ," he said smiling: "Planning and actuality are two different things. You see, I am sick, I got this leukemia . . ."

"You wrote about your plans in the late Seventies . . .," I said.

Bukowski faltered. Eventually he grinned: "Ah, well. Then, maybe I'll be on schedule . . . We'll see."

He wiped the sweat from his brow and leisurely adjusted his straw hat.

"That's it?"

"We haven't talked about Hemingway yet . . ."

"Oh, damn," Charles Bukowski said and slowly got up out of his garden chair. "I think we leave that for some other time. Let us better go out and grab something to eat."

Index

Books by SUN DOG PRESS

Steve Richmond, *Santa Monica Poems*

Steve Richmond, *Hitler Painted Roses*
(Foreword by Charles Bukowski and afterword by Mike Daily)

Steve Richmond, *Spinning Off Bukowski*

Neeli Cherkovski, *Elegy for Bob Kaufman*

Randall Garrison, *Lust in America*

Billy Childish, *Notebooks of a Naked Youth*

Dan Fante, *Chump Change*

Robert Steven Rhine, *My Brain Escapes Me*

Fernanda Pivano, *Charles Bukowski: Laughing With the Gods*

Howard Bone with Daniel Waldron, *Side Show: My Life with Geeks, Freaks & Vagabonds in the Carny Trade*

Jean-François Duval, *Bukowski and the Beats*

Dan Fante, *A gin-pissing-raw-meat-dual-carburetor-V8-son-of-a-bitch from Los Angeles*